SIMUL 2016

The Eighth International Conference on Advances in System Simulation

August 21 - 25, 2016

Rome, Italy

SIMUL 2016 Editors

Arash Ramezani, University of the Federal Armed Forces Hamburg, Germany

Carla Merkle Westphall, Federal University of Santa Catarina, Brazil

Printed from e-media with permission by:

Curran Associates, Inc.
57 Morehouse Lane
Red Hook, NY 12571

Some format issues inherent in the e-media version may also appear in this print version.

Printed by Curran Associates, Inc. (2016)

International Academy, Research, and Industry Association (IARIA)
412 Derby Way
Wilmington, DE 19810

Phone: (408) 893-6407
Fax: (408) 527-6351

petre@iaria.org

Additional copies of this publication are available from:

Curran Associates, Inc.
57 Morehouse Lane
Red Hook, NY 12571 USA
Phone: 845-758-0400
Fax: 845-758-2633
Email: curran@proceedings.com
Web: www.proceedings.com

TABLE OF CONTENTS

SIMUL 1: SIMULATION METHODOLOGIES

A Description Language for Environmental Fields Synthesis in Maritime Co-Simulation Scenarios 1
L. Wu, A. Hahn

Efficient Quantile Estimation When Applying Stratified Sampling and Conditional Monte Carlo, With Applications to Nuclear Safety 6
M. Nakayama

Computational Vibrational Spectroscopy of Hydrophilic Drug Irinotecan 11
B. Koteska, A. Mishev, M. Crcarevska, J. Ribarska, M. Dodov, L. Pejov

Numerical Simulation and Experimental Model-Validation for Fiber-Reinforced Plastics Under Impact Loading - Using the Example of Ultra-High Molecular Weight Polyethylene 17
A. Ramezani, H. Rothe

SIMUL 2: SIMULATION MODELS

A Comparison of Some Simple and Complex Surrogate Models: Make Everything as Simple as Possible? 26
W. Mulder, G. Molenberghs, G. Verbeke, B. Rengs, T. Fent

Pedestrian Activity Simulation in Shopping Environments: An Irregular Network Approach 33
J. Dijkstra, J. Jessurun

An Integrated Modelling Approach for Spatial-aware Federated Simulation 40
J. Xie, R. Kozik, N. Flourentzou

Agent-Based Model to Simulate Outpatient Consultations at the "Hospital de Clinicas" - Work-in-Progress Paper 46
R. Galeano, C. Villalba, D. Rexachs, E. Luque

SIMUL 3: APPLICATIONS SIMULATION

Simulation of Device Behavior for InAlAs/InGaAs HEMT under Optical Illumination 52
P. Sharma, J. Jogi, R. Gupta

UrMo Accessibility Computer: A Tool for Computing Contour Accessibility Measures 56
D. Krajzewicz, D. Heinrichs

Simulation of the Influence of Curb-Parking on the Efficiency of Designated Curb Bus Lanes 61
M. Bauer

Design and Control of a Mechatronic Vehicle Dynamics Simulator Pitch and Roll Dynamics 67
J. Lozoya-Santos, J. Salinas, E. Mendez, G. Gonzalez, J. Tudon-Martinez, R. Ramirez-Mendoza

SIMUL 4 / CAESD: COMPUTER-AIDED ENGINEERING SIMULATION FOR DEFENSE AND SECURITY

Developing an Interface between ANSYS and Abaqus to Simulate Blast Effects on High Security Vehicles 73
E. Hansen, N. Ehlers, A. Ramezani, H. Rothe

Modeling and Analyzing Enterprise Architectures to Examine the Feasibility of Network Centric Operations 77
O. Kroning, H. Rothe

Effects of Elevated Temperatures on Ballistic Resistance of Ultra High Molecular Weight Polyethylene 85
T. Heurich, A. Ramezani, H. Rothe

Author Index

SIMUL 2016

Forward

The Eighth International Conference on Advances in System Simulation (SIMUL 2016), held on August 21 - 25, 2016 in Rome, Italy, continued a series of events focusing on advances in simulation techniques and systems providing new simulation capabilities.

While different simulation events are already scheduled for years, SIMUL 2016 identified specific needs for ontology of models, mechanisms, and methodologies in order to make easy an appropriate tool selection. With the advent of Web Services and WEB 3.0 social simulation and human-in simulations bring new challenging situations along with more classical process simulations and distributed and parallel simulations. An update on the simulation tool considering these new simulation flavors was aimed at, too.

The conference provided a forum where researchers were able to present recent research results and new research problems and directions related to them. The conference sought contributions to stress-out large challenges in scale system simulation and advanced mechanisms and methodologies to deal with them. The accepted papers covered topics on social simulation, transport simulation, simulation tools and platforms, simulation methodologies and models, and distributed simulation.

We welcomed technical papers presenting research and practical results, position papers addressing the pros and cons of specific proposals, such as those being discussed in the standard forums or in industry consortiums, survey papers addressing the key problems and solutions on any of the above topics, short papers on work in progress, and panel proposals.

We take here the opportunity to warmly thank all the members of the SIMUL 2016 technical program committee as well as the numerous reviewers. The creation of such a broad and high quality conference program would not have been possible without their involvement. We also kindly thank all the authors that dedicated much of their time and efforts to contribute to the SIMUL 2016. We truly believe that thanks to all these efforts, the final conference program consists of top quality contributions.

This event could also not have been a reality without the support of many individuals, organizations and sponsors. We also gratefully thank the members of the SIMUL 2016 organizing committee for their help in handling the logistics and for their work that is making this professional meeting a success. We gratefully appreciate to the technical program committee co-chairs that contributed to identify the appropriate groups to submit contributions.

We hope the SIMUL 2016 was a successful international forum for the exchange of ideas and results between academia and industry and to promote further progress in simulation research. We also hope Rome provided a pleasant environment during the conference and everyone saved some time for exploring this beautiful historic city.

SIMUL 2016 Advisory Committee

Christoph Reinhart, Harvard University - Cambridge, USA
Amr Arisha, College of Business, DIT, Ireland

SIMUL 2016 Research Liaison Chairs

Tae-Eog Lee, KAIST, Korea
Marko Jaakola, VTT Technical Research Centre of Finland, Finland

SIMUL 2016 Industry Liaison Chairs

Shengnan Wu, American Airlines, USA
Tejas R. Gandhi, Virtua Health-Marlton, USA

SIMUL 2016 Special Area Chairs

Model-based system prediction
Georgiy Bobashev, RTI International -Research Triangle Park, USA
Aida Omerovic, SINTEF & University of Oslo, Norway

Process simulation
Ian Flood, University of Florida, USA
Gregor Papa, Jozef Stefan Institute - Ljubljana, Slovenia

SIMUL 2016 Publicity Chairs

Nuno Melão, Polytechnic Institute of Viseu, Portugal

SIMUL 2016

Committee

SIMUL Advisory Committee

Christoph Reinhart, Harvard University - Cambridge, USA
Amr Arisha, College of Business, DIT, Ireland

SIMUL 2016 Research Liaison Chairs

Tae-Eog Lee, KAIST, Korea
Marko Jaakola, VTT Technical Research Centre of Finland, Finland

SIMUL 2016 Industry Liaison Chairs

Shengnan Wu, American Airlines, USA
Tejas R. Gandhi, Virtua Health-Marlton, USA

SIMUL 2016 Special Area Chairs

Model-based system prediction
Georgiy Bobashev, RTI International -Research Triangle Park, USA
Aida Omerovic, SINTEF & University of Oslo, Norway

Process simulation
Ian Flood, University of Florida, USA
Gregor Papa, Jozef Stefan Institute - Ljubljana, Slovenia

SIMUL 2016 Publicity Chairs

Nuno Melão, Polytechnic Institute of Viseu, Portugal

SIMUL 2016 Technical Program Committee

Kareem Abdelgawadm, Heinz Nixdorf Institute - University of Paderborn, Germany
Carole Adam, University Grenoble-Alpes, France
Hossein Aghababa, University of Tehran, Iran
Petra Ahrweiler, EA European Academy of Technology and Innovation Assessment GmbH, Germany
Dimosthenis Anagnostopoulos, Harokopio University of Athens, Greece
Chrissanthi Angeli, Technological Institute of Piraeus - Athens, Greece
Thierry Antoine-Santoni, University of Corsica, France
Amr Arisha, College of Business - DIT, Ireland
Marek Bauer, Politechnika Krakowska, Poland
Ateet Bhalla, Independent Consultant, India

Kashif Bilal, COMSATS Institute of Information Technology, Pakistan
Paul-Antoine Bisgambiglia, Université de Corse, France
Keith Bisset, Virginia Tech, USA
Georgiy Bobashev, RTI International -Research Triangle Park, USA
Christos Bouras, University of Patras | Computer Technology Institute & Press «Diophantus», Greece
Christophe Bourdin, Université d'Aix-Marseille, France
Jan F. Broenink, University of Twente, Netherlands
Luigi Buglione, Engineering, Italy
Dilay Celebi, Istanbul Technical University, Turkey
Srinivas R. Chakravarthy, Kettering University, USA
Kuo-Hao Chang, National Tsing Hua University, Taiwan
E Jack Chen, BASF Corporation, USA
Soolyeon Cho, North Carolina State University - Raleigh, USA
Federico Ciccozzi, Mälardalen University, Sweden
Franco Cicirelli, Università della Calabria, Italy
Kendra Cooper, University of Texas at Dallas, USA
Duilio Curcio, University of Calabria - Rende (CS), Italy
Andrea D'Ambrogio, University of Roma "Tor Vergata", Italy
Yuya Dan, Matsuyama University, Japan
Saber Darmoul, King Saud University, Saudi Arabia
Jacinto Dávila, Universidad de Los Andes, Venezuela
Paula de Oliveira, University of Coimbra, Portugal
Luis Antonio de Santa-Eulalia, Université de Sherbrooke, Canada
Tom Dhaene, Ghent University - IBBT, Belgium
Jan Dijkstra, Eindhoven University of Technology, Netherlands
Atakan Dogan, Anadolu University, Turkey
Julie Dugdale, Université Pierre Mendès, France
Khaled S. El-Kilany, Arab Academy for Science - Alexandria, Egypt
Sabeur Elkosantini, Higher Institute of Computer Science of Mahdia - University of Monatir, Tunisia
Diego Encinas, Informatics Research Institute LIDI - National University of La Plata, Argentina
Zuhal Erden, Atılım University, Turkey
Zhou Fang, VR and Immersive Simulation Center - Renault DE-TD, France
Francisco Javier Otamendi Fernández de la Puebla, Universidad Rey Juan Carlos, Spain
Ian Flood, University of Florida, USA
Terrill L. Frantz, Peking University HSBC Business School, Shenzhen Campus, Guangdong, China
Jason Friedman, Tel Aviv University, Israel
Marco Furini, University of Modena and Reggio Emilia, Italy
José Manuel Galán, Universidad de Burgos, Spain
Tejas Gandhi, Medical Center of Central Georgia, USA
Siyang Gao, City University of Hong Kong, Hong Kong
Hector Miguel Gastelum Gonzalez, University of Guadalajara, Mexico
Petia Georgieva, University of Aveiro, Portugal
Charlotte Gerritsen, Netherlands Institute for the Study of Crime and Law Enforcement, Netherlands
Genady Grabarnik, St. John's University, USA
Antoni Grau, Technical University of Catalonia UPC, Spain
Francisco Grimaldo Moreno, Universitat de València, Spain
Christoph Grimm, TU Kaiserslautern, Germany
Amine Hamri, LSIS Marseille, France

Samer Hassan, Universidad Complutense de Madrid, Spain
Frank Herrmann, Regensburg Technical University of Applied Sciences, Germany
Tsan-sheng Hsu, Academia Sinica, Taiwan
Xiaolin Hu, Georgia State University, USA
Mauro Iacono, Seconda Università degli Studi di Napoli, Italy
Eric Innocenti, University of Corsica Pasquale Paoli, France
Joshua Ignatius, Universiti Sains Malaysia, Malaysia
Emilio Insfran, Universitat Politecnica de Valencia, Spain
Marko Jaakola, VTT Technical Research Centre of Finland, Finland
Cecilia Jaramillo, University Autonoma of Barcelona (UAB), Spain
András Jávor, Budapest University of Technology and Economics, Hungary
Emilio Jiménez Macías, University of La Rioja, Spain
Maria João Viamonte, ISEP - School of Engineering - Polytechnic of Porto, Portugal
Eugene John, University of Texas at San Antonio, USA
Waldemar Karwowski, University of Central Florida, USA
Mohammad Kazemifard, Razi University, Iran
Christina Kluever, University of Duisburg-Essen, Germany
Natallia Kokash, Centrum Wiskunde & Informatica (CWI), Netherlands
Sunil Kothari, HP Labs, USA
Claudia Krull, Otto-von-Guericke-University Magdeburg, Germany
Olexandr O. Kuzenkov, Khmelnitsky National University, Ukraine
Pierre L'Ecuyer, Université de Montréal, Canada
Herman Le Roux, Council for Scientific and Industrial Research, South Africa
SangHyun Lee, University of Michigan, USA
Fedor Lehocki, National Centre of Telemedicine Services / Slovak University of Technology in Bratislava, Slovakia
Jennie Lioris, CERMICS, France
Rong Liu, University of California, Los Angeles, USA
Francesco Longo, University of Calabria, Italy
Edwin Lughofer, Johannes Kepler University Linz, Austria
Johannes Lüthi, Fachhochschule Kufstein Tirol, Austria
Jose Machado, Universidade do Minho, Portugal
Tenreiro Machado, Institute of Engineering - Polytechnic of Porto, Portugal
Michael Manitz, Universität Duisburg/Essen, Germany
Ricardo Marcelín-Jiménez, Universidad Autónoma Metropolitana, Mexico
João Pedro Jorge Marques, University of Porto, Portugal
Goreti Marreiros, Engineering Institute - Polytechnic of Porto, Portugal
Stefano Marrone, Seconda Università di Napoli, Italy
Don McNickle, University of Canterbury - Christchurch, New Zealand
Nuno Melão, Polytechnic Institute of Viseu, Portugal
Jürgen Melzner, Bauhaus-University Weimar, Germany
Marco Mevius, HTWG Konstanz, Germany
Adel Mhamdi, RWTH Aachen University, Germany
Bożena Mielczarek, Wroclaw University of Technology, Poland
Saurabh Mittal, Dunip Technologies, USA
Owen Molloy, National University of Ireland, Galway, Ireland
Lars Mönch, University of Hagen, Germany
Roberto Montemanni, University of Applied Sciences of Southern Switzerland (SUPSI), Switzerland

Tingting Mu, University of Liverpool, UK
Àngela Nebot, Polytechnic University of Catalonia, Spain
Letizia Nicoletti, Cal-tek srl, Italy
Libero Nigro, Università della Calabria, Italy
Lialia Nikitina, Fraunhofer Institute for Algorithms and Scientific Computing, Germany
Mara Nikolaidou, Harokopio University of Athens, Greece
Halit Oguztuzun, Middle East Technical University, Ankara, Turkey
Aida Omerovic, SINTEF ICT, Norway
Tuncer Ören, University of Ottawa, Canada
Gregor Papa, Jozef Stefan Institute - Ljubljana, Slovenia
Laurent Perochon, VetaGro Sup, France
Claudine Picaronny, LSV ENS Cachan, France
Henri Pierreval, IFMA-LIMOS, France
François Pinet, Irstea, France
Marta Pla-Castells, Universitat de València, Spain
Katalin Popovici, MathWorks Inc., USA
Tomas Potuzak, University of West Bohemia, Czech Republic
Francesco Quaglia, Sapienza Universita' di Roma, Italy
Gauthier Quesnel, INRA, MIA Toulouse, France
Arash Ramezani, University of the Federal Armed Forces, Germany
Mohsen Ramezani, Monash University, Australia
Urvashi Rathod, Symbiosis Centre for Information Technology, India
Cláudia Ribeiro, INESC-ID Lisbon, Portugal
José Luis Risco Martín, Universidad Complutense de Madrid, Spain
Victor Romanov, Russian Plekhanov University of Economics, Russia
Agostinho Rosa, Technical University of Lisbon, Portugal
Rosaldo J. F. Rossetti, University of Porto, Portugal
Hendrik Rothe, Helmut Schmidt Universitat, Germany
Juliette Rouchier, LAMSADE, Paris-Dauphine, France
Manuel Filipe Santos, University of Minho, Portugal
Jean-Francois Santucci, University of Corsica, France
Federica Sarro, University College London, UK
Florence Sedes, Paul Sabatier University - Toulouse III | IRIT, France
Guodong Shao, National Institute of Standards and Technology - Gaithersburg, USA
Yuri N. Skiba, Centre for Atmospheric Sciences - Universidad Nacional Autónoma de México, Mexico
Frank Slomka, Ulm University, Germany
Jeffrey S. Smith, Auburn University, USA
Flavio Soares Correa da Silva, University of Sao Paulo, Brazil
Eric Solano, RTI International, USA
Yuri N. Sotskov, United Institute of Informatics Problems - National Academy of Sciences of Belarus, Belarus
Mu-Chun Su, National Central University, Taiwan
Nary Subramanian, University of Texas at Tyler, USA
Changho Sung, Korea Institute of Science and Technology Europe (KIST Europe), Germany
Magdalena Szmajduch, Cracow University of Technology, Poland
Elena Tànfani, University of Genova, Italy
Halina Tarasiuk, Institute of Telecommunications - Warsaw University of Technology, Poland
Alexander Tatashev, Moscow University of Communications and Informatics, Russia

Copyright Information

A Description Language for Environmental Fields Synthesis in Maritime Co-Simulation Scenarios

Liqun Wu, Axel Hahn
Department of Computing Science
Carl von Ossietzky Universität Oldenburg
Oldenburg, Germany
e-mail: {liqun.wu, axel.hahn}@uni-oldenburg.de

Abstract—**This paper introduces a Domain Specific Language (DSL) for describing the physical environment required in maritime co-simulation scenarios. This language helps simulation scenario modelers intuitively describe the physical environment which they wish their vessels to act in. The modelers can write programs to specify which environmental elements should be present in a simulation scenario, and how these elements should vary within the spatio-temporal span of the scenario. An environment synthesis framework is built based on this language. It uses programs written in this language to compose dynamic environmental fields. Thus, scenario modelers can focus on the simulation models they want to explore, while still have full control of the environment in their simulation scenarios.**

Keywords-Domain Specific Language; maritime co-simulation; environmental data synthesis; spatio-temporal field.

I. Introduction

Safety has been a significant challenge in constructing maritime traffic systems [1]. This is also true when applying eNavigation technology and assistance systems for navigators. Risk assessment of these systems is important to improve the safety of maritime eNavigation [2]. Research reveals that co-simulation platforms are appropriate for the assessment via running simulation scenarios. The co-simulation platforms distribute simulation tasks to different components. Each component focuses on one specific aspect of the simulation. All the components work collaboratively to accomplish the whole simulation. In this context, a vessel simulation component simulates vessel objects moving on the water. These objects need to receive information of influential environmental elements during the run of simulation scenarios, e.g., current and wind. The required environmental elements are assumed to be provided by another environment synthesis component, therefore vessel modelers can focus on modeling the behavior of vessels. The environment discussed here is particularly referred to the simulated physical environment in which the objects are situated and whose evolution is beyond the control of the objects [3].

To supply the information of the environmental elements, the environment synthesis component could either make use of existing observation datasets, or run a calculation model based on initial settings. However, edge cases, e.g., extreme weather conditions cannot be fully covered, although testing various conditions is crucial to assess safety issues. Furthermore, vessel modelers cannot fully control and modify the behavior of the environmental elements in simulation scenarios. Thus, they need a machine processable solution to specify the environment matching their scenarios. This solution should not require too much effort from vessel modelers that will cause distraction from their focuses on modeling vessels.

This paper proposes the Environmental Fields Description Language (EFDL) to describe the user-controlled environmental elements. It is a DSL that allows user to specify environmental element fields based on a simple and intuitive field structure. It aims to provide the formal language support for describing environment from requirement perspective. The scenario modelers can express what kind of physical environment their scenarios are situated in with domain abstractions in this language. Together with the EFDL, an environment synthesis framework is also proposed for composing dynamic environmental data that matches the EFDL description during simulation runs.

The rest of this paper is organized as follows: Section 2 illustrates the related work on DSL in simulation domain and remained problems; Section 3 introduces the conceptual structure and benefits of the proposed language, followed by Section 4 that describes how to implement and use this language in an environment synthesis framework. Section 5 concludes with discussion and future work.

II. Related Work

DSLs are computer languages specialized for certain domains [4]. A DSL has higher expressiveness than general computer languages in its target domain that allows domain experts to program with domain abstractions. Various guidelines have been developed for design and implementation of DSLs [4][5][6]. Modern Language Workbenches [7][8][9] assist in the development of DSLs.

DSLs have gained attention in spatio-temporal modeling and simulation. Maxwell and Costanza [10] have proposed the spatial modeling language (SML) to support modular simulation design. It mainly focuses on structuring and linking different modules for a model. SELES [11] landscape modeling framework provides a language to specify the model dynamics by defining how an event affects its neighborhood. It supports various raster data as input. Ocelet [12] uses an unusual approach that takes Service-Oriented Architecture (SOA) concepts to model processes in landscape. It relies on the evolving of the coded cases of the model actions, but does not include vocabularies to specify the spatio-temporal aspects.

More recent development takes the advantages of the model-driven methods and language workbenches. GAMA platform [13] provides a modeling language GAML to support the development of agent-based models. The GAML semantic is defined in a meta-model and implemented using XText [14] in a textual manner. It is an agent-oriented, typed language which allows to agentify Geographic Information System (GIS) data [15]. Environment can be specified by the modeler by a list of geometries in addition to being loaded from files and created as agents. It also supports to write equations linked to agent attributes imperatively. DSL3S [16] supports prototyping spatial simulation models using graphic notation. Its implementation utilizes the Eclipse Modeling Framework (EMF)-based graphic editor and an open source code generator. The DSL3S abstract syntax is defined as UML profiles, with each construct defined as a stereotype. This is a general level specification language with only 11 concepts. The "Spatial" concept provides means to load spatial environmental data files for the simulation.

All the above-mentioned DSLs focus on the description of the phenomenon that the simulation aims to explore. While most of them assume that the influential environmental information is available, GAML allows to input a list of user-defined environmental geometries. Nevertheless, it treats the influential environmental elements as agents, makes no conceptual distinction from the phenomenon that the simulation explores. It also does not emphasize the field-form environment, which is the common case in maritime domain. The researchers who developed ELMS [17] have realized the needs of the environment specification. They proposed the ELMS as a language to specify the simulated environment in multi-agent simulations. The objects which the agents' percept are defined as resources. However, their focuses remain in social simulation. Although the grid representation of the environment is mentioned, no means of defining resource variation among cells is provided.

III. ENVIRONMENTAL FIELD DESCRIPTION LANGUAGE

This paper proposes the EFDL to express the required change of the environmental elements in the simulated environment which the model objects act in. For each maritime simulation step, vessels perceive influential environmental elements, e.g., wind. Then, the received information is used as input to derive next actions of the model objects. Such an environmental element forms a field covering the space which the model objects move through and should be provided to the model objects during the simulation timespan, even at some locations its values could be zero or null. Vessel modelers also need to modify the variation of environmental fields matching different scenarios to test how their models react under different conditions. The EFDL allows modelers to write a formal description of these required environment fields with domain abstractions.

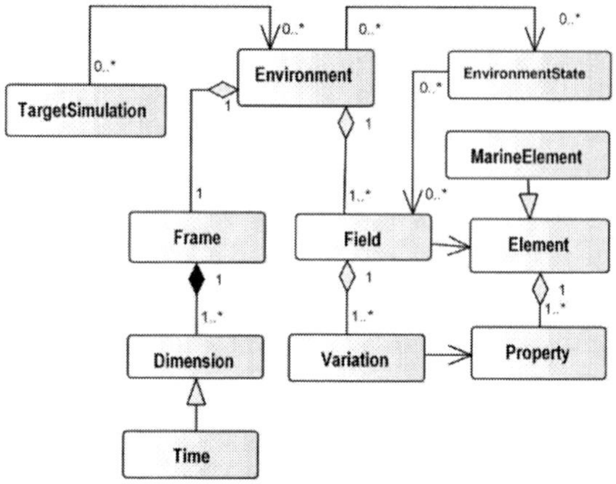

Figure 1. Conceptual structure of an environmental description.

The conceptual specification of the language has three modules: *Environment*, *Variation* and *Marine*. The *Environment* module defines the core structure of a description of the environment. The conceptualization is presented in Figure 1 leaving out the supporting concepts and attributes. It is explained in following paragraphs with examples of the formal definitions of the concepts, as well as a simple descriptive example of an environment with wind presented, required by scenarios to test how a 2D positioning system for maritime crafts endures different wind strengths.

The entry concept *Environment* is defined as a tuple consisting of one *Frame* and probably one or more *Fields*, formally as:

$$\begin{aligned}&\text{Environment} := \langle \text{frame, fields} \rangle,\\ &\quad \text{frame} \in \text{Frame, fields} \subset \text{Field.}\end{aligned} \quad (1)$$

All fields have a common *Frame* that represents the spatio-temporal span within which the target scenario is supposed be performed. Even if an element does not appear at some location, the user should be able to define this unavailability. *Frame* comprises of *Dimensions*. It is formally defined as in (2). The presented supporting function, i.e., *orthogonal: Dimension×Dimension→Boolean*, takes two instances of *Dimension* as input and returns true if they are orthogonal to each other.

$$\begin{aligned}&\text{Frame} := \langle \text{dimensions} \rangle\\ &\text{where dimensions} \subset \text{Dimension},\\ &|\text{dimensions}| \in \{1,2,3,4\},\\ &\forall\, d_i, d_j \in \text{dimensions: orthogonal}\left(d_i, d_j\right) = \text{true.}\end{aligned} \quad (2)$$

Dimensions in EFDL are limited to the physical spatio-temporal space. Each *Dimension* represents the spread of the *Frame* in one direction in the space. *Time* is defined as a subtype of the *Dimension* which is orthogonal to any spatial dimension. This concept is formally defined as following:

$$\text{Dimension} := \langle \vec{d}, \text{origin} \rangle. \quad (3)$$

The vector $\vec{d}$ represents the direction of the *Dimension*. After all, the *Frame* is conceptually an orthogonal spatio-temporal frame. The *Frame* is anchored by the *origins* of its *Dimensions*. The full definitions of the supporting concepts are omitted here. In practice, user can declaratively align one *Dimension* to an axis of common coordinate systems and define the *origins* using coordinates in the aligned system.

In our example, three *Dimensions* can be defined in the *Frame*, two of which are aligned to the axes of the WGS84 system. The other one is the time dimension referenced to the UTC+0 time. The defined *Frame* is grounded by setting the *origins* as the WGS84 coordinates of the most south-west point of the simulation region and the start time of the simulation. Having the above-introduced concepts, this can be done by simple declarations of instances of corresponding concepts and value assignments to the instances.

A *Field* represents the influential field of one environmental element whose information needs to be received by the model objects in the target scenario. Each *Field* is associated with an environmental *Element* and consists of one or more *Variations*. We define the supporting function *binding: Element×Field* to associate the *Field* to the corresponding *Element*. Each *Variation* in this field is associated with a *Property* of the *Element*. It defines how the values of the corresponding property should distribute. The formal definitions of the binding function and its input types described in this paragraph are represented in (4) leaving out the definitions of the support concepts. A similar function to associate the Variation to the Property is also provided.

$$\begin{aligned}
&\text{Field} := \langle \text{variations} \rangle \\
&\text{where}\ \ \text{properties} \sqsubset \text{Variation.} \\
\\
&\text{Element} := \langle \text{properties, name} \rangle \\
&\text{where}\ \ \text{properties} \sqsubset \text{Property, name} \in \text{String.} \qquad (4) \\
\\
&\text{binding: Element} \times \text{Field} \\
&\text{binding(element, field)} := \\
&\forall\ \text{variation} \in \text{field:} \\
&\text{propertyOf(variation)} \in \text{element} \land \\
&\text{elementOf(field)} = \text{element.}
\end{aligned}$$

Our example includes one *Field* (denoted as *f*) associated with *wind* element via *binding (f, wind)*. The *wind* element is defined in the *Marine* module which will be described in a later paragraph. The *Field f* has two *Variations* representing wind properties, namely the speed of x direction and of y direction. They are also defined in the *Marine* module.

Variation module express how the numerical values of an element property should fill the corresponding *Frame*. It does not focus on an accurate derivation based on available information, but on the easy expression of desired conditions. *Variation* can be defined in groups of one dimension (e.g., time) or of more dimensions (e.g., two spatial dimensions). Correlated groups can be further combined. Such a group is defined as a *Subvariation* consisting of a reference to the corresponding dimension(s) and a function with the coordinates in the dimension(s) as variables:

$$\text{Subvariation} := \langle \text{ref.dimensions, F(ref.dimensions)} \rangle \qquad (5)$$

Currently, we test two *Variation* types: pattern association is used to declare a typical pattern of an environmental element, which is pre-defined in the *Marine* module; customized grid allows user to divide the *Frame* into blocks by declaring the number of cells and the cell size along each dimension. The gridded blocks (cells) imply the desired resolution of the fields. Then the values distribution can be expressed with integer values based on the indexes of cells. As a simple illustration, the modelers could fix both wind speed values of cells with index 1 in time dimension (e.g., via mapping to a raster file) and declare that all the values should be linearly increased by a factor of 2 in time dimension.

An additional concept *EnviromentState* is used to specify which element values should be provided at each simulation step. It is defined in relation to the state of vessels such as their spatio-temporal location, neighborhood and offset. Most simply, user can state that all the element values at current vessel location should be provided to the vessels.

The *Marine* module is an application specific module with common types of involved environmental elements, such as the *wind* in the example. All the concrete environmental elements in this module are instances of the *MarineElement*, which itself is a subtype of the *Element*. It also includes typical patterns formation of these elements, which the *Variation* can refer to. Its separation from the other two core modules enhances the extensibility of this language. Further elements or application-specific modules can be added without modifying the core conceptualization of the simulated environment.

The EFDL brings three main benefits. First, EDFL descriptions are more intuitive from a "required condition" perspective. It distinguishes the controlled environmental variation from the phenomenon to be explored. This distinction avoids the need to transfer the conceptualization of environment into the conceptualization of active models similar to what the users investigate on, as some previously mentioned DSLs did. Second, it avoids the miscommunication between the component which requires information of certain environmental elements and the component which provides this information. As a computer language, the description written in the EFDL will be interpreted only in one way as defined in the semantic specification of the language. Third, the EFDL enables the user to control the environmental elements. It goes beyond indicating a dataset input directory and supports the users to describe their desired variation. This is especially useful when running scenarios with diverse conditions, which may require synthesis environmental fields.

IV. Implementation Apporach and Environment Synthesis Framework

The implementation of the EFDL uses an "abstract syntax first" approach. It means that the concepts and data structure holding the information of a program [6] as described in

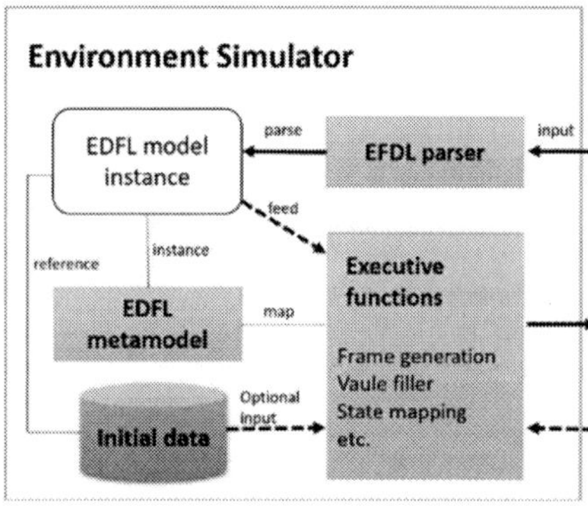

Figure 2. Environment synthesis framework.

Section 3 will be implemented at first. The concrete syntax containing the notations which is actually used to write the DSL program [6] will be defined based on the abstract syntax. While this language is domain-specific and usually needs to be combined with other general level tools to build a complete application, the most suitable notation format may be various in different situations. This way of implementation can have multiple concrete syntax that may needed for different applications without modifying the conceptualization in the abstract syntax.

We use the Eclipse Modeling Framework (EMF) [18] to define the abstract syntax. All the concepts and conceptual structure described in Section 3 will be stored in Ecore metamodels which can be easily integrated with widely-used EMF-based tools. A prototype editor will be developed as an Eclipse plug-in based on the metamodels using EMFText [19]. EMFText is an EMF-based Language Workbench that can define the textual syntax of DSLs. The grammar rules and the function signatures built on top of the conceptualization are defined in the concrete syntax using EMFText. EMFText maps them to the abstract syntax, i.e., the Ecore metamodels. The concrete syntax is used directly by users. Using the textual concrete syntax, users describe fields that are analogous to their description sentence in mind. The textual programs are also easier to be quantitatively compared with programs written in general purpose language for evaluation. The editor will be used to write the EFDL program in the concrete syntax.

The EFDL forms the base of our environment synthesis framework as shown in Figure 2. The EFDL editor comes with an execution engine that will be embedded in the environment synthesis component which we call environment simulator. It is one part of our maritime co-simulation platform. To run a scenario, the environment simulator loads a corresponding EFDL program. It parses the loaded program as an EFDL model which is an instance of the language metamodel. Then the content of this model is consumed by the corresponding executive functions to produce values of environmental elements. The values are mapped to the spatio-temporal locations specified in the *Frame* of the program model. Any data referenced in the model instance are also used by these functions. At each simulation step, the engine produces relevant element values based on current time and states (e.g., locations) of the vessel objects, as defined in the *EnvironmentState* of the model.

V. Conclusion and Future Work

Although various DSLs have been developed for spatio-temporal simulations, they focus on the phenomena to be investigated and assume the environmental elements that influence these phenomena to be given. This is not always true, especially for the safety critical simulations that have to run under various conditions. The modelers require the environment matching their scenarios. The EFDL proposed in this paper enables modelers to fully control the influential environmental elements by describing how they wish their fields vary using this language with an intuitive expression structure and domain abstractions. An environment synthesis framework is designed based on the EDFL to process the description written in this language and to compose the described environment for simulation scenarios.

This language separates the field structure and its value variation from the application-specific environmental elements. While the current usage is to support maritime co-simulations, the core field specification can be reused for simulations in other application domain combined with an application vocabulary extension. The implementation of this language takes advantage of language workbenches and allows multiple concrete syntax that adapted to different applications.

Currently, we are investigating on various formations of the element variations. The aim is to find the balance between the language simplicity and its expressiveness. This language should have the ability to express the environment with complicated change. The basic idea is to decompose its variation into simple facets (i.e., *the Subvariations*). Thus, how to correctly describe the combination of these facets in an easy way become crucial. It needs also to be investigated that to what extend the environment can be described under the conceptualization of the "field with a frame" as introduced in Section 3. When combining with the *Marine* module to express a specific environment, if all the environmental elements can be mapped into this conceptualization, or if additional conceptualization is needed, remain as open questions.

The developed language and framework will be tested with vessel modelers in the future by a series of test cases including generation of spatial varied (e.g., current), temporal varied fields (e.g., wind changing strength over time) and spatio-temporal varied fileds (e.g., current changing over time). The participating modelers will be asked to fill a questionnaire regarding the usability based on the test cases. The program length of these test cases will be compared to the program length of the same cases written in general purpose programing language to evaluate its productivity, following the approach from Kosar et al. [20].

The performance of the implemented simulator is beyond the scope of the research on the formal specification of the required environment description. However, it is important from the engineering point of view. While the specification is independent from the algorithms that creating values for specific fields, the efficiency of the simulator depends also on the chosen algorithms. The computational cost of the above-mentioned test cases should be also evaluated.

ACKNOWLEDGMENT

We thank the ministry of science and culture of Lower Saxony for supporting us with the graduate school Safe Automation of Maritime Systems (SAMS).

REFERENCES

[1] H. Gale and D. Patraiko, "Improving navigational safety - The role of e-Navigation," *Seaways*, pp. 4–8, Mar. 2007.

[2] C. Läsche, V. Gollücke, and A. Hahn, "Using an HLA Simulation Environment for Safety Concept Verification of Offshore Operations," in *Proceediings 27th European Conference on Modelling and Simulation*, Ålesund, Norway, pp. 156–162, 2013.

[3] F. Klügl, M. Fehler, and R. Herrler, "About the Role of the Environment in Multi-agent Simulations," in *Proceedings of First International Workshop, E4MAS 2004*, New Yourk, NY, USA, pp. 127–149, 2004.

[4] M. Mernik, J. Heering, and A. Sloane, "When and how to develop domain-specific languages," *ACM Comput. Surv. CSUR*, vol. 37, no. 4, pp. 316–344, Dec. 2005.

[5] G. Karsai, H. Krahn, C. Pinkernell, B. Rumpe, M. Schindler, and S. Völkel, "Design guidelines for domain specific languages," in *Proceedings of 9th OOPSLA Workshop on Domain-Specific Modeling (DSM' 09)*, Helsinki School of Economics. TR no B-108. Orlando, Florida, USA, arXiv:1409.2378, 2009.

[6] M. Völter, *DSL Engineering: Designing, Implementing and Using Domain-Specific Languages*. CreateSpace Independent Publishing Platform, 2013.

[7] M. Fowler, "Language Workbenches: The Killer-App for Domain Specific Languages?," 2005. [Online]. Available: http://www.martinfowler.com/articles/languageWorkbench.html. [Accessed: 01-Mar-2016].

[8] B. Merkle, "Textual modeling tools: overview and comparison of language workbenches," in *Proceedings of the ACM international conference companion on Object oriented programming systems languages and applications companion*, Reno/Tahoe, Nevada, USA, pp. 139–148, 2010.

[9] S. Erdweg, T. van der Storm, M. Völter, and M. Boersma, "The state of the art in language workbenches: conclusions from the Language Workbench Challenge," in *Proceedings of the International Conference on Software Language Engineering (SLE, 2013)*, USA, pp. 197–217, 2013.

[10] T. Maxwell and R. Costanza, "A language for modular spatio-temporal simulation," *Ecol. Model.*, vol. 103, no. 2–3, pp. 105–113, Nov. 1997.

[11] A. Fall and J. Fall, "A domain-specific language for models of landscape dynamics," *Ecol. Model.*, vol. 141, no. 1–3, pp. 1–18, Jul. 2001.

[12] P. Degenne, D. L. Seen, D. Parigot, and R. Forax, "Design of a domain specific language for modelling processes in landscapes," *Ecol. Model.*, vol. 220, no. 24, pp. 3527–3535, 2009.

[13] P. Taillandier, D. A. Vo, E. Amouroux, and A. Drogoul, "GAMA: A simulation platform that integrates geographical information data, agent-based modeling and multi-scale control.," in *Proceedings of the 13th International Conference on Principles and Practice of Multi-Agent Systems*, Kolkata, India, pp. 242–258, 2010.

[14] M. Eysholdt and H. Behrens, "Xtext: implement your language faster than the quick and dirty way," in *Proceedings of the ACM international conference companion on Object oriented programming systems languages and applications companion*, Reno, Nevada, USA, pp. 307–309, 2010.

[15] A. Grignard, P. Taillandier, B. Gaudou, D. A. Vo, N. Q. Huynh, and A. Drogoul, "GAMA 1.6: advancing the art of complex agent-based modeling and simulation," in *Proceedings of PRIMA 2013: Principles and Practice of Multi-Agent Systems*, vol. 829, pp. 117–131, 2013.

[16] L. de Sousa and A. R. da Silva, "A domain specific language for spatial simulation scenarios," *GeoInformatica*, vol. 20, no. 1, pp. 117–149, Jan. 2016.

[17] F. Okuyama, R. H. Bordini, and A. C. da Rocha Costa, "ELMS: An Environment Description Language for Multi-agent Simulation," in *Proceedings of First International Workshopt on Agent Environments for Multi-Agent Systems*, New Yourk, NY, USA, pp. 91–108, 2004.

[18] D. Steinberg, F. Budinsky, M. Paternostro, and E. Merks, *EMF: Eclipse Modeling Framework*, 2nd ed. Addison-Wesley Professional, 2008.

[19] "EMFText." [Online]. Available: http://www.emftext.org/index.php/EMFText. [Accessed: 01-Mar-2016].

[20] T. Kosar, P. E. M. López, P. A. Barrientos, and M. Mernik, "A preliminary study on various implementation approaches of domain-specific language," *Inf. Softw. Technol.*, vol. 50, no. 5, pp. 390–405, Apr. 2008.

Efficient Quantile Estimation When Applying Stratified Sampling and Conditional Monte Carlo, With Applications to Nuclear Safety

Marvin K. Nakayama

Dept. of Computer Science
New Jersey Institute of Technology
Newark, New Jersey 07102
Email: marvin@njit.edu

***Abstract*—We describe how to estimate a quantile when applying a combination of stratified sampling and conditional Monte Carlo, which are variance-reduction techniques for Monte Carlo simulations. We establish a central limit theorem for the resulting quantile estimator. We further prove that for any fixed stratification allocation, the asymptotic variance of the quantile estimator with a combination of stratified sampling and conditional Monte Carlo is no greater than that for stratified sampling alone. We explain how the methods may be used to efficiently perform a safety analysis of a nuclear power plant.**

Keywords–Monte Carlo; Variance Reduction; Risk Analysis; Value-at-Risk.

I. Introduction

For a given constant $0 < p < 1$, the p-quantile of a continuous random variable Y is the constant ξ such that p (resp., $1 - p$) of the mass of the distribution of Y lies to the left (resp., right) of ξ. An example is the median, which is the 0.5-quantile.

In many application areas, risk is measured by a p-quantile, with p close to 0 or 1. For example, in finance, a quantile is known as a *value-at-risk*, and there are banking regulations [1] that specify required cash reserves in terms of a 0.99-quantile of a loss distribution. In safety analyses of nuclear power plants (NPPs), the U.S. Nuclear Regulatory Commission (NRC) [2] requires that for a hypothesized event, such as a loss-of-coolant accident, the 0.95-quantile of the peak cladding temperature must lie below a given threshold.

When the random variable Y is the output of a complicated stochastic model, analytically computing a quantile of Y typically presents intractable challenges, so Monte Carlo simulation is instead often applied [3]. Quantile estimation via *simple random sampling* (SRS) has been well-studied; see Sections 2.3–2.6 of [4]. But SRS can produce quantile estimators with large statistical error, motivating the use of *variance-reduction techniques* (VRTs) to obtain more statistically efficient estimators; see Chapter V of [5] and Chapter 4 of [6] for overviews of VRTs to estimate a mean. Quantile estimation has also employed VRTs, including importance sampling (IS) [7][8][9][10], control variates (CV) [11][12][10], Latin hypercube sampling (LHS) [13][14], stratified sampling (SS) [8][15][10], and conditional Monte Carlo (CMC) [16]. The use of VRTs can be especially important when each simulation run takes substantial time to execute, limiting the sample size that can be obtained.

In this paper, we consider applying a combination of stratified sampling and conditional Monte Carlo, which we denote by SS+CMC, to estimate a quantile. We give a central limit theorem for the SS+CMC quantile estimator. Moreover, we prove that the asymptotic variance of the SS+CMC quantile estimator is no larger than that of the corresponding quantile estimator with SS alone. Thus, SS+CMC is guaranteed to do at least as well as SS for quantile estimation.

Stratified sampling plays a fundamental role in the so-called *risk-informed safety-margin characterization* (RISMC) for nuclear power plants [17][18]. Developed by an international effort of the Nuclear Energy Agency, RISMC analyzes a hypothesized accident of an NPP through Monte Carlo simulation with a detailed computer code. The computer code takes as input a random vector with specified joint distribution, where the random inputs may specify the timing, size, and location of events during the postulated accident. The progression of the accident is also modeled through an *event tree*, consisting of intermediate events that determine how the accident evolves, e.g., whether or not a safety relief valve is stuck open. The intermediate events have known probabilities of occurring, and a path through the event tree partitions the sample space into *scenarios*. The probability of each scenario is known, but the distribution of the output variable Y for a scenario is not known, although we can generate observations from the distribution by simulation with the computer code. The framework fits exactly into applying stratified sampling by using the scenarios as strata. Further incorporating CMC leads to additional improvements in statistical efficiency. This is critical because each code run entails numerically solving differential equations, which is computationally expensive.

The rest of the paper unfolds as follows. Section II provides a list of acronyms used in the paper. Section III reviews how to apply SRS for quantile estimation. Section IV describes previous work on estimating a quantile via stratified sampling. In Section V, we combine SS with conditional Monte Carlo. We provide concluding remarks in Section VI. Throughout the paper, we give details on how the methods can be applied to perform a RISMC safety analysis of a nuclear power plant.

II. List of Acronyms

CDF	cumulative distribution function
CLT	central limit theorem
CMC	conditional Monte Carlo
CV	control variates

EDF	empirical distribution function
IS	importance sampling
LHS	Latin hypercube sampling
NPP	nuclear power plant
NRC	Nuclear Regulatory Commission
PCT	peak cladding temperature
RISMC	risk-informed safety-margin characterization
SBO	station blackout
SRS	simple random sampling
SS	stratified sampling
VRT	variance-reduction technique

III. Background and Simple Random Sampling

Let Y be a real-valued random variable with cumulative distribution function (CDF) F, i.e., $F(y) = P(Y \le y)$. For a fixed real number p with $0 < p < 1$, we define $\xi \equiv F^{-1}(p) \equiv \inf\{y : F(y) \ge p\}$ as the p-quantile of F (or equivalently, of Y); see Fig. 1. We assume that F is not analytically nor numerically tractable, but we have a computer code that can generate independent and identically distributed (i.i.d.) observations from F. The goal is to estimate ξ via Monte Carlo simulation. The typical approach, and the one we will follow, first estimates the CDF using simulation, and then inverts it to obtain a quantile estimator. Throughout the paper, we will use the following example to motivate and explain the different methods we consider.

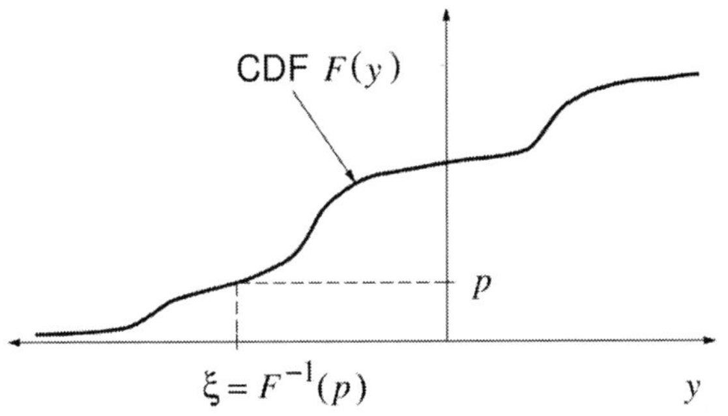

Figure 1. CDF F and p-quantile ξ.

Example 1. Consider a safety analysis of a nuclear power plant, in which a detailed computer code is used to model the progression of a hypothesized event, such as a loss-of-coolant accident or a station blackout. The computer code is run with random inputs having specified distributions, and the code outputs a *load* L representing the peak cladding temperature (PCT). The NRC [2] currently requires that the 0.95-quantile of L lies below a *fixed capacity* $C = 2200$°F. But the recent RISMC formulation [17][18] models the capacity C as a *random variable* to account for important changes in NPPs, e.g., aging components, extended operating licenses, and power uprates (i.e., operating an NPP at a higher level to produce more electricity). The papers [17][18] assume that the capacity C (in °F) has a triangular$(1800, 2200, 2600)$ distribution, and the computer code also generates an observation of C each time it is run. The RISMC problem requires that the probability that the load exceeds capacity is small, i.e., $P(L \ge C) \le \alpha$ for some specified small α, say, $\alpha = 0.05$. We can formulate the requirement in terms of a quantile by letting $Y = C - L$, and stipulating that the α-quantile of Y is nonnegative, i.e., $\xi \ge 0$.

We start by describing how to use simple random sampling to estimate ξ; see Section 2.3 of [4] for an overview. We first generate a sample of n i.i.d. observations $Y_1, Y_2, \ldots, Y_n$ from F. Then we estimate the CDF F via the *empirical distribution function* (EDF) $\hat{F}_n$ defined by

$$\hat{F}_n(y) = \frac{1}{n} \sum_{i=1}^{n} I(Y_i \le y),$$

where $I(\cdot)$ is the indicator function, which takes on the value 1 (resp., 0) when its argument is true (resp., false). Because the true p-quantile is $\xi = F^{-1}(p)$, this suggests estimating it by

$$\hat{\xi}_{\mathrm{SRS}}(n) = \hat{F}_n^{-1}(p), \tag{1}$$

which we call the *SRS p-quantile estimator*. The SRS quantile estimator can be refined through interpolation [13] or smoothing techniques [19], but for simplicity, we only consider $\hat{\xi}_{\mathrm{SRS}}(n)$.

We can equivalently compute $\hat{\xi}_{\mathrm{SRS}}(n)$ via *order statistics*. Let $Y_{(1)} \le Y_{(2)} \le \cdots \le Y_{(n)}$ be the order statistics of the sample $Y_1, Y_2, \ldots, Y_n$. Then $\hat{\xi}_{\mathrm{SRS}}(n) = Y_{(\lceil np \rceil)}$, where $\lceil \cdot \rceil$ is the ceiling function; see Fig. 2.

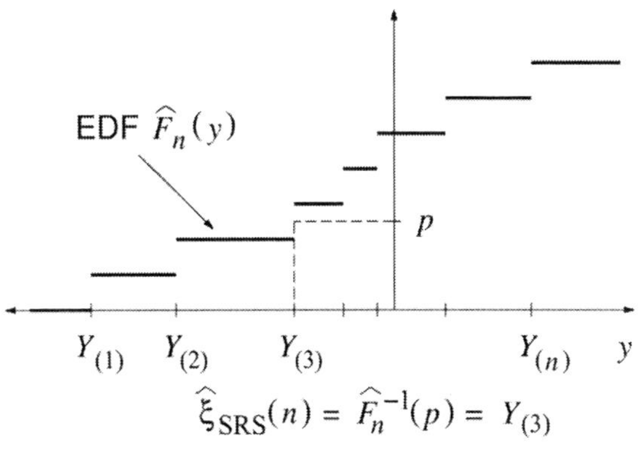

Figure 2. EDF $\hat{F}_n$ and the SRS p-quantile estimator $\hat{\xi}_{\mathrm{SRS}}(n)$.

The SRS quantile estimator $\hat{\xi}_{\mathrm{SRS}}(n)$ satisfies a central limit theorem (CLT), for which we give the following heuristic derivation. Let f denote the derivative (when it exists) of the CDF F, and suppose that $f(\xi) > 0$. For large n, we have that $\hat{F}_n \approx F$, so it is plausible that $\hat{\xi}_{\mathrm{SRS}}(n) = \hat{F}_n^{-1}(p) \approx F^{-1}(p) = \xi$. Consequently,

$$\begin{aligned} F(\xi) &\approx F(\hat{\xi}_{\mathrm{SRS}}(n)) \approx F(\xi) + f(\xi)[\hat{\xi}_{\mathrm{SRS}}(n) - \xi] \\ &\approx \hat{F}_n(\xi) + f(\xi)[\hat{\xi}_{\mathrm{SRS}}(n) - \xi], \end{aligned}$$

where the second step uses a Taylor approximation, and the last step follows because $\hat{F}_n \approx F$. Rearranging terms and scaling by $\sqrt{n}$ then yields

$$\sqrt{n}[\hat{\xi}_{\mathrm{SRS}}(n) - \xi] \approx \frac{\sqrt{n}}{f(\xi)}[F(\xi) - \hat{F}_n(\xi)]. \tag{2}$$

The ordinary CLT (e.g., Theorem 1.9.1A of [4]) ensures that

$$\sqrt{n}[F(\xi) - \hat{F}_n(\xi)] \Rightarrow N(0, \psi^2_{\text{SRS}}) \tag{3}$$

as $n \to \infty$, where $\Rightarrow$ denotes convergence in distribution (see Section 1.2.4 of [4]),

$$\psi^2_{\text{SRS}} = \text{Var}[I(Y \leq \xi)] = p(1-p), \tag{4}$$

and $N(a, b^2)$ represents a normal random variable with mean a and variance b^2. Finally, dividing the left side of (3) by $f(\xi)$ gives the right side of (2), suggesting that $\hat{\xi}_{\text{SRS}}(n)$ obeys the CLT

$$\sqrt{n}[\hat{\xi}_{\text{SRS}}(n) - \xi] \Rightarrow N(0, \kappa^2_{\text{SRS}}) \tag{5}$$

as $n \to \infty$, where

$$\kappa^2_{\text{SRS}} = \eta^2 \psi^2_{\text{SRS}} \tag{6}$$

is the *asymptotic variance* in the CLT, and

$$\eta = \frac{1}{f(\xi)} \tag{7}$$

is known as the *quantile density*. For a rigorous proof of the CLT in (5), see, e.g., p. 77 of [4].

IV. Stratified Sampling

Stratified sampling partitions the sample space into strata, and then allocates a fixed proportion of the overall sample size to each stratum. Section 4.3 of [6] provides an overview of SS to estimate a mean, and [15] considers quantile estimation combining SS with CV. Also, [8][10] combine SS with IS to estimate a quantile.

Suppose there is an auxiliary random variable Z, which could be generated in the process of generating the output variable Y, and we will use Z as a *stratification variable*. One possibility is $Z = Y$. Another is $Z = h(X)$ when the output variable $Y = v(X)$, where h and v are real-valued functions and X is some multidimensional random variable with known joint distribution; here, the function h may be more analytically tractable than v.

We partition the support R of Z into $R = \cup_{s=1}^t R_s$ for some fixed $t \geq 1$, with $R_s \cap R_{s'} = \emptyset$ for $s \neq s'$. Assume that we know the value of $\lambda = (\lambda_1, \lambda_2, \ldots, \lambda_t)$, where $\lambda_s = P(Z \in R_s)$ for $s = 1, 2, \ldots, t$. We call each R_s (or s) a *stratum*, which is also known as a *scenario*. Thus, for each $y \in \Re$, the CDF F of Y satisfies

$$F(y) = P(Y \leq y) = \sum_{s=1}^t P(Z \in R_s) P(Y \leq y | Z \in R_s)$$
$$= \sum_{s=1}^t \lambda_s F_{[s]}(y) \tag{8}$$

by the law of total probability, where

$$F_{[s]}(y) = P(Y \leq y | Z \in R_s) \tag{9}$$

is the conditional CDF of Y given $Z \in R_s$. In (8), the λ_s are known, but not the $F_{[s]}$, which we will estimate via Monte Carlo. Define a random variable $Y_{[s]} \sim F_{[s]}$, i.e., $Y_{[s]}$ has the conditional distribution of Y given $Z \in R_s$. We thus estimate $F_{[s]}$ by generating observations of $Y_{[s]}$, which we assume can be done for each stratum s, and using an empirical distribution.

Example 1 (cont). *Event trees* play an important role in a RISMC study, and Fig. 3 depicts an event tree from [17] of a hypothesized station blackout (SBO) at a nuclear power plant. The intermediate events E_1, E_2, E_3, which have known

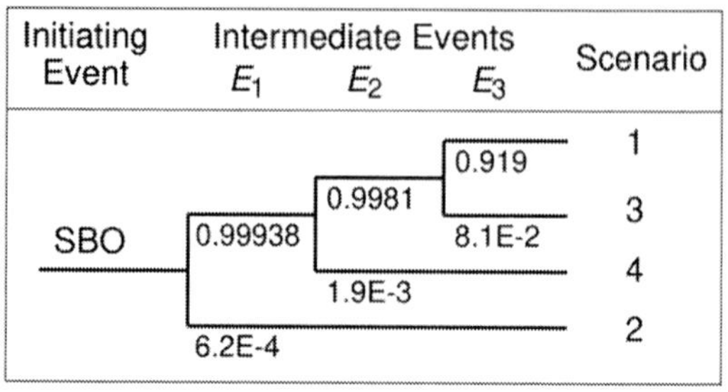

Figure 3. Event tree of a hypothesized station blackout at a nuclear power plant.

branching probabilities, as shown, determine how the accident progresses. For example, the lower (resp., upper) branch of E_2 represents the event that a safety relief valve is stuck open (resp., closes properly), which occurs with probability 0.0019 (resp., 0.9981). Paths from left to right through the event tree partition the state space into scenarios, and let Z denote a random chosen scenario. The support of Z is the set $R = \{1, 2, 3, 4\}$, and we can partition R into $t = 4$ strata $R_s = \{s\}$, $s = 1, 2, 3, 4$. We compute the probability λ_s of each scenario by multiplying the branching probabilities along its path, e.g., $\lambda_4 = 0.99938 \times 0.0019$. Each scenario s has a computer code that generates an observation of a load $L_{[s]}$ and a capacity $C_{[s]}$. Thus, we define the output $Y_{[s]} \sim F_{[s]}$ as $Y_{[s]} = C_{[s]} - L_{[s]}$ for scenario s.

To apply SS with an overall sample size n to estimate ξ, we allocate a fraction γ_s to stratum s, where $0 < \gamma_s < 1$ and $\sum_{s=1}^t \gamma_s = 1$. One possibility is to take $\gamma_s = \lambda_s$ for each s, but we also allow other allocations. Let $\gamma = (\gamma_1, \gamma_2, \ldots, \gamma_t)$, and $n_s = \gamma_s n$ be the sample size for stratum s, where we assume that n_s is integer-valued; if not, we set $n_s = \lfloor \gamma_s n \rfloor$, where $\lfloor \cdot \rfloor$ is the floor function. Let $Y_{[s],1}, Y_{[s],2}, \ldots, Y_{[s],n_s}$ be a sample of n_s i.i.d. observations of $Y_{[s]}$. Then, we can estimate $F_{[s]}$ via

$$\hat{F}_{[s],n,\gamma}(y) = \frac{1}{n_s} \sum_{i=1}^{n_s} I(Y_{[s],i} \leq y)$$

for each y. By (8), we then obtain the SS estimator $\tilde{F}_{n,\gamma}$ of the CDF F as

$$\tilde{F}_{n,\gamma}(y) = \sum_{s=1}^t \lambda_s \hat{F}_{[s],n,\gamma}(y).$$

The *SS quantile estimator* is then $\hat{\xi}_{\text{SS},\gamma}(n) = \tilde{F}_{n,\gamma}^{-1}(p)$. When there is only $t = 1$ stratum for SS with $\lambda_1 = \gamma_1 = 1$, the SS quantile estimator $\hat{\xi}_{\text{SS},\gamma}(n)$ reduces to the SRS quantile estimator $\hat{\xi}_{\text{SRS}}(n)$.

The SS quantile estimator $\hat{\xi}_{\text{SS},\gamma}(n)$ satisfies a CLT

$$\sqrt{n}[\hat{\xi}_{\text{SS},\gamma}(n) - \xi] \Rightarrow N(0, \kappa^2_{\text{SS},\gamma}) \tag{10}$$

as $n \to \infty$, where the asymptotic variance is

$$\kappa^2_{\text{SS},\gamma} = \eta^2 \psi^2_{\text{SS},\gamma}, \tag{11}$$

η is the quantile density in (7),

$$\psi^2_{\mathrm{SS},\gamma} = \sum_{s=1}^{t} \frac{\lambda_s^2}{\gamma_s} \zeta^2_{\mathrm{SS},[s]}, \tag{12}$$

$$\zeta^2_{\mathrm{SS},[s]} = \mathrm{Var}[I(Y_{[s]} \leq \xi)] = F_{[s]}(\xi)[1 - F_{[s]}(\xi)]; \tag{13}$$

see [15][8][10]. (The last two papers consider the combination of importance sampling and SS for quantile estimation, but SRS is a special case of IS, so they cover the setting of SS-alone.)

The SS asymptotic variance $\kappa^2_{\mathrm{SS},\gamma}$ in (11) is the product of two terms. The first, η^2, is the same as in the SRS asymptotic variance κ^2_{SRS} in (6), and the value of η^2 is unaffected by the particular Monte Carlo method employed to estimate ξ. But the second factor $\psi^2_{\mathrm{SS},\gamma}$ does depend on how ξ is estimated. The choice of the stratification allocation γ_s, $s = 1, 2, \ldots, t$, also affects the asymptotic variance $\kappa^2_{\mathrm{SS},\gamma}$ in the CLT (10) through $\psi^2_{\mathrm{SS},\gamma}$ in (12).

One possible choice for γ is the *proportional allocation*, in which $\gamma = \lambda$. As shown on p. 217 of [6], the proportional allocation for any choice of $t \geq 2$ strata $R_1, R_2, \ldots, R_t$, is guaranteed to reduce variance compared to SRS. To see why, let S be a discrete random variable such that $S = s$ if and only if $Z \in R_s$, $s = 1, 2, \ldots, t$, so $P(S = s) = \lambda_s$. (In Example 1 we have $S = Z$.) Thus, because $\zeta^2_{\mathrm{SS},[s]} = \mathrm{Var}[I(Y \leq \xi) | S = s]$, it follows that when $\gamma = \lambda$, we have that

$$\begin{aligned}\psi^2_{\mathrm{SS},\lambda} &= \sum_{s=1}^{t} \lambda_s \zeta^2_{\mathrm{SS},[s]} = E[\mathrm{Var}[I(Y \leq \xi)|S]] \\ &\leq E[\mathrm{Var}[I(Y \leq \xi)|S]] + \mathrm{Var}[E[I(Y \leq \xi)|S]] \\ &= \mathrm{Var}[I(Y \leq \xi)] = \psi^2_{\mathrm{SRS}},\end{aligned}$$

where the inequality holds because of the nonnegativity of a variance, the next step follows from a variance decomposition, and the last equality holds by (4). Hence, (6) and (11) imply the proportional allocation for SS leads to no larger asymptotic variance for the quantile estimator than SRS; also see [15].

For a given set of t strata $R_1, R_2, \ldots, R_t$, the optimal allocation γ that minimizes the asymptotic variance $\kappa^2_{\mathrm{SS},\gamma}$ of the SS quantile estimator is $\gamma^* = (\gamma_1^*, \gamma_2^*, \ldots, \gamma_t^*)$ with

$$\gamma_s^* = \frac{\lambda_s \zeta_{\mathrm{SS},[s]}}{\sum_{s'=1}^{t} \lambda_{s'} \zeta_{\mathrm{SS},[s']}}, \quad s = 1, 2, \ldots, t;$$

see, e.g., [15] and p. 217 of [6]. The allocation γ^* typically cannot be implemented directly in practice because $\zeta_{\mathrm{SS},[s]}$ and $F_{[s]}(\xi)$, $s = 1, 2, \ldots, t$, are unknown. The paper [15] provides an adaptive two-stage approach to asymptotically achieve the minimal SS asymptotic variance, where the first stage estimates the optimal γ^*, which is then used for the sampling in the second stage.

V. Combining SS With Conditional Monte Carlo

Conditional Monte Carlo, which is also known as the conditional-expectation method, reduces variance by analytically integrating out some of the variability; see Section V.4 of [5] for an overview of applying CMC to estimate a mean. Recall that for SS, we assumed that Z was a stratification variable with strata R_s for $s = 1, 2, \ldots, t$. Now, we assume that for each s, we have another auxiliary random variable $X_{[s]}$. We can then write the (conditional) CDF $F_{[s]}$ in (9) of $Y_{[s]}$ as

$$F_{[s]}(y) = P(Y_{[s]} \leq y) = E[P(Y_{[s]} \leq y | X_{[s]})] \tag{14}$$

by conditioning on $X_{[s]}$. Thus, assuming that

$$\begin{aligned} q_{[s]}(x, y) &\equiv P(Y_{[s]} \leq y | X_{[s]} = x) &(15)\\ &= E[I(Y_{[s]} \leq y) | X_{[s]} = x] &(16)\end{aligned}$$

can be computed, analytically or numerically, then (14) and (15) suggest that we can estimate $F_{[s]}(y)$ by averaging copies of $q_{[s]}(X_{[s]}, y)$, which we note is only a function of the conditioning variable $X_{[s]}$ and y as $Y_{[s]}$ has been integrated out through the conditional probability.

Example 1 (cont). The initial RISMC studies [17][18] have that the load $L_{[s]}$ and the capacity $C_{[s]}$ are independent random variables, which we will also assume. The independence assumption is reasonable from a modeling standpoint because the load is determined by how the hypothesized accident progresses, whereas the capacity depends on material properties of the components. Let $G_{[s]}$ denote the marginal CDF of the capacity $C_{[s]}$ in scenario s, i.e., $G_{[s]}(z) = P(C_{[s]} < z)$. As noted before, [17][18] assume that $G_{[s]}$ is a triangular distribution; the papers actually further assume that $G_{[s]}$ is the same for all scenarios s, but we do not require that here. For each scenario s, take the conditioning variable as $X_{[s]} = L_{[s]}$, and because the output is $Y_{[s]} = C_{[s]} - L_{[s]}$, we can write (15) as

$$\begin{aligned} q_{[s]}(x, y) &= P(C_{[s]} - L_{[s]} \leq y | L_{[s]} = x) \\ &= P(C_{[s]} \leq L_{[s]} + y | L_{[s]} = x) = G_{[s]}(x + y)\end{aligned}$$

by the independence of $L_{[s]}$ and $C_{[s]}$. In this case, $q_{[s]}(x, y)$ is only a function of the observed load $L_{[s]} = x$ and y because the random capacity $C_{[s]}$ has been integrated out, replaced by its marginal CDF $G_{[s]}$. When $G_{[s]}$ is a triangular CDF, as in [17][18], the function $q_{[s]}$ can be easily computed, as we previously required.

To implement the combination SS+CMC to estimate ξ, let $X_{[s],i}$, $i = 1, 2, \ldots, n_s$, be i.i.d. copies of $X_{[s]}$, where $n_s = \gamma_s n$ as before with SS allocation γ_s. Then, as suggested by (14) and (15), our CMC estimator of the CDF $F_{[s]}$ is given by

$$\tilde{F}_{[s],n,\gamma}(y) = \frac{1}{n_s} \sum_{i=1}^{n_s} q_{[s]}(X_{[s],i}, y).$$

Then, as in (8), we combine the $\tilde{F}_{[s],n}$, $s = 1, 2, \ldots, t$, to obtain the SS+CMC estimator of the CDF F of Y as

$$\tilde{F}_{n,\gamma}(y) = \sum_{s=1}^{t} \lambda_s \tilde{F}_{[s],n,\gamma}(y).$$

We finally obtain the SS+CMC p-quantile estimator as $\hat{\xi}_{\mathrm{SS+CMC},\gamma}(n) = \tilde{F}^{-1}_{n,\gamma}(p)$, which satisfies the following result.

Theorem 1. *If $f(\xi) > 0$, then*

$$\sqrt{n}[\hat{\xi}_{SS+CMC,\gamma}(n) - \xi] \Rightarrow N(0, \kappa^2_{SS+CMC,\gamma}) \tag{17}$$

as $n \to \infty$ for any SS allocation γ, where

$$\kappa^2_{SS+CMC,\gamma} = \eta^2 \psi^2_{SS+CMC,\gamma}, \quad (18)$$

$$\psi^2_{SS+CMC,\gamma} = \sum_{s=1}^{t} \frac{\lambda_s^2}{\gamma_s} \zeta^2_{SS+CMC,[s]}, \quad (19)$$

$$\zeta^2_{SS+CMC,[s]} = Var[q_{[s]}(X_{[s]}, \xi)], \quad (20)$$

and η is the quantile density in (7). Moreover, when SS and SS+CMC use the same stratification allocation γ, we have that

$$\kappa^2_{SS+CMC,\gamma} \le \kappa^2_{SS,\gamma}, \quad (21)$$

where $\kappa^2_{SS,\gamma}$ in (11) is the asymptotic variance in the CLT (10) for the SS quantile estimator.

Proof: By applying ideas from the proofs in [10], we can formally show that the SS+CMC quantile estimator satisfies a Bahadur representation [20], which then implies the CLT in (17). To establish (21), we apply a variance decomposition to (13) to obtain

$$\begin{aligned}\zeta^2_{SS,[s]} &= \mathrm{Var}[I(Y_{[s]} \le \xi)] \\ &= \mathrm{Var}[E[I(Y_{[s]} \le \xi)|X_{[s]}]] + E[\mathrm{Var}[I(Y_{[s]} \le \xi)|X_{[s]}]] \\ &\ge \mathrm{Var}[E[I(Y_{[s]} \le \xi)|X_{[s]}]] = \mathrm{Var}[q_{[s]}(X_{[s]}, \xi)] \\ &= \zeta^2_{SS+CMC,[s]}\end{aligned}$$

by (16) and (20). Thus, (19) and (12) imply that $\psi^2_{SS+CMC,\gamma} \le \psi^2_{SS,\gamma}$, from which (21) follows by (11) and (18). ■

VI. Conclusion and Future Work

We described how to estimate a quantile when applying a combination SS+CMC of stratified sampling and conditional Monte Carlo. We provided a central limit theorem for the SS+CMC quantile estimator. We further proved that the SS+CMC quantile estimator has asymptotic variance that is no greater than that of the SS quantile estimator, when both approaches use the same stratification allocation. We also explained how SS+CMC can be employed to efficiently perform a risk-informed safety-margin characterization of a nuclear power plant.

A direction for future work is to develop confidence intervals for ξ when applying SS+CMC. One approach is to use a finite difference to consistently estimate the asymptotic variance $\kappa^2_{SS+CMC,\gamma}$ in (18) in the CLT (17), as is done in [10] for other variance-reduction techniques. Another possibility applies *sectioning*, an approach that is closely related to batching (also known as subsampling) and was originally proposed in Section III.5a of [5] for SRS; [21] extends sectioning to IS and CV.

Acknowledgments

This work has been supported in part by the National Science Foundation under Grants No. CMMI-1200065, DMS-1331010, and CMMI-1537322. Any opinions, findings, and conclusions or recommendations expressed in this material are those of the author and do not necessarily reflect the views of the National Science Foundation.

References

[1] Basel Committee on Banking Supervision, "Basel II: International convergence of capital measurement and capital standards: a revised framework," tech. rep., Bank for International Settlements, Basel, Switzerland, 2004.

[2] U.S. Nuclear Regulatory Commission, "Acceptance criteria for emergency core cooling systems for light-water nuclear power reactors," Title 10, Code of Federal Regulations Section 50.46 (10CFR50.46), U.S. Nuclear Regulatory Commission, Washington, DC, 2010.

[3] L. J. Hong, Z. Hu, and G. Liu, "Monte Carlo methods for value-at-risk and conditional value-at-risk: A review," *ACM Trans. Mod. Comp. Sim.*, vol. 24, p. Article 22 (37 pages), 2014.

[4] R. J. Serfling, *Approximation Theorems of Mathematical Statistics*. New York: John Wiley and Sons, 1980.

[5] S. Asmussen and P. Glynn, *Stochastic Simulation: Algorithms and Analysis*. New York: Springer, 2007.

[6] P. Glasserman, *Monte Carlo Methods in Financial Engineering*. New York: Springer, 2004.

[7] P. W. Glynn, "Importance sampling for Monte Carlo estimation of quantiles," in *Mathematical Methods in Stochastic Simulation and Experimental Design: Proceedings of the 2nd St. Petersburg Workshop on Simulation*, pp. 180–185, Publishing House of St. Petersburg Univ., St. Petersburg, Russia, 1996.

[8] P. Glasserman, P. Heidelberger, and P. Shahabuddin, "Variance reduction techniques for estimating value-at-risk," *Management Science*, vol. 46, pp. 1349–1364, 2000.

[9] L. Sun and L. J. Hong, "Asymptotic representations for importance-sampling estimators of value-at-risk and conditional value-at-risk," *Operations Research Letters*, vol. 38, pp. 246–251, 2010.

[10] F. Chu and M. K. Nakayama, "Confidence intervals for quantiles when applying variance-reduction techniques," *ACM Transactions On Modeling and Computer Simulation*, vol. 36, pp. Article 7 (25 pages plus 12–page online–only appendix), 2012.

[11] J. C. Hsu and B. L. Nelson, "Control variates for quantile estimation," *Management Science*, vol. 36, pp. 835–851, 1990.

[12] T. C. Hesterberg and B. L. Nelson, "Control variates for probability and quantile estimation," *Management Science*, vol. 44, pp. 1295–1312, 1998.

[13] A. N. Avramidis and J. R. Wilson, "Correlation-induction techniques for estimating quantiles in simulation," *Operations Research*, vol. 46, pp. 574–591, 1998.

[14] H. Dong and M. K. Nakayama, "Constructing confidence intervals for a quantile using batching and sectioning when applying Latin hypercube sampling," in *Proceedings of the 2014 Winter Simulation Conference* (A. Tolk, S. D. Diallo, I. O. Ryzhov, L. Yilmaz, S. Buckley, and J. A. Miller, eds.), pp. 640–651, Institute of Electrical and Electronics Engineers, 2014.

[15] C. Cannamela, J. Garnier, and B. Iooss, "Controlled stratification for quantile estimation," *Annals of Applied Statistics*, vol. 2, no. 4, pp. 1554–1580, 2008.

[16] M. K. Nakayama, "Quantile estimation when applying conditional Monte Carlo," in *SIMULTECH 2014 Proceedings*, pp. 280–285, 2014.

[17] D. A. Dube, R. R. Sherry, J. R. Gabor, and S. M. Hess, "Application of risk informed safety margin characterization to extended power uprate analysis," *Reliability Engineering and System Safety*, vol. 129, pp. 19–28, 2014.

[18] R. R. Sherry, J. R. Gabor, and S. M. Hess, "Pilot application of risk informed safety margin characterization to a total loss of feedwater event," *Reliability Engineering and System Safety*, vol. 117, pp. 65–72, 2013.

[19] M. P. Wand and M. C. Jones, *Kernel Smoothing*. London: Chapman and Hall, 1995.

[20] R. R. Bahadur, "A note on quantiles in large samples," *Annals of Mathematical Statistics*, vol. 37, pp. 577–580, 1966.

[21] M. K. Nakayama, "Confidence intervals using sectioning for quantiles when applying variance-reduction techniques," *ACM Transactions on Modeling and Computer Simulation*, vol. 24, p. Article 19, 2014.

Computational Vibrational Spectroscopy of Hydrophilic Drug Irinotecan

Bojana Koteska, Anastas Mishev
Faculty of Computer Science and Engineering
Skopje, Macedonia
email:bojana.koteska@finki.ukim.mk
email:anastas.mishev@finki.ukim.mk

Ljupco Pejov
Institute of Chemistry
Faculty of Natural Sciences and Mathematics
Skopje, Macedonia
email:ljupcop@pmf.ukim.mk

Maja Simonoska Crcarevska, Jasmina Tonic Ribarska, Marija Glavas Dodov
Institute of Pharmaceutical Technology, Center of Pharmaceutical Nanotechnology
Faculty of Pharmacy
Skopje, Macedonia
email:msimonoska@ff.ukim.edu.mk
email:jato@ff.ukim.edu.mk
email:magl@ff.ukim.edu.mk

***Abstract*—A computational study of structural and vibrational spectroscopic properties of hydrophilic drug irinotecane was carried out. Both static and dynamical approaches to the problem have been implemented. In the static ones, vibrational spectra of the title system were computed within the double harmonic approximation, diagonalizing the mass-weighted Hessian matrices. These were calculated for the minima on AM1, PM3, PM6 and B3LYP/6-31G(*d,p*) potential energy surfaces. Within the dynamical approach, atom-centered density matrix propagation scheme was implemented at AM1 level of theory. From the computed molecular dynamics trajectories at series of temperatures (ranging from 10 to 300 K), velocity-velocity autocorrelation function was calculated and the vibrational density of states was sequentially obtained by Fourier transformation. Comparison with the experimental data revealed that the employed density functional level of theory exhibited remarkable performances. Of all semiempirical theoretical levels, PM6 was found to perform best, comparable to B3LYP/6-31G(*d,p*) when lower-frequency region is in question.**

Keywords-theoretical vibrational spectroscopy; high-performance computing; computational modelling; drugs; density functional theory.

I. INTRODUCTION

The classical paradigm in pharmaceutical sciences concerning drug delivery systems has changed significantly upon the advent of nanoscience and nanotechnology [1]. This emerging research area has opened quite new possibilities in achieving appropriate administration and targeting of pharmacologically active substances. Appropriate drug delivery is of essential importance in medical treatment of diseases, as it can affect most important aspects of drugs' pharmacological activity, such as its pharmacokinetics, distribution, metabolism, as well as the direct therapeutic effect itself.

The field of drug delivery along with the efforts directed towards controlled release have exhibited a significant evolution in the last few decades: starting from matrix-incorporated, hydrogel-encapsulated and finally nanoparticle-encaged drug paradigm. In the context of previous discussion, finding the most appropriate system for drug administration and targeted delivery is of essential importance in current research in pharmaceutical sciences [1].

In the last period, it has been shown that complex delivery systems built up when a hydrophilic drug is entrapped into a nanoparticle composed of hydrophobic polymer exhibit remarkably controllable properties.

Recently [2], the hydrophilic drug irinotecane (in the form of hydrochloride) has been incorporated into nanoparticles built up by poly lactic-co-glycolic acid copolymer (PLGA) and co-adsorbed PEO-PPO-PEO (polyethylene oxide – polypropylene – polyethylene oxide) copolymer. The formulations were designed by a planned experiment approach, and the nanoparticle-drug interaction upon encapsulation was studied by differential scanning calorimetry (DSC) and Fourier transform infrared (FTIR) spectroscopy. Subtle changes in the IR spectral properties of predominantly the co-polymer part of this complex system were used to derive conclusions about the drug incorporation into the nanoparticles and the nature of nanoparticle-drug interactions. Due to the inherent complexity and size of this multi-component system, to get an in-depth understanding of the mentioned phenomena, it is of essential importance to carry out theoretical simulations along with the spectroscopic experiments. In the course of the main aim to understand the vibrational spectroscopic, as well as energetic aspects of the nanoparticle-drug interactions, in the present study we carry out a computational study of vibrational dynamics of the hydrophilic drug irinotecane. We rely on the contemporary theoretical approaches to the mentioned issue, which are yet computationally feasible for studies of the drug molecule itself, as well as the drug incorporated into the nanoparticle cage.

In Section 2, we describe the two computational methodologies – static and dynamic. Section 3 presents the results from the implementation of both computational methods and a short discussion. In Section 4, we provide the conclusion.

II. Computational Details

To be able to get an insight into the changes of geometry and vibrational force field of the irinotecan molecule upon its inclusion in the PLGA/PEO-PPO-PEO nanoparticles, one has to explore in details the corresponding aspects in the case of free molecular system. For that purpose, we have adopted the following computational methodology. Two computational approaches were actually implemented in our current study: static and dynamic one.

Within the static approach, the geometry of neutral irinotecan molecule was first optimized using Schlegel's gradient optimization algorithm [3]. This was done at density functional level of theory (DFT), as well as using semiempirical AM1 [4], PM3 [5] and PM6 [6] Hamiltonians.

DFT calculations were performed employing a combination of Becke's three-parameter adiabatic connection exchange functional (B3 [7]) with the Lee-Yang-Parr correlation functional (LYP [8]); this computational approach is denoted by the (B3-LYP) acronym in the computational chemistry literature. The Pople-style basis set 6-31G(*d,p*) was used for orbital expansion in solving the Kohn-Sham equations, which was done in an iterative manner. This basis set is flexible enough to account for necessary structural specificity of the studied molecule; it contains a set of *d*-type polarization functions on "heavy" (*i.e.,* non-hydrogen) atoms and set of *p*-type polarization functions on all hydrogen atoms. It has been already demonstrated in numerous studies that DFT results exhibit a remarkably good convergence with the basis set size and double-zeta quality basis sets (as the one implemented in the current study) are often quite sufficient for a wide variety of purposes. For numerical integration in the course of DFT calculations, we have used the pruned (75,302) grid, consisting of 75 radial shells and 302 angular points per shell (leading to approximately 7000 points per atom). Subsequently to location of the stationary points on the molecular potential energy hypersurfaces (PESs), we have performed vibrational frequency calculations for the corresponding geometries. These computations were carried out within the harmonic approximation (diagonalizing the mass-weighted Hessian matrix). The aim of harmonic vibrational analysis was two-fold: to examine the character of the located stationary point on the corresponding PES, as well as to compute the intramolecular vibrational frequencies. The absence of imaginary frequencies (*i.e.,* negative eigenvalues of the Hessian matrices) served as an indication that a true (real) minimum has been located on the corresponding PES (instead of a saddle-point, *i.e.,* transition structure).

Within the dynamical approach, we have used the atom-centered density-matrix propagation scheme (ADMP) quantum molecular dynamics methodology [9]. A series of ADMP simulations were carried out for the irinotecan molecule, under constant temperature conditions, employing semiempirical AM1 method. The temperature was kept constant by velocity scaling at each step of the dynamical simulation. Dynamical simulations of the studied system were carried out at 10, 100, 200 and 300 K. Dynamical vibrational spectral characteristics of the title system were computed from the results of dynamical simulations as explained further in the paper. Each dynamical simulation consisted of 2000 steps, and the initial kinetic energy was set to 51297 microHartrees. The fictitious electronic mass was set to 0.1 amu; simulation step size was set at 0.2 fs.

All quantum mechanical calculations in the present study were carried out with the Gaussian09 series of codes [10].

III. Results and Discussion

In this Section, we provide the results from the static and dynamic approaches for finding the vibrational spectroscopy of hydrophilic drug irinotecan.

A. *Static approach*

The optimized geometry of irinotecan molecule at the B3LYP/6-31G(*d,p*) level of theory (*i.e.,* the minimum on the corresponding PES) is shown in Fig. 1.

Figure 1. Optimized geometry of irinotecan at B3LYP/6-31G(*d,p*) level of theory.

As can be seen from Fig. 1, the structure of neutral free irinotecan is characterized by an intramolecular O-H...O hydrogen bond. The H...O distance in this intramolecular contact is 2.0054 Å.

Semiempirical levels of theory give quite similar structures for free irinotecan molecule, the main predicted structural differences being in the conformationally flexible intramolecular degrees of freedom. The structures corresponding to real minima on the AM1, PM3 and PM6 PESs of free irinotecane molecule are shown in Fig. 2. Perhaps the most notable difference in the predicted minimum-energy structures at the implemented semiempirical levels of theory is the conformational flexibility of the OH group. As can be seen from Fig. 2, both AM1 and PM3 levels of theory predict minimum energy structures in which the proton from the OH group is far below the plane in which the C-C=O fragment (containing the carbonyl group oxygen atom) lies. Such arrangement does not conform to an arrangement of atoms characteristic for a hydrogen bond. Obviously, therefore, these two semiempirical levels of theory fail to predict the existence of intramolecular hydrogen bond of the O-H...O type.

Contrary to AM1 and PM3 levels, however, the results obtained with the PM6 semiempirical Hamiltonian are similar with this respect to the DFT results. We are therefore apt to conclude that the PM6 semiempirical level of theory should be regarded as more reliable that AM1 and PM3 when structural consequences of specific intramolecular interactions are in question. Concerning the conformational flexibility of the mostly-aliphatic part of the molecule (with sp^3 hybridized carbon atoms), on the other hand, all levels of theory predict different conformational landscape generated by rotations around the C-O and O-N bonds. However, due to the absence of specific intramolecular interactions in this part of the molecule, such flexibility is in fact expected. Moreover, in presence of relatively low barriers to intramolecular torsional motions (*i.e.*, hindered rotations) of the mentioned types, the actual molecular structure may be an average of the thermally-induced dynamically interchanging configurations.

a)

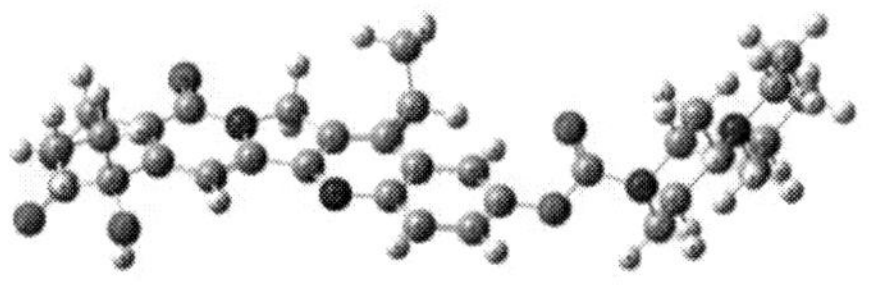

b)

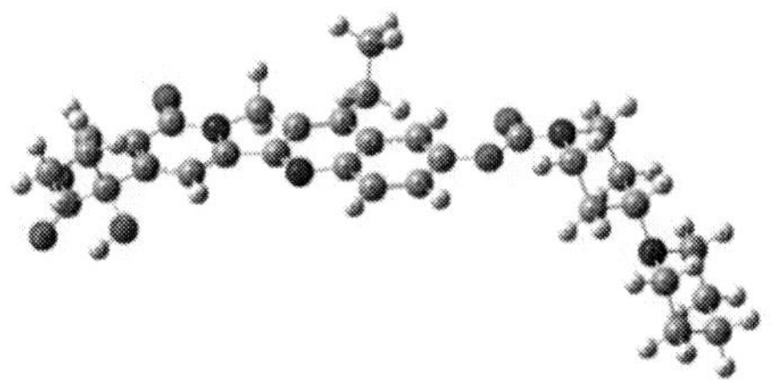

c)

Figure 2. Optimized geometry of irinotecan at semiempirical AM1 (a), PM3 (b) and PM6 (c) levels of theory.

The main aim of the present study is to establish a reliable computational methodology for prediction of vibrational spectroscopic properties of free irinotecan molecule, which could later be used for prediction of spectral changes as a consequence of inclusion of this molecule within PLGA/PEO-PPO-PEO nanoparticles, followed by subsequent adsorption on the inner, hydrophilic wall thereof.

We have therefore further computed the IR spectra of the title molecule at the employed theoretical levels, by diagonalization of mass-weighted Hessian matrix. Since this procedure essentially gives the harmonic vibrational frequencies, to account for the known systematic differences between experimental (anharmonic) values and the theoretical ones, as well as to account for the known systematic errors due to inherent assumptions to each of the employed theoretical models, we have scaled the initially computed vibrational wavenumbers with the established scaling factors [11]. The resulting IR spectra obtained by convoluting the delta-function spectra with Lorentzian functions with a half-width of 4 cm^{-1} are presented in Fig. 3.

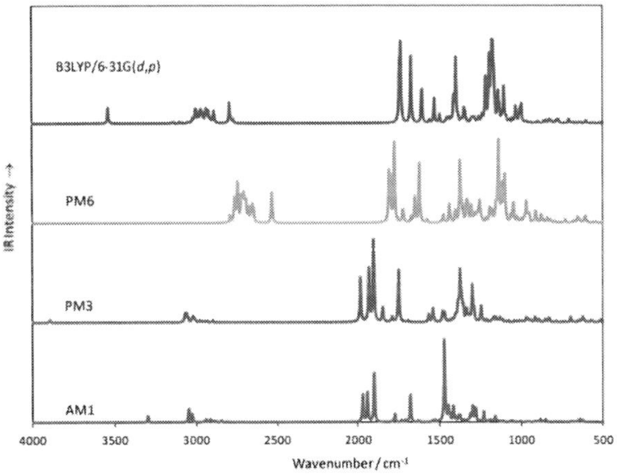

Figure 3. Theoretical IR spectra of free irinotecan in the MIR region computed at semiempirical AM1, PM3 and PM6, as well as at DFT B3LYP/6-31G(*d,p*) levels of theory.

As can be seen, the methods exhibit rather different performances when vibrational modes appearing above and around 3000 cm^{-1} are in question. However, as the experimental spectroscopic data have usually been collected in the region below 2500 (or 2000) cm^{-1}, this is the region that may be considered to be of primary importance in the context of present and also of upcoming studies of this molecular system, either isolated (gas-phase) or embedded within a condensed phase environment. When one considers the mentioned region, however, it becomes obvious even from visual inspection of the theoretical spectra that PM6 semiempirical approach performs rather comparably to the B3LYP/6-31G(*d,p*) "model chemistry", and thus is the method of choice for further studies of vibrational spectroscopic properties of irinotecan incorporated in PLGA/PEO-PPO-PEO nanoparticles. Such nanoparticles are rather large from computational viewpoint, with rather disordered structure viewed at molecular level. It is therefore of substantial interest to compare the performances of various computational methods with this respect. If the performances of a method with lower computational cost are comparable to those of a well-established computational approach (such as, e.g., B3LYP/6-31G(*d,p*)), it could be of high significance for prediction of changes of the vibrational spectroscopic signature of irinotecan molecule upon its incorporation (encapsulation)/inner wall adsorption within the mentioned nanoparticles serving as drug-carriers. Finally, we compare the experimental ATR FTIR spectra of irinotecan hydrochloride with the B3LYP/6-31G(*d*,*p*) theoretical one in Fig. 4.

As can be seen, the agreement between theory and experiment is remarkable.

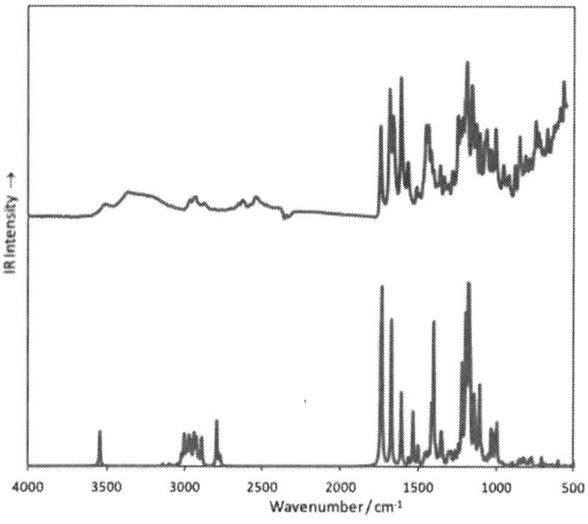

Figure 4. Theoretical IR spectrum of free irinotecan computed at DFT B3LYP/6-31G(*d*,*p*) level of theory (lower curve), together with the experimental ATR FTIR spectrum of irinotecan hydrochloride.

While the spectral region above and around 3000 cm^{-1} is dominated by bands due to OH and CH stretching vibrations, the lower frequency region (usually below 2000 cm^{-1}) is a bit more complex and contains the so-called molecular fingerprint region. This spectral region is dominated by bands due to carbonyl (C=O) stretching vibrations in two spatially distant segments of irinotecan molecule, appearing at about 1744, 1737 and 1674 cm^{-1} in the B3LYP/6-31G(*d*,*p*) theoretical spectrum (IR intensities are 349, 503 and 469 km mol^{-1} respectively). The carbonyl stretching band appearing at lowest frequencies is due to the carbonyl group attached to the heterocyclic aromatic ring. Therefore, partial delocalization of electronic density into the aromatic ring leads to lowering of the corresponding C=O bond force constant value and consequently lower C=O stretching vibration as compared to the other intramolecular carbonyl moieties which are not attached to aromatic systems. Note that the band appearing at about 1608 cm^{-1} (with IR intensity of about 204 km mol^{-1}) is due to a mode containing a significant contribution of the C=O stretching coordinate (along with the C=C stretching ones and in-plane CCH bending one – δ(CCH)). Yet another band due to the aromatic C=C stretching mode appearing at about 1532 cm^{-1} is of appreciable IR intensity (~175 km mol^{-1}). The lower-frequency part of the spectrum is dominated by intensive bands due to CH and CH_2 bending, scissoring and wagging modes appearing at 1414 and 1401 cm^{-1} (IR intensities being 151 and 447 km mol^{-1} respectively) and further at about 1220, 1198, 1180, 1170, 1143 and as low as about 1000 cm^{-1} (with IR intensities varying from 100 to about 400 km mol^{-1}).

B. Dynamical approach

In a realistic system relevant to the present study, the molecules are not static, and the processes take place at temperatures high above absolute zero. The static quantum chemical approximation is therefore insufficient to account for all dynamical features related to drug incorporation and adsorption on the inner walls of nanoparticles. In the present pilot study, we employ the atom centered density matrix propagation approach (ADMP) to study the dynamical aspects of the tackled problem. In comparison to other studies related to theoretical vibrational spectroscopy of drug molecules, one of the main aims of the present study is to make a thorough comparison of the performances of variety of static methodologies (based on exploration of molecular PES and subsequent computation of the second derivative matrix) with the dynamical ones, such as the presently implemented ADMP one. From a fundamental viewpoint, ADMP methodology is an extended Lagrangian approach to molecular dynamics, based on usage of Gaussian basis functions, in which it is the density matrix that is being propagated [9]. The system's extended Lagrangian is written in the form:

$$L = \frac{1}{2}Tr\left(V^T MV\right) + \frac{1}{2}\mu Tr(WW) - E(R,P) - Tr[\Lambda(PP-P)] \quad (1)$$

In (1), *M*, *R* and *V* represent the nuclear masses, positions and velocities; *P*, *W* and μ denote the density matrix, density matrix velocity and the fictitious mass for the electronic degrees of freedom, correspondingly. Λ, on the other hand, is a Lagrangian multiplier matrix, used to impose the constraints on the total number of electrons in the system and on the idempotency of the density matrix. The Euler-Lagrange equations for density matrix propagation may subsequently be obtained applying the principle of stationary action. These equations can be written in the form:

$$\mu \frac{d^2P}{dt^2} = -\left[\left.\frac{\partial E(R,P)}{\partial P}\right|_R + \Lambda P + P\Lambda - \Lambda\right] \quad (2)$$

$$M \frac{d^2R}{dt^2} = -\left.\frac{\partial E(R,P)}{\partial R}\right|_P \quad (3)$$

Equations (2) and (3) were integrated in the present study by the velocity Verlet algorithm, under the conditions described technically in the Computational details section. Since we deal with a finite-size molecular system, periodic boundary conditions have not been imposed in the present study.

From the computed ADMP molecular dynamics trajectory, we have subsequently computed the velocity-velocity autocorrelation function, defined as [12]:

$$C(t)=\frac{\langle \vec{v}(0)\cdot \vec{v}(t)\rangle}{\langle \vec{v}(0)\cdot \vec{v}(0)\rangle} \tag{4}$$

From the last quantity, the vibrational density of states power spectrum $\Phi(\omega)$ may be computed as a squared $F(\omega)$, where $F(\omega)$ is Fourier transform of $C(t)$:

$$F(\omega)=\frac{1}{\sqrt{2\pi}}\int_{-\infty}^{+\infty} C(t)\cdot \exp(i\omega t)dt \tag{5}$$

In the presently studied case, we have computed $F(\omega)$ by fast Fourier transformation technique (FFT), using Welch window function of the form:

$$w(n)=1-\left(\frac{n-\frac{1}{2}(N-1)}{\frac{1}{2}(N+1)}\right)^2 \tag{6}$$

where N denotes the total number of data points, and n is the n-th data point. Computations of Fourier transformation using the mentioned window function were carried out with the OriginPro 2016 program [13].

Throughout the quantum molecular dynamics simulation the total angular momentum of the system was conserved to an exceptionally high degree (< 10^{-11} $\hbar$) – Fig. 5, as a consequence of the usage of projection methods to remove the residual angular forces.

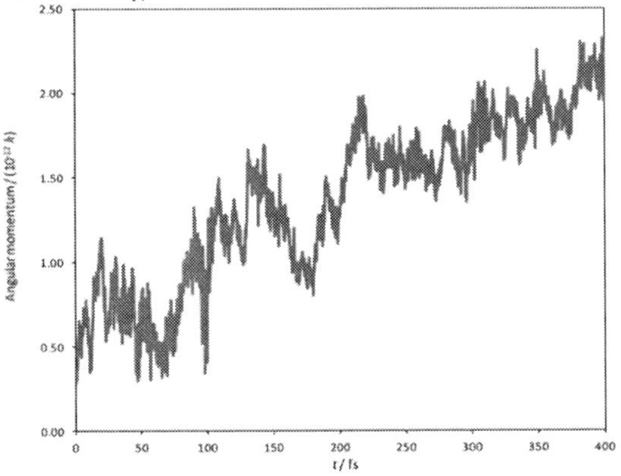

Figure 5. The total angular momentum of the studied system as a function of simulation time.

The RMS idempotency was conserved to better than 10^{-12} throughout all the simulation steps at all simulation temperatures. Fig. 6, Fig. 7 and Fig. 8 depict the time evolution of electronic kinetic energy (*i.e.*, density matrix kinetic energy), nuclear kinetic energy, as well as total energy in case of ADMP simulation of free irinotecane at temperature of 100 K.

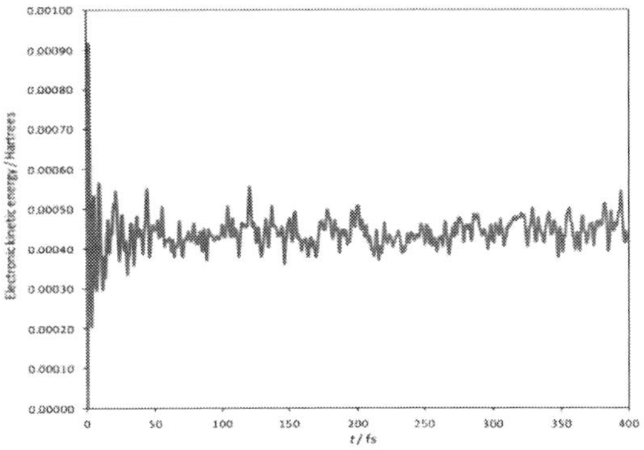

Figure 6. Time evolution of the electronic kinetic energy (density matrix kinetic energy).

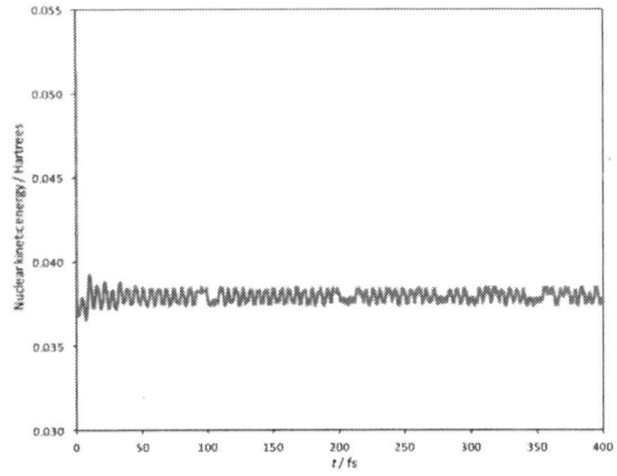

Figure 7. Time evolution of the nuclear kinetic energy.

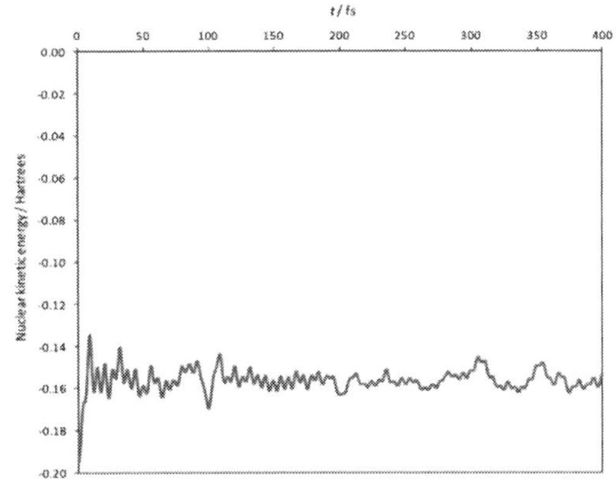

Figure 8. Time evolution of the total energy.

Fig. 9 and Fig. 10 depict the vibrational spectra of free irinotecane molecule computed by Fourier transformation of the velocity-velocity autocorrelation functions at 100 and 300 K.

As we are primarily interested in the appearance of the lower-frequency spectral region of the title molecular system, only the spectral range below 2000 cm^{-1} is presented in these figures.

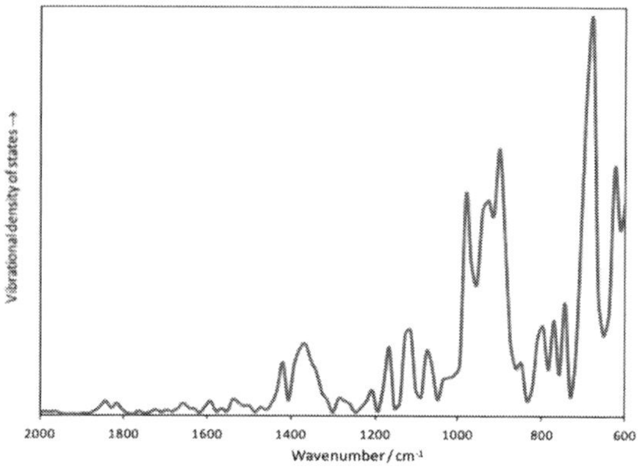

Figure 9. Vibrational spectrum of irinotecane computed from the ADMP simulation at 300 K.

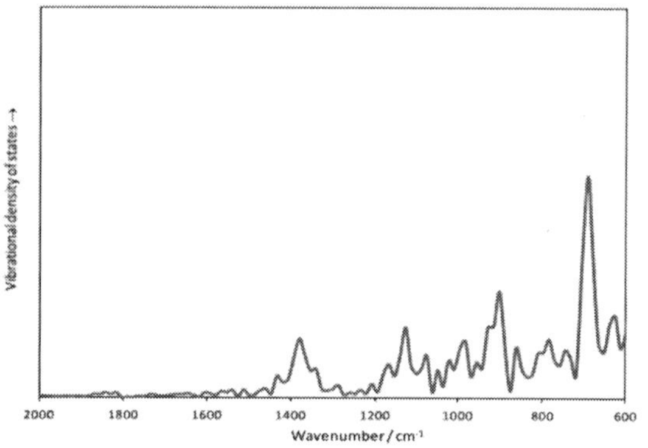

Figure 10. Vibrational spectrum of irinotecane computed from the ADMP simulation at 100 K.

IV. Conclusions and Directions For Further Work

In the present study, we have carried out a theoretical vibrational spectroscopic study of hydrophilic drug irinotecane. Semiempirical AM1, PM3 and PM6 levels of theory were applied, along with the B3LYP/6-31G(*d*,*p*) DFT level. The DFT level was found to reproduce remarkably well the experimental FTIR spectra of the title system. Of all semiempirical levels the PM6 approach was found to perform comparable to B3LYP. Vibrational spectra were also computed from ADMP molecular dynamics simulations at series of temperatures. The conclusions derived have established an appropriate choice of computational methodologies for upcoming studies of irinotecan molecule entrapped in PLGA/PEO-PPO-PEO nanoparticles. The approach elaborated in this paper has two main advantages. The first one concerns the computational cost of the prediction of IR spectral features of drug molecules (such as the presently studied one), which is significantly reduced by using appropriate semiempirical Hamiltonian, while the results remain of DFT-like (B3LYP) quality. The second advantage is the explicit account of dynamical features in computation of the vibrational spectra of the title system by using ADMP methodology.

Acknowledgment

This work was supported in part by the European Union's Horizon 2020 research and innovation programme, project Virtual Research Environment for Regional Interdisciplinary Collaboration in Southeast Europe and Eastern Mediterranean VI-SEEM [675121].

References

[1] M. W. Tibbitt, J. E. Dahlman, and R. Langer, "Emerging Frontiers in Drug Delivery", Journal of the American Chemical Society, vol. 138, 2016, pp. 704-717, doi: 10.1021/jacs.5b09974.

[2] M. Simonoska Crcarevska et al., "Definition of formulation design space, in vitro bioactivity and in vivo biodistribution for hydrophilic drug loaded PLGA/PEO–PPO–PEO nanoparticles using OFAT experiments", European Journal of Pharmaceutical Sciences, vol. 49, 2013, pp. 65-80, doi:10.1016/j.ejps.2013.02.004.

[3] H. B. Schlegel, "Optimization of equilibrium geometries and transition structures", Journal of Computational Chemistry, vol. 3, 1982, pp. 214-218, doi: 10.1002/jcc.540030212.

[4] M. J. S. Dewar and W. Thiel, "Ground states of molecules. 38. The MNDO method. Approximations and parameters", Journal of the American Chemical Society, vol. 99, 1977, pp. 4899-4907, doi: 10.1021/ja00457a004.

[5] J. J. P. Stewart, "Optimization of parameters for semiempirical methods I. Method", Journal of Computational Chemistry, vol. 10, 1989, pp. 209-220, doi: 10.1002/jcc.540100208.

[6] J. J. P. Stewart, "Optimization of parameters for semiempirical methods V: modification of NDDO approximations and application to 70 elements", Journal of Molecular Modeling, vol. 13, 2007, pp. 1173-1213, doi: 10.1007/s00894-007-0233-4.

[7] A. D. Becke, "Density-functional exchange-energy approximation with correct asymptotic behavior", Physical Review A, vol. 38, 1988, pp. 3098-3100, doi:http://dx.doi.org/10.1103/PhysRevA.38.3098.

[8] C. Lee, W. Yang, and R. G. Parr, "Development of the Colle-Salvetti correlation-energy formula into a functional of the electron density", Physical Review B, vol. 37, 1988, pp. 785-789, doi: 10.1103/PhysRevB.37.785.

[9] S. S. Iyengar et al., "Ab initio molecular dynamics: Propagating the density matrix with Gaussian orbitals. II. Generalizations based on mass-weighting, idempotency, energy conservation and choice of initial conditions", Journal of Chemical Physics, vol. 115, 2001, pp. 10291-10302, doi: 10.1063/1.1416876.

[10] M. J. Frisch et al., Gaussian 09, Revision A.1, Gaussian, Inc., Wallingford CT, 2009.

[11] National Institute of Standards and Technology, Precomputed Vibrational Scaling Factors, http://cccbdb.nist.gov/vibscalejust.asp (accessed 15.04.2016).

[12] D. A. McQuarrie, Statistical Mechanics, Harper&Row, New York, 1976.

[13] OriginPro 2016, 1991-2015 OriginLab Corporation. [Online]. Available from: http://www.originlab.com/2016 .

Numerical Simulation and Experimental Model-Validation for Fiber-Reinforced Plastics Under Impact Loading

Using the Example of Ultra-High Molecular Weight Polyethylene

Arash Ramezani and Hendrik Rothe
Chair of Measurement and Information Technology
University of the Federal Armed Forces
Hamburg, Germany
Email: ramezani@hsu-hh.de, rothe@hsu-hh.de

Abstract—**In the security sector, the partly insufficient safety of people and equipment due to failure of industrial components are ongoing problems that cause great concern. Since computers and software have spread into all fields of industry, extensive efforts are currently made in order to improve the safety by applying certain numerical solutions. This work presents a set of numerical simulations of ballistic tests which analyze the effects of composite armor plates. The goal is to improve fiber-reinforced plastics in order to be able to cope with current challenges. Of course, the maximization of security is the primary goal, but keeping down the costs is becoming increasingly important. This is why numerical simulations are more frequently applied than experimental tests which are thus being replaced gradually.**

Keywords-solver technologies; simulation models; fiber-reinforced plastics; optimization; armor systems.

I. INTRODUCTION

This work will focus on composite armor structures consisting of several layers of ultra-high molecular weight polyethylene (UHMW-PE), a promising ballistic armor material due to its high specific strength and stiffness. The goal is to evaluate the ballistic efficiency of UHMW-PE composite with numerical simulations, promoting an effective development process.

Due to the fact that all engineering simulation is based on geometry to represent the design, the target and all its components are simulated as CAD models. The work will also provide a brief overview of ballistic tests to offer some basic knowledge of the subject, serving as a basis for the comparison of the simulation results. Details of ballistic trials on composite armor systems are presented. Instead of running expensive trials, numerical simulations should identify vulnerabilities of structures. Contrary to the experimental result, numerical methods allow easy and comprehensive studying of all mechanical parameters. Modeling will also help to understand how the fiber-reinforced plastic armor schemes behave during impact and how the failure processes can be controlled to our advantage. By progressively changing the composition of several layers and the material thickness, the composite armor will be optimized. There is every reason to expect possible weight savings and a significant increase in protection, through the use of numerical techniques combined with a small number of physical experiments.

After a brief introduction and description of the different methods of space discretization in Section III, there is a short section on ballistic trials where the experimental set-up is depicted, followed by Section V describing the analysis with numerical simulations. The paper ends with a concluding paragraph in Section VI.

II. STATE-OF-THE-ART

The numerical modeling of composite materials under impact can be performed at a constituent level (i.e., explicit modeling of fibre and matrix elements, e.g., [1]), a meso-mechanical level (i.e., consolidated plies or fibre bundles, e.g., [2]), or macromechanically in which the composite laminate is represented as a continuum.

In [3–6] a non-linear orthotropic continuum material model was developed and implemented in a commercial hydrocode (i.e., ANSYS® AUTODYN®) for application with aramid and carbon fibre composites under hypervelocity impact. The non-linear orthotropic material model includes orthotropic coupling of the material volumetric and deviatoric responses, a non-linear equation of state (EoS), orthotropic hardening, combined stress failure criteria and orthotropic energy-based softening. For more detail refer to [7].

Lässig et al. [8] conducted extensive experimental characterization of Dyneema® HB26 UHMW-PE composite for application in the continuum non-linear orthotropic material model, and validated the derived material parameters through simulation of spherical projectile impacts at hypervelocity. The target geometry is homogenized. The projectile is an aluminum ball in simplified terms. However, homogenized target geometries with orthotropic material models are not able to reproduce different modes of failure. The results are valid for aluminum spherical-shaped projectiles in hypervelocity range only.

Nguyen et al. [9] evaluated and refined the modeling approach and material model parameter set developed in [8] for the simulation of impact events from 400 m/s to 6600 m/s. Across this velocity range the sensitivity of the numerical output is driven by different aspects of the material model, e.g., the strength model in the ballistic regime and the equation of state (EoS) in the hypervelocity regime. Here, the target geometry is divided into sub-laminates joined by bonded contacts breakable through a combined tensile and shear stress failure criterion.

The models mentioned above are valid for blunt FSP´s from a velocity range of 400 to 6600 m/s. They show considerable shortcomings in simulating pointed projectiles and thick HB26-composites.

This paper will present an optimal solution of this problem with an enhanced model for ultra-high molecular weight polyethylene under impact loading. For the first time, composite armor structures consisting of several layers of fiber-reinforced plastics are simulated for all the current military threats.

III. Methods of Space Discretization

To deal with problems involving the release of a large amount of energy over a very short period of time, e.g., explosions and impacts, there are three approaches: as the problems are highly non-linear and require information regarding material behavior at ultra-high loading rates which is generally not available, most of the work is experimental and thus may cause tremendous expenses. Analytical approaches are possible if the geometries involved are relatively simple and if the loading can be described through boundary conditions, initial conditions or a combination of the two. Numerical solutions are far more general in scope and remove any difficulties associated with geometry [10]. They apply an explicit method and use very small time steps for stable results.

For problems of dynamic fluid-structure interaction and impact, there typically is no single best numerical method which is applicable to all parts of a problem. Techniques to couple types of numerical solvers in a single simulation can allow the use of the most appropriate solver for each domain of the problem.

The goal of this paper is to evaluate a hydrocode, a computational tool for modeling the behavior of continuous media. In its purest sense, a hydrocode is a computer code for modeling fluid flow at all speeds [11]. For that reason a structure will be split into a number of small elements. The elements are connected through their nodes (see Fig. 1).

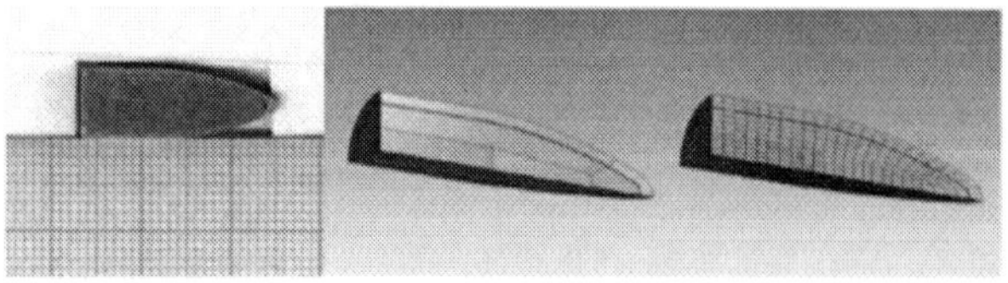

Figure 1. Example grid.

The behavior (deflection) of the simple elements is well-known and may be calculated and analyzed using simple equations called shape functions. By applying coupling conditions between the elements at their nodes, the overall stiffness of the structure may be built up and the deflection/distortion of any node – and subsequently of the whole structure – can be calculated approximately [12].

Using a CAD-neutral environment that supports bidirectional, direct, and associative interfaces with CAD systems, the geometry can be optimized successively [13]. Therefore, several runs are necessary: from modeling to calculation to the evaluation and subsequent improvement of the model (see Fig. 2).

Bullet-resistant materials are usually tested by using a gun to fire a projectile from a set distance into the material in a set pattern. Levels of protection (see Fig. 3) are based on the ability of the target to stop a specific type of projectile traveling at a specific speed.

IV. Ballistic Trials

Ballistics is an essential component for the evaluation of our results. Here, terminal ballistics is the most important sub-field. It describes the interaction of a projectile with its target. Terminal ballistics is relevant for both small and large caliber projectiles. The task is to analyze and evaluate the impact and its various modes of action. This will provide information on the effect of the projectile and the extinction risk.

Given that a projectile strikes a target, compressive waves propagate into both the projectile and the target. Relief waves propagate inward from the lateral free surfaces of the penetrator, cross at the centerline, and generate a high tensile stress. If the impact was normal, we would have a two-dimensional stress state. If the impact was oblique, bending stresses will be generated in the penetrator. When the compressive wave reached the free surface of the target, it would rebound as a tensile wave. The target may fracture at this point. The projectile may change direction if it perforates (usually towards the normal of the target surface).

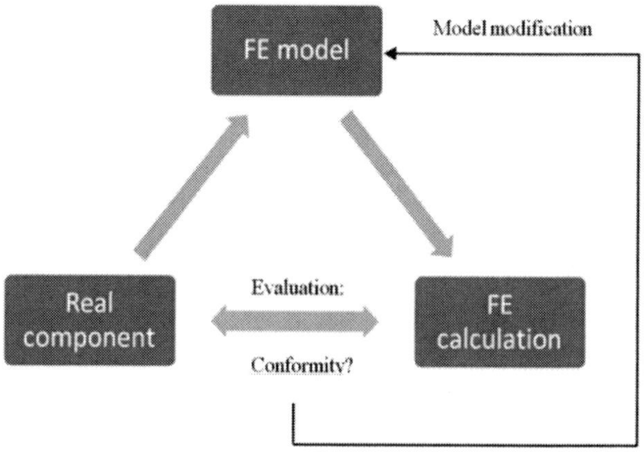

Figure 2. Basically iterative procedure of a FE analysis [12].

Because of the differences in target behavior based on the proximity of the distal surface, we must categorize targets into four broad groups. A semi-infinite target is one where there is no influence of distal boundary on penetration. A thick target is one in which the boundary influences penetration after the projectile is some distance into the target. An intermediate thickness target is a target where the boundaries exert influence throughout the impact. Finally, a thin target is one in which stress or deformation gradients are negligible throughout the thickness.

There are several methods by which a target will fail when subjected to an impact. The major variables are the target and penetrator material properties, the impact velocity, the projectile shape (especially the ogive), the geometry of the target supporting structure, and the dimensions of the projectile and target.

In order to develop a numerical model, a ballistic test program is necessary. The ballistic trials are thoroughly documented and analyzed – even fragments must be collected. They provide information about the used armor and the projectile behavior after fire, which must be consistent with the simulation results (see Fig. 4).

In order to create a data set for the numerical simulations, several experiments have to be performed. Ballistic tests are recorded with high-speed videos and analyzed afterwards. The experimental set-up is shown in Fig. 5. Testing was undertaken at an indoor ballistic testing facility. The target stand provides support behind the target on all four sides. Every ballistic test program includes several trials with different composites. The set-up has to remain unchanged.

	Protection Level \ Projectile	9 x 19 mm	.357 Magnum	.44 Rem. Mag.	5,56x45 mm	7,62x39 mm	7,62x51 mm	7,62x54 mm R	.50 BMG
		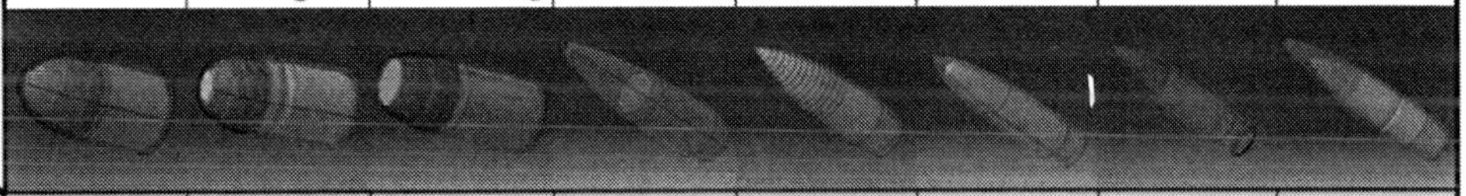							
1	PM 1 / VR 1								
2	PM 2 / VR 2	$v = 360 \pm 10 \frac{m}{s}$ $E = 518J$							
3	PM 3 / VR 3	$v = 415 \pm 10 \frac{m}{s}$ $E = 689J$							
4	PM 4 / VR 4		$v = 430 \pm 10 \frac{m}{s}$ $E = 943J$	$v = 440 \pm 10 \frac{m}{s}$ $E = 1510J$					
5	PM 5 / VR 5		$v = 580 \pm 10 \frac{m}{s}$ $E = 1194J$						
6	PM 6 / VR 6					$v = 720 \pm 10 \frac{m}{s}$ $E = 2074J$			
7	PM 7 / VR 7 *STANAG Level 1*				$v = 950 \pm 10 \frac{m}{s}$ $E = 1805J$		$v = 830 \pm 10 \frac{m}{s}$ $E = 3289J$		
8	PM 8 / VR 8 *STANAG Level 2*					$v = 740 \pm 10 \frac{m}{s}$ $E = 2108J$			
9	PM 9 / VR 9						$v = 820 \pm 10 \frac{m}{s}$ $E = 3261J$		
10	PM 10 / VR 10 *STANAG Level 3*							$v = 860 \pm 10 \frac{m}{s}$ $E = 3846J$	
11	PM 11 *STANAG Level 3*						$v = 930 \pm 10 \frac{m}{s}$ $E = 3633J$		
12	PM 12						$v = 810 \pm 10 \frac{m}{s}$ $E = 4166J$		
13	PM 13								$v = 930 \pm 10 \frac{m}{s}$ $E = 18595J$

Figure 3. The APR 2006 resistance classification and related CAD models [14].

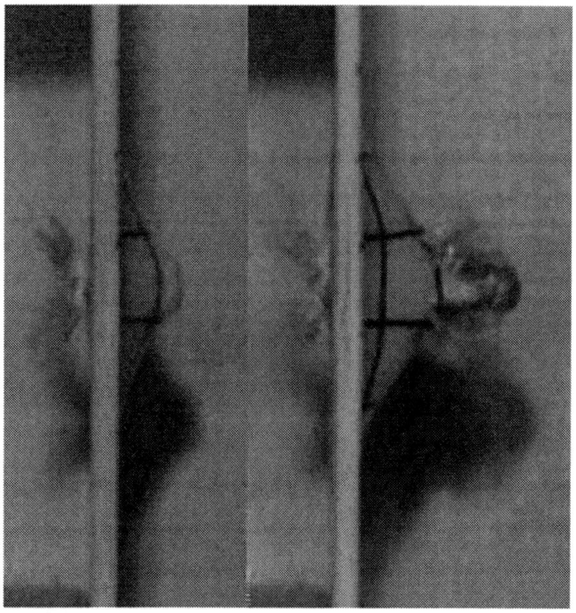

Figure 4. Ballistic tests and the analysis of fragments.

The camera system is a PHANTOM v1611 that enables fast image rates up to 646,000 frames per second (fps) at full resolution of 1280 x 800 pixels. The use of a polarizer and a neutral density filter is advisable, so that waves of some polarizations can be blocked while the light of a specific polarization can be passed.

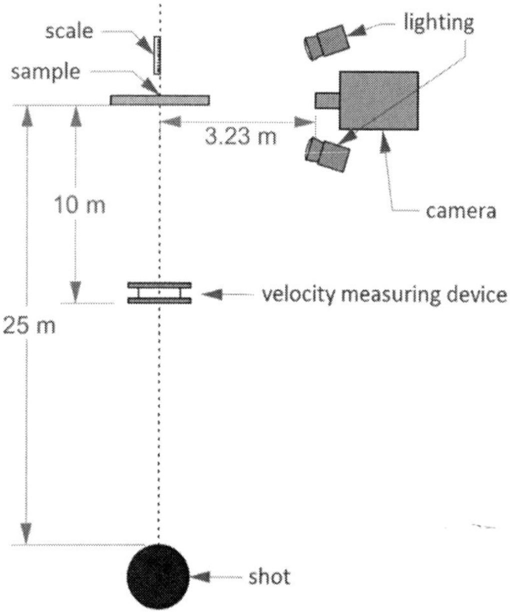

Figure 5. Experimental set-up.

Several targets of different laminate configurations were tested to assess the ballistic limit (V_{50}). The ballistic limit is considered the velocity required for a particular projectile to reliably (at least 50% of the time) penetrate a particular piece of material [15]. After the impact, the projectile is examined regarding any kind of change it might have undergone.

V. Numerical Simulation

The ballistic tests are followed by computational modeling of the experimental set-up. Then, the experiment is reproduced using numerical simulations. Fig. 1 shows a cross-section of the projectile and a CAD model. The geometry and observed response of the laminate to ballistic impact is approximately symmetric to the axis through the bullet impact point.

Numerical simulation of modern armor structures requires the selection of appropriate material models for the constituent materials and the derivation of suitable material model input data. The laminate system studied here is an ultra-high molecular weight polyethylene composite. Lead and copper are also required for the projectiles.

The projectile was divided into different parts - the jacket and the base - which have different properties and even different meshes. These elements have quadratic shape functions and nodes between the element edges. In this way, the computational accuracy, as well as the quality of curved model shapes increases. Using the same mesh density, the application of parabolic elements leads to a higher accuracy compared to linear elements (1st order elements).

A. *Modelling*

In [8], numerical simulations of 15 kg/m^2 Dyneema® HB26 panels impacted by 6 mm diameter aluminum spheres between 2052 m/s to 6591 m/s were shown to provide very good agreement with experimental measurements of the panel ballistic limit and residual velocities, see Fig. 6. The modelling approach and material parameter set from [8] were applied to simulate impact experiments at velocities in the ballistic regime (here considered as < 1000 m/s). In Fig. 6 the results of modelling impact of 20 mm fragment simulating projectiles (FSPs) against 10 mm thick Dyneema® HB26 are shown. The model shows a significant under prediction of the ballistic limit, 236 m/s compared to 394 m/s.

B. *Simulation Results*

Relatively newer numerical discretization methods, such as Smoothed Particle Hydrodynamics (SPH), have been proposed that rectifies the issue of grid entanglement. The SPH method has shown good agreement with high velocity impact of metallic targets, better predictions of crack propagation in ceramics and fragmentation of composites under hypervelocity impact (HVI) compared to grid-based Lagrange and Euler methods. Although promising, SPH suffers from consistency and stability issues that lead to lower accuracy and instabilities under tensile perturbation. The latter makes it unsuitable for use with UHMW-PE composite under ballistic impact, because this material derives most of its resistance to penetration when it is loaded in tension. For these types of problems, the grid-based Lagrangian formulation still remains the most feasible for modeling UHMW-PE composite.

3D numerical simulations were performed of the full target and projectile, where both were meshed using 8-node hexahedral elements. The projectile was meshed with 9 elements across the diameter. The target is composed of sub-laminates that are one element thick, separated by a small gap to satisfy the master-slave contact algorithm (external gap in AUTODYN®) and bonded together as previously discussed. The mesh size of the target is approximately equal to the projectile at the impact site. The mesh was then graded towards the edge, increasing in coarseness to reduce the computational load of the model. Since UHMW-PE composite has a very low coefficient of friction, force fit clamping provides little restraint.

High speed video of ballistic impact tests typical showed the action of loosening and moving clamps upon impact. As such no boundary conditions were imposed on the target. The FSP material was modelled as Steel S-7 from the AUTODYN® library described using a linear EoS and the Johnson-Cook strength model [16]. The aluminum sphere was modelled using AL1100-O from the AUTODYN® library that uses a shock EoS and the Steinburg Guinan strength model [17]. The master-slave contact algorithm was used to detect contact between the target and projectile.

The sub-laminate model with shock EoS was applied to the aluminum sphere hypervelocity impact series and 20 mm FSP ballistic impact series presented in Fig. 6, the results of which are shown in Fig. 7. The sub-laminate model is shown to provide a significant improvement in predicting the experimental V_{50} of 394 m/s for the FSP ballistic impacts (377 m/s) compared to the monolithic model (236 m/s).

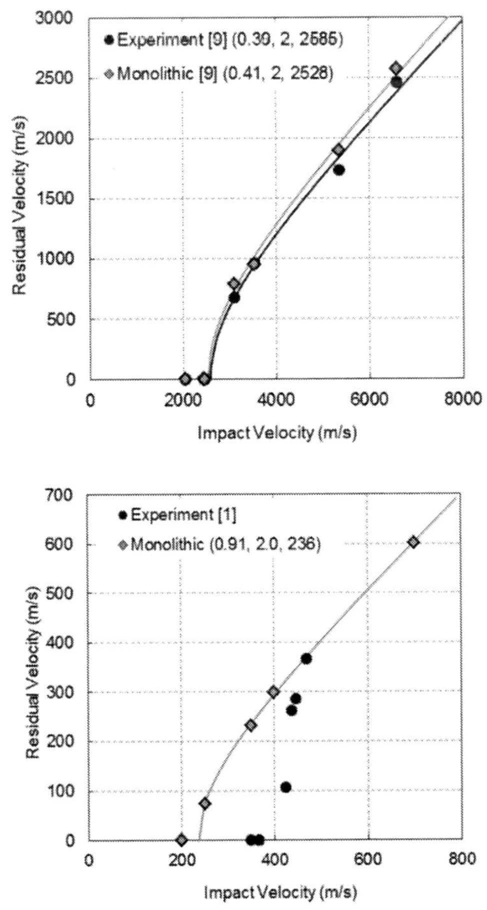

Figure 6. Experimental and numerical impact residual velocity results for impact of 6 mm diameter aluminum spheres against 15 kg/m2 Dyneema® HB26 at normal incidence (left) and impact of 20 mm fragment simulating projectiles against 10 mm thick Dyneema® HB26 at normal incidence (right). Lambert-Jonas parameters (a, p, V_{bl}) are provided in the legend.

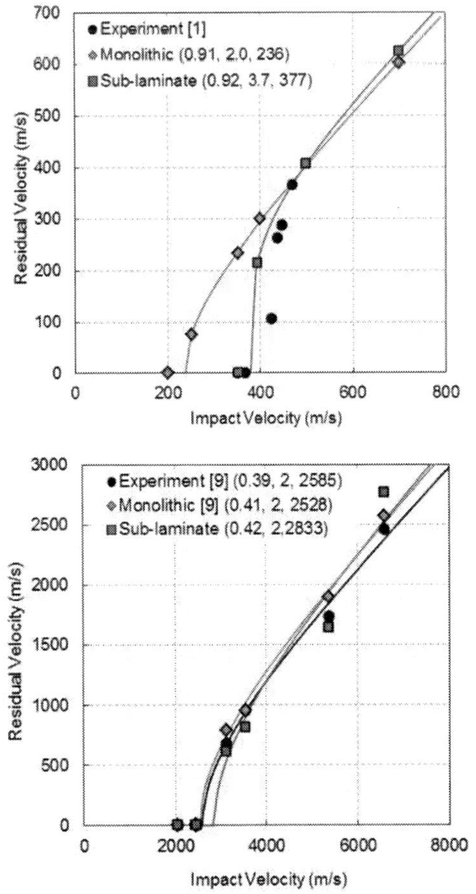

Figure 7. Comparison of the experimental results with the two numerical models for impact of 20 mm fragment simulating projectiles against 10 mm thick Dyneema HB26® at normal incidence (left) , and impact of 6 mm diameter aluminium spheres against 15 kg/m2 Dyneema® HB26 at normal incidence (right). Lambert-Jonas parameters (a, p, Vbl) are provided in the legend.

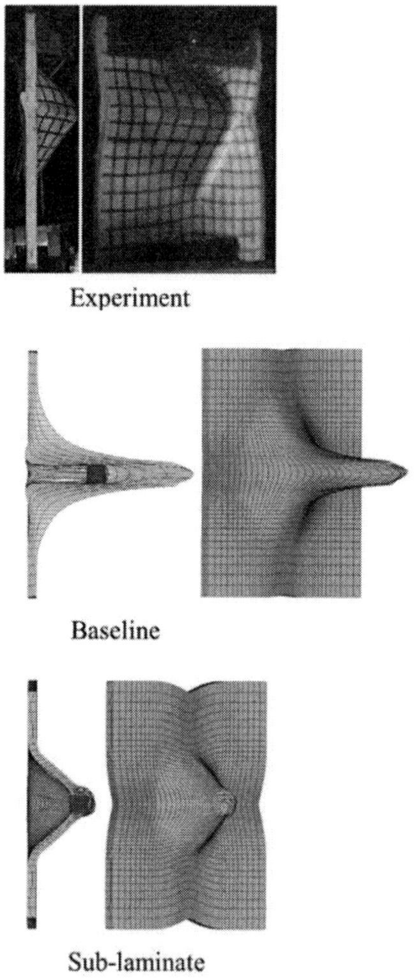

Figure 8. Bulge of a 10 mm target impact by a 20 mm FSP at 365 m/s (experiment) and 350 m/s (simulations), 400 µs after the initial impact.

The ballistic limit and residual velocity predicted with the sub-laminate model for the hypervelocity impact case are shown to be comparable with the original monolithic model. For conditions closer to the ballistic limit, the sub-laminate model is shown to predict increased target resistance (i.e., lower residual velocity). For higher overmatch conditions there is some small variance between the two approaches.

In Fig. 8, a qualitative assessment of the bulge formation is made for the 10 mm panel impacted at 365 m/s (i.e., below the V_{50}) by a 20 mm FSP. Prediction of bulge development is important as it is characteristic of the material wave speed and is also a key measure in defence applications, particularly in personnel protection (i.e., vests and helmets). The sub-laminate model is shown to reproduce the characteristic pyramid bulge shape and drawing of material from the lateral edge. In comparison, the bulge prediction of the baseline model is poor, showing a conical shape with the projectile significantly behind the apex. In the baseline model penetration occurs through premature through-thickness shear failure around the projectile rather than in-plane tension (membrane) which would allow the formation of a pyramidal bulge as the composite is carried along with the projectile. Furthermore, in the baseline model the extremely small through thickness tensile strength (1.07 MPa) in the bulk material leads to early spallation/delamination of the back face. This allows the material on the target back face to fail and be accelerated ahead of the projectile. In the sub-laminate model, these two artifacts are addressed, and so a more representative bulge is formed.

C. *Further Validations*

The material model developed in [8] and [9] has some shortcomings regarding the simulation of handgun projectiles (see Fig. 9). The ballistic limit was significantly under predicted. Evaluation of the result suggests that the failure mechanisms, which drive performance in the rear section of the target panel (i.e., membrane tension) were not adequately reproduced, suggesting an under-estimate of the material in-plane tensile performance.

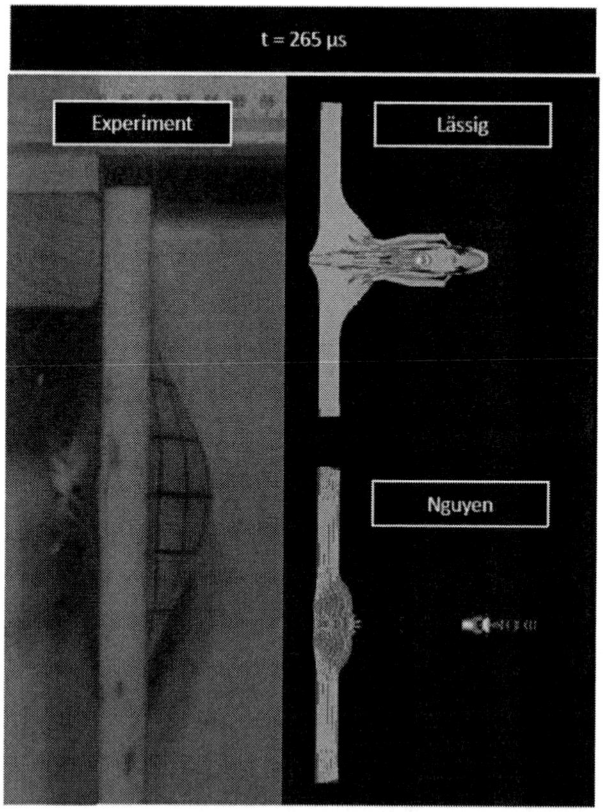

Figure 9. Comparing experimantal results with the previous simulation models of Lässig [8] and Nguyen [9], 265 µs after impact (grey = plastic deformation, green = elastic deformation, orange = material failure); projectile velocity: 674 m/s; target thickness: 16.2 mm (60 layers of HB26).

A major difficulty in the numerical simulation of fibre composites under impact is the detection of failure processes between fibre and matrix elements as well as between the individual laminate layers (delamination). One promising approach is the use of "artificial" inhomogeneities on the macroscale. Here, an alternative simulation model has been developed to overcome these difficulties. Using sub-laminates and inhomogeneities on the macroscale, the model does not match the real microstructure, but allows a more realistic description of the failure processes mentioned above.

Approaches based on the continuum or macroscale present a more practical alternative to solve typical engineering problems. However the complexity of the constitutive equations and characterization tests necessary to describe an anisotropic material at a macro or continuum level increases significantly.

When considering the micromechanical properties of the orthotropic yield surface with a non-linear hardening description, a non-linear shock equation of state, and a three-dimensional failure criterion supplemented by a linear orthotropic softening description should be taken into account. It is important to consider all relevant mechanisms that occur during ballistic impact, as the quality of the numerical prediction capability strongly depends on a physically accurate description of contributing energy dissipation mechanisms. Therefore, a combination of ballistic experiments and numerical simulations is required. Predictive numerical tools can be extremely useful for enhancing our understanding of ballistic impact events. Models that are able to capture the key mechanical and thermodynamic processes can significantly improve our understanding of the phenomena by allowing time-resolved investigations of virtually every aspect of the impact event. Such high fidelity is immensely difficult, prohibitively expensive or near impossible to achieve with existing experimental measurement techniques.

The thermodynamic response of a material and its ability to carry tensile and shear loads (strength) is typically treated separately within hydrocodes such that the stress tensor can be decomposed into volumetric and deviatoric components. Since the mechanical properties of fibre-reinforced composites are anisotropic (at least at the meso- and macroscale level), the deviatoric and hydrostatic components are coupled. That is deviatoric strains will produce a volumetric dilation and hydrostatic pressure leads to non-uniform strains in the three principal directions.

The strength and failure model was investigated by modeling single elements under normal and shear stresses. It was found that under through-thickness shear stress, the element would fail prematurely below the specified through-thickness shear failure stress. It was found that if the through-thickness tensile strength was increased, failure in through-thickness shear was delayed. This evaluation study shows the importance of the strength, failure and erosion models for predicting performance in the ballistic regime.

Previous material models for fiber-reinforced plastics were adjusted and the concept has been extended to different calibers and projectile velocities. Composite armor plates between 5.5 and 16.2 mm were tested in several ballistic trials and high-speed videos were used to analyze the characteristics of the projectile – before and after the impact.

The simulation results with the modified model are shown in Fig. 10. The deformation of the projectile, e.g., 7.62×39 mm, is in good agreement with the experimental observation. Both delamination and fragmentation can be seen in the numerical simulation.

Compared to the homogeneous continuum model, fractures can be detected easily. Subsequently, the results of experiment and simulation in the case of perforation were compared with reference to the projectile residual velocity. Here, only minor differences were observed.

It should be noted that an explicit modeling of the individual fibres is not an option, since the computational effort would go beyond the scope of modern server systems (see Fig. 11).

VI. Conclusions

This work demonstrated how a small number of well-defined experiments can be used to develop, calibrate, and validate solver technologies used for simulating the impact of projectiles on complex armor systems and composite laminate structures.

Existing material models were optimized to reproduce ballistic tests. High-speed videos were used to analyze the characteristics of the projectile – before and after the impact. The simulation results demonstrate the successful use of the coupled multi-solver approach and new modeling techniques. The high level of correlation between the numerical results and the available experimental or observed data demonstrates that the coupled multi-solver approach is an accurate and effective analysis method.

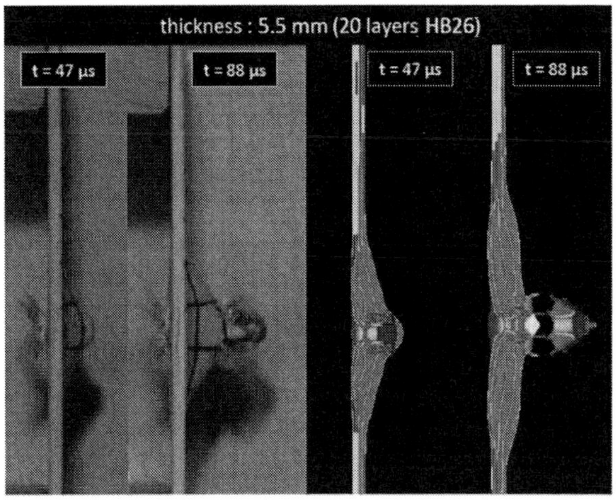

Figure 10. Effect of a 5.5 mm target impact by a 7.62×39 mm bullet at 686 m/s, 47 µs and 88 µs after the initial impact.

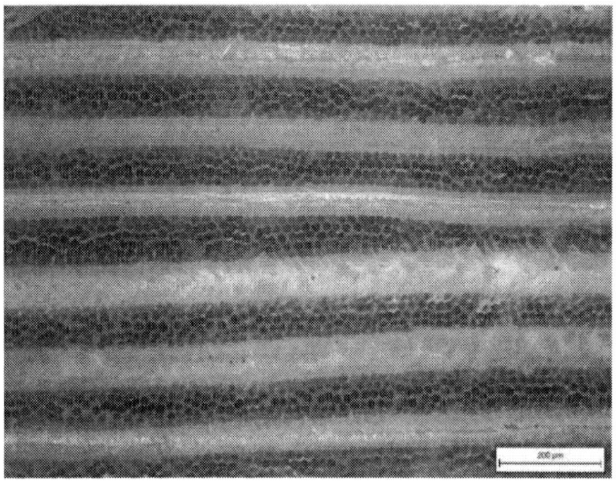

Figure 11. Cross section of a Dyneema® HB26 panel.

A non-linear orthotropic continuum model was evaluated for UHMW-PE composite across a wide range of impact velocities. Although previously found to provide accurate results for hypervelocity impact of aluminum spheres, the existing model and dataset revealed a significant underestimation of the composite performance under impact conditions driven by through-thickness shear performance (ballistic impact of fragment simulating projectiles). The model was found to exhibit premature through thickness shear failure as a result of directional coupling in the modified Hashin-Tsai failure criterion and the large discrepancy between through-thickness tensile and shear strength of UHME-PE composite. As a result, premature damage and failure was initiated in the through-thickness shear direction leading to decreased ballistic performance. By de-coupling through-thickness tensile failure from the failure criteria and discretizing the laminate into a nominal number of kinematically joined sub-laminates through the thickness, progresses in modelling the ballistic response of the panels was improved.

New concepts and models can be developed and easily tested with the help of modern hydrocodes. The initial design approach of the units and systems has to be as safe and optimal as possible. Therefore, most design concepts are analyzed on the computer.

FEM-based simulations are well-suited for this purpose. Here, a numerical model has been developed, which is capable of predicting the ballistic performance of UHMW-PE armor systems. Thus, estimates based on experience are being more and more replaced by software.

The gained experience is of prime importance for the development of modern armor. By applying the numerical model a large number of potential armor schemes can be evaluated and the understanding of the interaction between laminate components under ballistic impact can be improved.

The most important steps during an FE analysis are the evaluation and interpretation of the outcomes followed by suitable modifications of the model. For that reason, ballistic trials are necessary to validate the simulation results. They are designed to obtain information about

- the velocity and trajectory of the projectile prior to impact,
- changes in configuration of projectile and target due to impact,
- masses, velocities, and trajectories of fragments generated by the impact process.

Ballistic trials can be used as the basis of an iterative optimization process. Numerical simulations are a valuable adjunct to the study of the behavior of metals subjected to high-velocity impact or intense impulsive loading. The combined use of computations, experiments and high-strain-rate material characterization has, in many cases, supplemented the data achievable by experiments alone at considerable savings in both cost and engineering man-hours.

REFERENCES

[1] D. B. Segala and P. V. Cavallaro, "Numerical investigation of energy absorption mechanisms in unidirectional composites subjected to dynamic loading events," in Computational Materials Science 81, pp. 303–312, 2014.

[2] S. Chocron et al., "Modeling unidirectional composites by bundling fibers into strips with experimental determination of shear and compression properties at high pressures," in Composites Science and Technology 101, pp. 32–40, 2014.

[3] C. J. Hayhurst, S. J. Hiermaier, R. A. Clegg, W. Riedel, and M. Lambert, "Development of material models for nextel and kevlar-expoxy for high pressures and strain rates," in International Journal of Impact Engineering 23, pp. 365–376, 1999.

[4] R. A. Clegg, D. M. White, W. Riedel, and W. Harwick, "Hypervelocity impact damage prediction in composites: Part I—material model and characterisation," in International Journal of Impact Engineering 33, pp. 190–200, 2006.

[5] W. Riedel, H. Nahme, D. M. White, and R. A. Clegg, "Hypervelocity impact damage prediction in composites: Part II—experimental investigations and simulations," in International Journal of Impact Engineering 33, pp. 670–80, 2006.

[6] M. Wicklein, S. Ryan, D. M. White, and R. A. Clegg, "Hypervelocity impact on CFRP: Testing, material modelling, and numerical simulation," in International Journal of Impact Engineering 35, pp.1861–1869, 2008.

[7] ANSYS. *AUTODYN Composite Modelling Release 15.0.* [Online]. Available from: http://ansys.com/ 2016.07.08.

[8] T. Lässig et al., "A non-linear orthotropic hydrocode model for ultra-high molecular weight polyethylene in impact simulations," in International Journal of Impact Engineering 75, pp. 110–122, 2015.

[9] L. H. Nguyen et al., "Numerical Modelling of Ultra-High Molecular Weight Polyethylene Composite Under Impact Loading," in Procedia Engineering 103, pp. 436–443, 2015.

[10] J. Zukas, Introduction to hydrocodes. Elsevier Science, 2004.

[11] G.-S. Collins, An Introduction to Hydrocode Modeling. Applied Modelling and Computation Group, Imperial College London, 2002.

[12] P. Fröhlich, FEM Application Practice. Vieweg Verlag, 2005.

[13] H.-B. Woyand, FEM with CATIA V5. J. Schlembach Fachverlag, 2007.

[14] R. Frieß, "General basis for ballistic material, construction and product testing," presented at the Ballistic Day in Ulm, 2008.

[15] D. E. Carlucci and S. S. Jacobson, Ballistics: Theory and Design of guns and ammunition. CRC Press, 2008.

[16] G. Johnson and W. Cook, "A constitutive model and data for metals subjected to large strains, high strain rates and high temperatures," in 7th International Symposium on Ballistics, pp. 541–547, 1983.

[17] D. Steinberg, Equation of state and strength properties of selected materials. California, 1996.

A Comparison of Some Simple and Complex Surrogate Models: Make Everything as Simple as Possible?

Wim De Mulder
and Geert Molenberghs
and Geert Verbeke
Leuven Biostatistics and
Statistical Bioinformatics Centre
KU Leuven and Hasselt University, Belgium
Email: wim.demulder@cs.kuleuven.be,
geert.molenberghs@uhasselt.be,
geert.verbeke@med.kuleuven.be

Bernhard Rengs
and Thomas Fent
Wittgenstein Centre (IIASA, VID/ÖAW, WU)
VID/ÖAW
Vienna, Austria
Email: bernhard.rengs@oeaw.ac.at,
thomas.fent@oeaw.ac.at

***Abstract*—In this paper, we compare three surrogate models on a highly irregular, yet real-world data set. The three methods strongly vary in mathematical sophistication and computational complexity. First, inverse distance weighting, a very intuitive method whose single parameter can be readily determined via basic, albeit nonlinear, optimization. Secondly, radial basis function networks, for which some parameters can be determined via simple matrix algebra, although determination of other parameters require cluster analysis and nonlinear optimization. Thirdly, Gaussian process emulation, a statistical technique having a technical mathematical formulation and where specification of parameter values rely on complex and time-consuming optimization. It comes as a complete surprise that inverse distance weighting performs best on our complex data set. Our work encourages to moderate the extreme optimism about and overly use of very advanced methods. The commonplace a priori assumption that simple, intuitive methods underperform on complex data sets is not always justified, and such methods still have their place in the current era of highly advanced computational and mathematical models.**

Keywords–Gaussian process emulation; Radial basis function networks; Inverse distance weighting; Agent-based models; Cluster analysis.

I. INTRODUCTION

Ideally, any model of a real-world phenomenon explains observed data very well, has a rigorous mathematical formulation and is practically useful in the sense that it is computationally cheap to run it as many times as desired on a sequence of given inputs. However, as any researcher is aware of, these widely acclaimed properties are often conflicting by their very nature. As just one example, complex biological phenomena such as cancer can often be accurately represented using mathematically sound signaling network models in which the model equations contain parameters that are mechanistically descriptive of direct or indirect interactions in the system [1]. Yet this comes at the price of computational intractability, as the combinatorial explosion in the number of possible network models, which defines the solution space, makes model inference problems of this type NP-hard [2]. Thus, the repeated application of such computer models, for example by running the model under different parameter settings to find the parameter values that ensure the closest fit to empirical data, is practically limited to much fewer runs than accurate empirical analysis or other research objectives require.

One popular solution adopted by researchers who have to apply computationally expensive computer models for varying values of a certain variable (typically a variable in input or parameter space) is to approximate the complex model by a simpler, fast-running surrogate model [3]. Surrogate models are a particular instance of approximation methods that mimic the behavior of the simulation model while being computationally cheaper to evaluate. They are typically constructed by applying the expensive model to a limited number of values of the variable of interest, and then using the obtained input-output pairs, known as the training data set, to find a suitable fast-running approximation.

Agent-based models, which are briefly reviewed in Section II-E, often belong to the class of computationally expensive methods as they require the repeated simulation of nonlinear interactions between basic entities, and this during consecutive time steps, until a stable state is reached. Consequently, a researcher will often rely on surrogate techniques in applications where the agent-based model is to be applied to a very large number of input points. In this work, we compare the performance of three well-established surrogate techniques that have been developed in the literature, namely inverse distance weighting, radial basis function networks and Gaussian process emulation. These methods are very different in nature, e.g., Gaussian process emulation is a statistical technique that also provides a measure for the uncertainty in the approximation, while inverse distance weighting and radial basis function networks have been developed by nonstatisticians. However, in the context of this paper we will especially emphasize their disparity from another perspective, namely in terms of their complexity. The term complexity is used here to cover conceptual complexity as well as computational complexity related both to optimization of the parameters of the surrogate model and to the calculation of the output of the surrogate technique for a given input point. We elaborate on this term below. If we imagine all surrogate models lying on a spectrum defined in terms of complexity, then, loosely speaking, Gaussian process emulation and inverse distance weighting are at opposite ends while radial basis function networks have their place somewhere in the middle. Their very different positions in this spectrum makes it an interesting research question of how this exactly translates into performance.

The various methods that play a role in our work are reviewed in Section II. First, the three above surrogate techniques mentioned above. Second, agent-based models, which are used as the case study system to be approximated by the considered surrogate methods. Finally, cluster analysis, a dimensionality reduction technique that is essential in our implementations of Gaussian process emulation and radial basis function networks, due to the fact that our data set to train these models is very large. The training data set is described in Section III-A. Section III describes implementation details of the surrogate models, as well as of the cluster analysis that was applied to our training data set. Results are presented in Section IV and an extensive discussion follows in Section V. The final section concludes and suggests some future research questions.

II. Related Methodology

This section describes the various methods that play a role in this paper.

A. Gaussian process emulation

Gaussian process (GP) emulation provides an approximation, called the emulator, to a mapping $\nu : \mathbb{R}^n \to \mathbb{R}^m$. The rationale behind the development of GP emulation was to provide fast-running approximations to slow-running computer models, such that tasks requiring many executions of ν (e.g., calibration) can be performed with respect to the emulator rather than by relying on ν, thereby ensuring that the considered task ends within a reasonable time. For our case study below it holds that $m = 1$.
The steps in constructing an emulator are as follows. In the first step, it is assumed that nothing is known about ν. The value $\nu(\mathbf{x})$ for any $\mathbf{x}$ is then modeled via a Gaussian distribution with mean $m(\mathbf{x}) = \sum_{i=1}^{q} \beta_i \, h_i(\mathbf{x})$, where β_i are unknown coefficients and where h_i represent linear regression functions. The covariance between $\nu(\mathbf{x})$ and $\nu(\mathbf{x}')$, with $\mathbf{x}$ and $\mathbf{x}'$ being arbitrary input vectors in $\mathbb{R}^n$, is modeled as $\mathrm{Cov}\Big(\nu(\mathbf{x}), \nu(\mathbf{x}') \,|\, \sigma^2\Big) = \sigma^2 \, c(\mathbf{x}, \mathbf{x}')$, where σ^2 denotes a constant variance parameter and where $c(\mathbf{x}, \mathbf{x}')$ denotes a function that models the correlation between $\nu(\mathbf{x})$ and $\nu(\mathbf{x}')$. We adopt the most common choice for c:

$$c(\mathbf{x}, \mathbf{x}') \;=\; \exp\Big[-\sum_i \Big((x_i - x_i')/\delta_i\Big)^2\Big] \qquad (1)$$

with x_i and x_i' as the ith component of $\mathbf{x}$ and $\mathbf{x}'$, respectively, and where the δ_i represent parameters that can be optimized via maximum likelihood [4]. In plain words, before the training data set is taken into account it is assumed that $\nu(\mathbf{x})$ can be well approximated as a linear combination of user-chosen regression functions h_i and that a Gaussian distribution is a good model to represent the uncertainty in this approximation.
In the second step, training data $(\mathbf{x}_1, \nu(\mathbf{x}_1)), \ldots, (\mathbf{x}_n, \nu(\mathbf{x}_n))$ are taken into account. The information encapsulated in the training data set is used to improve the initial approximation as well as the model for the uncertainty in this approximation. This is done via a Bayesian analysis. It can be shown that this results in adjusting the Gaussian distributions to Student's t-distributions [5]. The mean of the Student's t-distribution in $\mathbf{x}$ is then considered the best approximation to $\nu(\mathbf{x})$. Therefore, we refer to this mean as $\hat{\nu}(\mathbf{x})$. It is given by

$$\hat{\nu}(\mathbf{x}) \;=\; m(\mathbf{x}) + U^T(\mathbf{x})A^{-1}([\nu(\mathbf{x}_1), \ldots, \nu(\mathbf{x}_n)]^T - H\boldsymbol{\beta})$$

with

$$\boldsymbol{\beta} \;=\; (\beta_1, \ldots, \beta_q)^T$$
$$H \;=\; \begin{bmatrix} h_1(\mathbf{x}_1) & \ldots & h_q(\mathbf{x}_1) \\ \ldots & & \\ h_1(\mathbf{x}_n) & \ldots & h_q(\mathbf{x}_n) \end{bmatrix}$$

and where $U(\mathbf{x})$ contains the correlations, as given by (1), between $\mathbf{x}$ and each of the training data points $\mathbf{x}_i$, and where A is the correlation matrix, containing the correlations between $\mathbf{x}_i$ and $\mathbf{x}_j$ for $i, j = 1, \ldots, n$. It is worth paying some attention to the role of $U(\mathbf{x})$. The ith element of this vector is $c(\mathbf{x}_i, \mathbf{x})$. From (1) it follows that the closer $\mathbf{x}$ to $\mathbf{x}_i$ in input space, the larger $c(\mathbf{x}_i, \mathbf{x})$. Therefore, the vector $U(\mathbf{x})$ is a weight vector, meaning that the closer $\mathbf{x}$ to $\mathbf{x}_i$, the higher the influence of the ith training data point in determining the approximation to $\nu(\mathbf{x})$.
The formula for $\hat{\nu}(\mathbf{x})$ above shows that the Bayesian analysis adds a correction term to the prior mean $m(\mathbf{x})$ by taking into account the information encapsulated in the training data set. A crucial entity in the correction term is A^{-1}, the inverse of the correlation matrix. We found that the inversion operation for our very large training data set, described in Section III-A below, is computationally intractable. We resolved this by dividing the training data set into smaller subsets using cluster analysis (a method briefly reviewed in Section II-D) and then training an emulator for each small subset. Approximations generated by these emulators can then be combined into a final, unique approximation as outlined in Section III-C.
Values for the β_i and for σ^2 can be determined by optimization principles in Hilbert space, and analytical formulae are given in [5] and [6]. For a more detailed account on GP emulation we also refer to the cited works.

GP emulation is an advanced method, having a very sound mathematical basis, where Bayesian statistics, Hilbert space methods and approximation theory all play a role [7]. A thorough understanding thus requires knowledge of several advanced mathematical concepts. As so often happens, the conceptual complexity translates into computational intractability. In particular, optimizing the parameters δ_i, β_i and σ^2 can be very time-consuming. For example, each parameter δ_i corresponds to one input component and the presence of even a few input components often makes this multidimensional nonlinear optimization task computationally very hard. A final aspect of complexity is the computational complexity of evaluating $\hat{\nu}(\mathbf{x})$, which is dominated by the evaluation of the correction term, resulting in an overall computational complexity of $O(n^3)$.

B. Radial basis function networks

A radial basis function network (RBFN) relies on so-called basis functions ϕ_j that are radially symmetric around a chosen center $\boldsymbol{\mu}_j \in \mathbb{R}^n$. A common choice for ϕ_j is

$$\phi_j(\mathbf{x}) \;=\; \exp\left(-\left(\frac{||\mathbf{x} - \boldsymbol{\mu}_j||}{\rho}\right)^T\right) \qquad (2)$$

where $\rho > 0, \tau > 0$ are parameters and where $||.||$ represents the Euclidean norm. The parameter ρ is often called the width of the basis function and determining a value for it amounts to finding a compromise between locality and smoothness of $\hat{\nu}(\mathbf{x})$ given by (3) below [8].
The points $\boldsymbol{\mu}_j$ are called the centers of the basis functions and are typically determined by one of the heuristic methods described in [9]. One popular way, which we take here, is to use cluster analysis to determine the number of centers r and to specify a value for $\boldsymbol{\mu}_1, \ldots, \boldsymbol{\mu}_r$, as outlined in Section II-D. These centers have an intuitive interpretation: they can be considered prototypical elements of the different parts of the input space. That is to say, cluster analysis divides the input space into smaller regions, ideally such that ν has a distinctive behavior in each region, and the distance from a given input point $\mathbf{x}$ to the jth region is calculated as $||\mathbf{x} - \boldsymbol{\mu}_j||$.
The value of ν in any $\mathbf{x}$ is then approximated as a shifted linear combination of the outputs of the basis functions:

$$\hat{\nu}(\mathbf{x}) \quad = \quad \gamma + \sum_{j=1}^{r} w_j \phi_j(\mathbf{x}) \qquad (3)$$

where γ and $\mathbf{w} = [w_1, \ldots, w_r]^T$ are parameters that are typically determined as a least-squares solution to the minimization problem $\min \sum_{i=1}^{n} (\nu(\mathbf{x}_i) - \hat{\nu}(\mathbf{x}_i))^2$, as described in [9]. Notice that the centers $\boldsymbol{\mu}_j$ are obtained via unsupervised learning, while the other parameters involve supervised learning.
From a conceptual point of view, an RBFN is an artificial neural network where the centers $\boldsymbol{\mu}_j$ play the role of the nodes of the hidden layer [8]. The activation of the jth hidden node is determined by $\phi_j(\mathbf{x})$ and the closer an input $\mathbf{x}$ to $\boldsymbol{\mu}_j$, the more the jth hidden node is triggered. The output layer then combines the activations of all hidden nodes into one final value that is used as the approximation to $\nu(\mathbf{x})$. This is illustrated in Figure 1 where several output components are allowed.

Informally speaking, the complexity of RBFN is lower than that of GP emulation. A good conceptual understanding does not require more than a basic knowledge of artificial neural networks and of approximation theory. While an understanding of artificial neural networks helps to internalize a visual representation of a RBFN, some insight in approximation theory, e.g., polynomial approximation and Fourier series, is needed to appreciate that a complex, but reasonable, function can often be approximated in terms of simpler functions, provided that certain conditions are fulfilled. As for the computational complexity of optimizing the parameters, three stages are involved. First, centers are determined using, e.g., k-means. While the general version of k-means is NP-hard, there are numerous approximation algorithms, some of which run in time polynomial in n and r [10]. The second optimization task concerns optimizing a nonlinear function to determine ρ and τ. As only two parameters are involved, this task can often be completed in a very reasonable time. Some researchers prefer to associate a different ρ with each ϕ_j, resulting in the much harder task of optimizing a nonlinear function depending on $r + 1$ variables. Alternatively, there are researchers who simply assign a heuristic value to ρ, e.g., $\rho = d_{\max}/\sqrt{2r}$, with $d_{\max}$ being the maximum distance between all pairs of centers [11]. Finally, determining γ and $\mathbf{w}$ comes at almost no computational cost, as they are the solution of a least-squares problem which is essentially obtained by inverting a matrix,

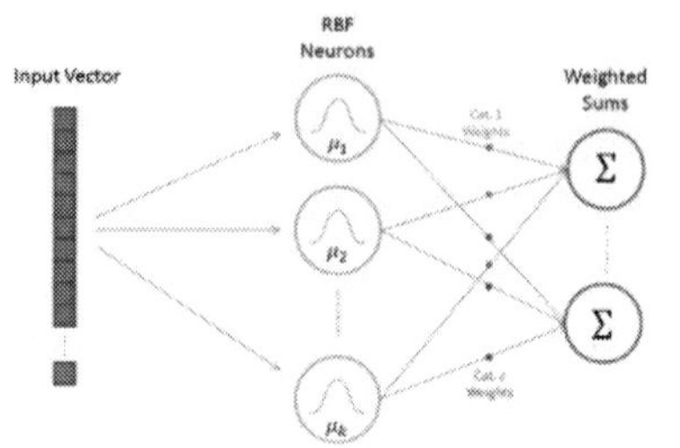

Figure 1. RBFN as artificial neural network [12]

and this matrix is only of dimension $(r + 1) \times (r + 1)$, i.e., only quadratic in the number of clusters. Since the essence of cluster analysis is dimensionality reduction, r is typically much smaller than n. It is seen from (3) that the computational complexity of evaluating $\hat{\nu}(\mathbf{x})$ is only $O(r^2)$.

C. Inverse distance weighting

Inverse distance weighting (IDW) is an approximation method in a metric space setting, originally developed by Shepard in the context of spatial analysis and geographic information systems [13]. Although the method is very simple, it is still used nowadays, for example to estimate spatial rainfall distribution, where the unknown spatial rainfall data is approximated from the known data of sites that are adjacent to the unknown site (see, e.g., [14] and [15]).
IDW approximates the unknown value of ν in a given point $\mathbf{x}$ as:

$$\hat{\nu}(\mathbf{x}) \quad = \quad \sum_{i=1}^{n} \frac{w_i(\mathbf{x})}{\sum_{j=1}^{n} w_j(\mathbf{x})} \nu(\mathbf{x}_i) \qquad \text{if } d(\mathbf{x}, \mathbf{x}_i) \neq 0 \ \forall i \ (4)$$

$$\quad = \quad \nu(\mathbf{x}_i) \qquad \text{otherwise} \qquad (5)$$

with

$$w_i(\mathbf{x}) \quad = \quad \frac{1}{d(\mathbf{x}, \mathbf{x}_i)^{\alpha}}$$

where d is any metric and where α is a constant larger than zero.

The above formulation shows that IDW is very intuitive: obtain an approximation for the output in $\mathbf{x}$ as a weighted average of known outputs $\nu(\mathbf{x}_i)$, and give more weight to outputs that have been mapped from training data input points that are closer to $\mathbf{x}$. No advanced mathematical principle is involved. Optimization can be avoided by simply choosing $\alpha = 1$. Alternatively, α can be determined as the solution to the same minimization problem as in RBFN, namely $\min \sum_{i=1}^{n} (\nu(\mathbf{x}_i) - \hat{\nu}(\mathbf{x}_i))^2$. Although this is a nonlinear optimization task, there is only one parameter, α, involved. The computational complexity of evaluating $\hat{\nu}(\mathbf{x})$ is $O(n^2)$, which is higher than that of a RBFN, but provided that the number of training data points is not extremely large, this evaluation can be done very fast as only simple multiplications and additions are involved.

D. Cluster analysis

Cluster analysis is the unsupervised partitioning of a data set into groups, also called clusters, such that data elements which are members of the same group have a higher similarity

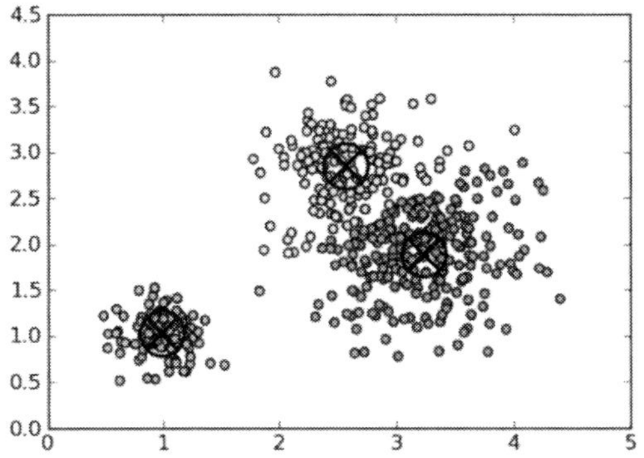

Figure 2. Illustration of k-means with $k = 3$ [18]

than data elements which are members of different groups [16]. Similarity is typically expressed in terms of a user-defined distance measure, such as the commonly used Euclidean distance. Arguably the best known clustering algorithm is k-means [17], an iterative algorithm that not only determines clusters but also centers (sometimes called centroids) for the obtained clusters. Given the number of clusters, k, and a data set $D = \{\mathbf{x}_1, \ldots, \mathbf{x}_n\}$, the algorithm chooses the clusters $C_i (i = 1, \ldots, k)$ such that $\sum_{i=1}^{k} \sum_{\mathbf{x} \in C_i} ||\mathbf{x} - \boldsymbol{\mu}_i||^2$ is minimal, where $\boldsymbol{\mu}_i$ is the center of the ith cluster. The clusters C_i are simply subsets of the given data set with $C_i \cap C_j = \emptyset$ if $i \neq j$ and $\cup_{i=1}^{n} C_i = D$. Each center $\boldsymbol{\mu}_i$ readily follows from the construction of the clusters, as it is the average of all points belonging to C_i. An illustration is provided in Figure 2. We have used k-means for two purposes. First, due to the very large size of our training data set and the related instabilities in inverting the correlation matrix, direct application of GP emulation turned out to be infeasible. Thus we applied cluster analysis, thereby creating smaller training data sets, each of them being a subset of the original training data set. A separate emulator was then trained with each of these small data sets. Second, the number of clusters that was determined with k-means gave at once the number of basis functions in our RBFN, i.e. the parameter r in (3), and the cluster centers were used as the centers of the basis functions, i.e., the parameters $\boldsymbol{\mu}_1, \ldots, \boldsymbol{\mu}_r$ in (2). The result of the performed cluster analysis is outlined in Section III-B.

E. Agent-based models

An agent-based model (ABM) is a computational model that simulates the behavior and interactions of autonomous agents. A key feature is that population level phenomena are studied by explicitly modeling the interactions of the individuals in these populations [19][20]. The systems that emerge from such interactions are often complex and might show regularities that were not expected by researchers in the field who solely relied on their background knowledge about the characteristics of the lower-level entities to make predictions about the higher-level phenomena. ABMs are especially popular among sociologists who model social life as interactions among adaptive agents who influence one another in response to the influence they receive [21].

In previous work, we developed an agent-based model to

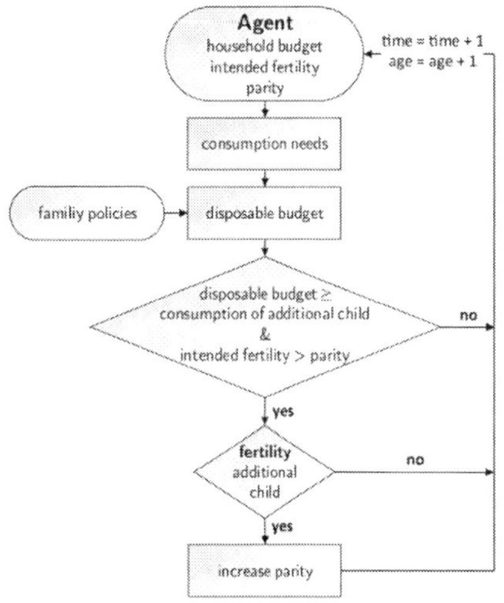

Figure 3. The decision making process in a household

analyze the effectiveness of family policies under different assumptions regarding the social structure of a society [22]. The agents represent the female partner in a household. They are heterogeneous with respect to age, household budget, parity, and intended fertility. A network of mutual links connects the agents to a small subset of the population to exchange fertility preferences. Figure 3 illustrates the decision making process in a household. The agents are endowed with a certain budget of time and money which they allocate to satisfy their own and their children's needs. We assume that the agent's and their children's consumption levels depend on the household budget but increase less than linearly with household budget. Thus, wealthier households have a higher savings rate. If the household's intended fertility exceeds the actual parity and the disposable budget suffices to cover the consumption needs of another child, the household is subject to the appropriate age-specific fertility. Hence the household is exposed to having an additional child depending on the outcome of a random process. If an additional child is born, other agents may update their intended fertility.

We considered two components of family policies: 1. the policymaker provides a fixed amount of money or monetary equivalent per child to each household and 2. a monetary or non-monetary benefit proportional to the household income is transferred to the household. Any policy mix greater than zero supports the household in covering the dependent children's consumption needs.

The output at the aggregate level that is produced by the ABM consists of the cohort fertility, the intended fertility, and the fertility gap. The inputs include the level of fixed and income-dependent family allowances, denoted by b^f and b^v, and parameters that determine the social structure of a society, such as a measure for the agents' level of homophily α, and the strength of positive and negative social influence, denoted by pr_3 and pr_4 resp. The results of the application of our ABM and the related sociological findings can be found in the cited work. The purpose of this paper is to generate a training data set by application of the ABM to selected input points and then using this data set to empirically compare GP emulation, RBFN and IDW. The training data set we created is described in the next section.

III. IMPLEMENTATION

We describe our data set and the implementation details of the methods that are compared to each other.

A. Data set

The input variables of our ABM are given equidistant values from the input domain and the ABM is applied to generate the corresponding outputs. As input domain, we considered the variables b^f, b^v, α, pr_3 and p_4, a selection of the larger amount of variables that were used in the ABM. These five variables were found to have the greatest influence on the outcomes. On the output side, we restrict attention to one variable, namely cohort fertility. The ABM was applied to 10,732 vectors in the input domain, which gives a very large training data set. A test data set containing 500 input–output pairs was generated to compare the performance of the three methods under study.

B. Cluster analysis

In clustering the training data set containing 10,732 data points we performed trial and error to determine a suitable number of clusters. A highly desired objective is that the clusters are kept relatively small, since an emulator is to be trained for each cluster and numerical instabilities arise when the number of training data points that are used in constructing an emulator becomes large, as explained in Section II-A. In previous work [23], we found that numerical instabilities can be avoided by constraining the result of k-means such that the largest cluster has no more than about 500 training data points. The main characteristics of a suitable set of clusters that was obtained in this previous work are as follows: 34 clusters, largest cluster size equal to 500, smallest cluster size equal to 15.

C. Description of the implemented methods

We implemented 8 methods instantiated from the domains of IDW, GP emulation and RBFN.

The first two methods are based on GP emulation and cluster analysis. As outlined above, a GP emulator was trained for each of the 34 clusters, each containing a part of the full training data set. The first method, hereafter referred to as GP-closest, computes an approximation to $\nu(\mathbf{x})$ by finding the cluster that is closest to $\mathbf{x}$ and taking the output of the corresponding emulator in $\mathbf{x}$ as the sought-after value. The distance between a point and a cluster is hereby taken as the Euclidean distance between that point and the center of the given cluster. The second GP emulation method, which we call GP-average, determines the approximation as a weighted average of the outputs of all emulators in the given input point. Each weight is taken as an inverse measure of the distance between the given input point and the specified cluster. That is, we use the formulation of IDW, given by (4)-(5), choosing $\alpha = 1$ in (6), and where $\nu(\mathbf{x}_i)$ is replaced by the output of the emulator corresponding to the ith cluster.

The next five methods are RBFNs, with different values for the parameters ρ and τ in (2). The chosen values are displayed in Table I. To make reference to a specific method convenient, we labeled these methods RBFN-1,..., RBFN-5.

The 8th and last method is a simple IDW, as given by (4)-(5).

TABLE I. PARAMETER VALUES FOR THE DIFFERENT RBFNS.

Method	ρ	τ
RBFN-1	1	2
RBFN-2	1	1
RBFN-3	1	0.5
RBFN-4	2	2
RBFN-5	4	2

IV. RESULTS

We now discuss the measure that is used to evaluate our results and we analyze the outputs of this measure.

A. Evaluation measure

Given a test input point $\mathbf{x}$ with corresponding true output $\nu(\mathbf{x})$ and an approximation $\hat{\nu}(\mathbf{x})$ produced by one of the methods described in the previous section, we evaluate the quality of the approximation as the relative difference between $\nu(\mathbf{x})$ and $\hat{\nu}(\mathbf{x})$, as follows:

$$RD(\mathbf{x}) = \left| \frac{\hat{\nu}(\mathbf{x}) - \nu(\mathbf{x})}{1/2(\hat{\nu}(\mathbf{x}) + \nu(\mathbf{x}))} \right|$$

The average relative difference for a particular method, denoted ARD, is then the average of $RD(\mathbf{x})$ over all 500 test points.

B. Results and analysis

The ARD is calculated for each of the methods described in Section III-C and results are shown in Table II.

Let us first restrict attention to the RBFN methods. The results show that the choice of parameter values is of crucial importance for the performance. The ARD varies from 0.165 for RBFN-1 to 0.235 for RBFN-3. The fact that the best result is obtained for RBFN-1 where $\tau = 2$ supports the common practice to set τ at this value in applications. On the other hand, the parameter ρ should be part of the learning process, as results for $\tau = 2$ widely vary, from 0.165 to 0.227. However, the price to be paid for the resulting substantial rise in performance is high, as the determination of a suitable ρ amounts to a nonlinear optimization task.

Turning attention to a global comparison, a remarkable observation is that all ARDs are high, with at least a 14.6% difference, on average, between the approximations and the true outputs. Since the ARD is high for all considered methods and since these methods come from very different domains, varying in mathematical and computational complexity, it is conceivable that the training data set is highly complex, displaying many irregularities. This makes it even more interesting to compare the methods, as empirical comparisons are too often based on either artificially created data sets or real-world data sets that are well understood and not exceedingly complex. A multidimensional and exceptionally complex, but still real-world, data set as ours is useful to evaluate performance in a less typical situation than those appearing in the mainstream literature and to check the limits of surrogate modeling techniques.

However, the most striking observation is that IDW, by far the simplest of the considered techniques, is also by far the best method. The difference of the ARD of IDW and that of the second best performing, RBFN-4, is substantial. This is not only surprising because of the simplicity of IDW, but also because the training data set is very complex. One would expect an irregular data set to call for more advanced techniques.

TABLE II. PERFORMANCE OF THE IMPLEMENTED METHODS ON THE TEST DATA SET.

Method	*ARD*
GP-closest	0.212
GP-average	0.293
RBFN-1	0.165
RBFN-2	0.197
RBFN-3	0.235
RBFN-4	0.190
RBFN-5	0.227
IDW	0.146

V. DISCUSSION

Above, we have compared three surrogate models on a highly complex, irregular real-world data set. The three methods strongly vary in mathematical sophistication and computational complexity. IDW is a very simple and intuitive method, requiring only limited optimization efforts, and the resulting approximation function can be quickly evaluated on a given input point. RBFNs require to choose basis functions and to determine suitable centers for these functions. The centers of the basis functions are typically obtained by applying k-means, an algorithm that in many practical applications turns out to converge very fast. If this is not the case, one may decide to rely on one of the approximation algorithms that have been developed that run in polynomial time. Determination of the parameters ρ and τ associated to the basis functions require nonlinear optimization. Although nonlinear optimization is known to be computationally hard, the fact that only two parameters are involved ensures that this task can typically still be fulfilled in a very reasonable time. Some researchers prefer to increase flexibility by associating a different ρ to each basis function, which drastically increases computational complexity. At the other extreme, it is also possible to assign ρ a fixed, heuristic value. The remaining parameters to be optimized in RBFNs are the weights in the linear combination of the basis functions, which can be determined quickly via the inversion of a matrix of, for most applications, small dimensions. GP emulation is a statistical technique and has a deep and refined mathematical foundation. Optimization is typically very complex and time-consuming: determination of the parameters δ_i calls for nonlinear optimization of a likelihood function, while the posterior mean of the generated Student's t-distribution, to be used as approximation for the output in a given input point, requires inverting a correlation matrix having dimensions that are quadratic in the number of training data points.
If we vaguely define the overall complexity of a method as the sum of its conceptual complexity, the computational complexity of optimizing the parameters involved and the computational complexity of calculating the approximate output for a given input point, the above discussion shows that the arrow of increasing complexity runs along IDW, RBFN and GP .

One is inclined to assume that the most advanced method will perform best. In fact, it has become commonplace among researchers to select a method from the set of advanced approximation or machine learning techniques whenever confronted with a complex data set (as an illustration, we refer to [24] and [25]). Furthermore, when experimentally comparing machine learning algorithms, it is typically advanced methods that are given a role in this process, leaving out simple techniques under the a priori assumption that these will underperform anyway (see, e.g., [26] and [27]). And new machine learning algorithms appearing in the literature are almost always a sophistication of an already sophisticated algorithm (examples are [28] and [29]). That is, *most advanced* and *best* are used almost interchangeably.

To many researchers it will thus come as a complete surprise that a very simple method like IDW performed better than two much more advanced approximation methods on our complex training data set generated by an ABM.

VI. CONCLUSION AND FUTURE WORK

Although it might be objected that the three considered surrogate models were applied to only one data set, our answer is that the purpose of our work is obviously *not* to demonstrate that simpler methods are better than more advanced ones. Rather, we have shown that *there are* complex problems for which simple methods work better than much more advanced techniques.

Therefore, our work is meant as a cautionary note that the meaning of the term *best approximation method* is still that it performs best on a given application. Although intuition says that a more advanced technique will often deliver better results, there is no strict guarantee that this will be the case for a specific problem at hand. Indeed, methods having a sophisticated mathematical foundation always rely on assumptions about the given training data set and the function to be approximated. It is all too often ignored that these assumptions might not hold in practice or too quickly assumed that deviations from mathematical assumptions are small enough, and that the considered method will still perform properly.

Our findings should not be seen as a discouragement to apply advanced methods. Rather, we interpret our results as an invitation to always evaluate a very simple method on a given data set alongside one or more advanced techniques. This comes at almost no cost, as simple methods like IDW can be easily implemented and are computationally very cheap. It is also important to notice that IDW does not make any assumption about the given data set, thus applying it in a setting where it is strictly speaking not applicable (as is often the case for advanced methods) is not an issue. When such simple methods do perform better than other, more sophisticated methods, their return on investment is therefore incredibly high. As often attributed to Einstein: "everything should be made as simple as possible ..." This is, of course, not to say that advanced methods are useless. In many situations a more complex problem cannot be handled by simple intuition and then a more advanced method should be applied. Or, as Einstein continues, "... but not simpler".

Possible future research questions include:

- Can we improve the RBFNs by associating a different ρ with each basis function to the extent that these RBFNs become better than IDW?
- What specific characteristics of the data set are responsible for the fact that IDW performs better than GP emulation and RBFN?

- Are the obtained results sensitive to the number of clusters?

REFERENCES

[1] E. Molinelli et al., "Perturbation biology: inferring signaling networks in cellular systems," PLoS Computational Biology, vol. 9, 2013.

[2] V. Chandrasekaran, N. Sebro, and P. Harsha, "Complexity of inference in graphical models ," in Proceedings of the 24th Conference on Uncertainty in Artificial Intelligence, 2008.

[3] S. Koziel and L. Leifsson, Eds., Surrogate-based modeling and optimization. Springer, 2013.

[4] I. Andrianakis and P. G. Challenor, "The effect of the nugget on Gaussian process emulators of computer models," Computational Statistics and Data Analysis, vol. 56, 2012, pp. 4215–4228.

[5] A. O'Hagan, "Bayesian analysis of computer code outputs: A tutorial," Reliability Engineering & System Safety, vol. 91, 2006, pp. 1290–1300.

[6] J. Oakley and A. O'Hagan, "Bayesian inference for the uncertainty distribution of computer model outputs," Biometrika, vol. 89, 2002, pp. 769–784.

[7] W. De Mulder, G. Molenberghs, and G. Verbeke, "A mathematical review of the standard Gaussian process emulator," *Submitted to:* International Statistical Review.

[8] N. Benoudjit and M. Verleysen, "On the kernel widths in radial-basis function networks," Neural Processing Letters, vol. 18, 2003, pp. 139–154.

[9] C. Bishop, Ed., Neural networks for pattern recognition. Clarendon Press, 1996.

[10] M. Song and S. Rajasekaran, "Fast k-means algorithms with constant approximation," in Lecture Notes in Computer Science. Springer-Verlag, 2005.

[11] S. Haykin, Ed., Neural networks: a comprehensive foundation. Prentice-Hall, 1999.

[12] C. McCormick, "Radial basis function network (RBFN) tutorial," http://mccormickml.com/2013/08/15/radial-basis-function-network-rbfn-tutorial/, 2013.

[13] D. Shepard, "A two-dimensional interpolation function for irregularly-spaced data," in Proceedings of the 1968 ACM National Conference.

[14] P. Goovaerts, "Geostatistical approaches for incorporating elevation into the spatial interpolation of rainfall," Journal of Hydrology, vol. 228, 2000, pp. 113–129.

[15] F. Chen and C. Liu, "Estimation of the spatial rainfall distribution using inverse distance weighting (IDW) in the middle of Taiwan," Paddy and Water Environment, vol. 10, 2012, pp. 209–222.

[16] A. Jain, M. Murty, and P. Flynn, "Data clustering: a review," ACM Computing Surveys, vol. 31, 1999, pp. 264–323.

[17] A. Jain and R. Dubes, Eds., Algorithms for clustering data. Prentice Hall College Div, 1988.

[18] M. Pacula, "K-means clustering example," http://blog.mpacula.com/2011/04/27/k-means-clustering-example-python/.

[19] N. Gilbert, Ed., Agent-based models: quantitative applications in the social sciences. SAGE Publications, Inc, 2007.

[20] F. C. Billari, T. Fent, A. Prskawetz, and J. Scheffran, Eds., Agent–Based Compuational Modelling: Applications in Demography, Social, Economic, and Environmental Sciences, ser. Contributions to Economics. Springer, 2006.

[21] M. Macy and R. Willer, "From factors to factors: computational sociology and agent-based modeling," Annual Review of Sociology, vol. 28, 2002, pp. 143–166.

[22] T. Fent, B. Aparicio Diaz, and A. Prskawetz, "Family policies in the context of low fertility and social structure," Demographic Research, vol. 29, 2013, pp. 963–998.

[23] W. De Mulder, B. Rengs, G. Molenberghs, T. Fent, and G. Verbeke, "Statistical emulation applied to a very large data set generated by an agent-based model," in Proceedings of the Seventh International Conference on Advances in System Simulation.

[24] A. Khazaee, A. Ebrahimzadeh, and A. Babajani-Feremi, "Application of advanced machine learning methods on resting-state fMRI network for identification of mild cognitive impairment and Alzheimers disease," Brain Imaging and Behavior, 2015, pp. 1–19.

[25] J. Behmann, A. Mahlein, T. Rumpf, and L. Plümer, "A review of advanced machine learning methods for the detection of biotic stress in precision crop protection," Precision Agriculture, vol. 16, 2015, pp. 239–260.

[26] N. Williams, S. Zander, and G. Armitage, "A preliminary performance comparison of five learning algorithms for practical IP traffic flow classification," ACM SIGCOMM Computer Communication Review, vol. 36, 2006, pp. 7–15.

[27] A. Morton, E. Marzban, G. Giannoulis, A. Patel, R. Aparasu, and I. Kakadiaris, "A comparison of supervised machine learning techniques for predicting short-term in-hospital length of stay among diabetic patients," in 13th International Conference on Machine Learning and Applications.

[28] I. Rojas et al., "A new radial basis function networks structure: application to time series prediction," in Proceedings of the International Joint Conference on Neural Networks, 2000, pp. 449–454.

[29] X. Hong and S. Billings, "Dual-orthogonal radial basis function networks for nonlinear time series prediction," Neural Networks, vol. 11, 1998, pp. 479–493.

Pedestrian Activity Simulation in Shopping Environments

An Irregular Network Approach

Jan Dijkstra and Joran Jessurun
Information Systems in the Built Environment,
Department of the Built Environment
Eindhoven University of Technology
Eindhoven, The Netherlands
e-mail: {j.dijkstra,a.j.jessurun}@tue.nl

Abstract—**Micro-scale agent-based modeling can be used for the simulation of pedestrian movement for low and high density scenarios and of the effect of changes in an environment. Such models can also be used for pedestrian dynamics in city centers to show the design effects in the shopping environment. This paper focuses on the generation of the movement network and the underlying behavioral rules that conducts the activation of pedestrians on the network representing a shopping environment. The store visits will be realized by Monte Carlo simulation.**

Keywords- Monte Carlo Simulation; Activity Agenda; Agent Based Simulation Modeling; Pedestrian Dynamics; Irregular Network .

I. INTRODUCTION

Agent-based modeling is a computational methodology that allows us to create, analyze, and experiment with artificial virtual worlds populated by agents. A specific research area is micro-scale agent-based modeling that can be used for the simulation of pedestrian movement for low and high density scenarios and for the effect of changes in the environment. Such kind of models can also be used for pedestrian dynamics in city centers to show the design effects in the shopping environment. In this context, Ali and Moulin [1] describe their multi-agent simulation prototype of customers' shopping behavior in a mall. The basis of this paper is an agent based model to simulate pedestrian dynamic destination, route and scheduling behavior. This agent based model is under development, where the simulation of movement patterns is embedded in a more comprehensive model of activity behavior.

Representation is a substantial issue in simulating pedestrian dynamics. One can distinguish the representation of the pedestrian environment and the representation of pedestrians. In the domain of a city center, representation of a pedestrian environment includes the geometry of the shopping environment such as stores and streets, the network as a cellular grid, and pedestrian objects. Pedestrian representation includes socioeconomic characteristics, speed, goals, familiarity with the environment, and an agenda of activities. This activity agenda includes planned activities and can be rescheduled by unplanned activities. It is assumed that pedestrians perceive their environment and that they are supposed to carry out a set of activities. For completing an activity, pedestrians spend time in stores. As a consequence, time duration influences their movement behavior over the network.

In this way, we want to achieve the full potential of an agent based model. Also, that it involves explicitly the modeling of the dynamics of the individual pedestrians. Such models are called agent-based simulation models [2]. In our case, the pedestrians are the agents in the agent-based simulation model.

Although a 3D presentation of pedestrian movement is the ultimate goal, it is nevertheless meaningful to test the underlying principles in an appropriate 2D representation of pedestrians and their environment. Repast Simphony [3] and NetLogo [4] can be used as modeling and simulation toolkit because they provide a suitable simulation framework that supports skeletons of agents and their environment, and their interoperability (e.g., Geographic Information System, also called GIS). In our approach, we use Repast as guideline for the theoretical framework of the simulation process. On the other hand, we will use NetLogo for the actual simulation because it easily allows the empirical testing of the principles of the simulation approach. Also, we will use shape-file information of the environment and a network structure for visualizing the 2D environment.

The realization of pedestrian movement uses a choice network approach. Herein, the network is an irregular lattice of cells and the choice of movement direction is determined by activation of pedestrians' activities. The domain of the agent-based modeling approach is pedestrian behavior in a shopping environment and the choice mechanism that are involved. It shows some similarity with other models that investigate pedestrian movement with fine-scale considerations and pedestrians' shop-around behavior (e.g., [5]), or principles of bounded rationality [6]. In tackling the combined 'Multi Agent System (MAS) – Cellular Automata (CA)' approach, the inspiring 'situated cellular agents' approach [7] is worth mentioning. Rooted on basic principles of CA, this approach takes into account the heterogeneity of agents and provides interaction between agents locally and at-a-distance interaction; also, the notion of perception and action is included in affective agents [8].

Our model distinguishes itself from other similar models because store visit is included in the pedestrian movement behavior in the shopping environments. To our knowledge, this has not been done in this way.

This paper shows some similarities with previously published works (e.g., [9][10]) , but this paper makes it consistent with each other. Moreover, improvements have been made, in particular the mathematical underpinnings of the irregular network approach.

This paper discusses successively pedestrian agent and its environment in Section II, the engineering basis of the simulation process in Section III, the simulation of store visits in Section IV, and the simulation of pedestrian activity and pedestrian movement in Section V, called simulation pedestrian dynamics. A discussion about the conclusions and future directions will conclude this paper in Section VI.

II. Pedestrian Agent and Environment

The basis for a pedestrian agent structure includes methods like *perceive*, *interpret* and *updEnv*, where the pedestrian agent has its own control. The behavior represents the set of possible attitudes.

The environment consists of streets, a set of stores, and pedestrians represented by agents. Streets are presented as an irregular lattice of cells (cellular network), which is used to simulate agent movement. A pedestrian agent moves with his own behavior and personal characteristics. At each time, there is an update of pedestrian agents' positions (*updEnv*). In fact, each cell in the cellular network can be considered as an information container object; it contains information about the area size, street or store characteristics, and agents' positions. We regard a restricted environment of a pedestrian agent in the cellular network. The cellular network provides percepts (*perceive*) and the pedestrian agent perform actions in them (*interpret*).

The pedestrian behavioral aspects are shown in Fig. 1. Perceptual fields, which guide which stores an pedestrian agent will perceive, may vary according to the agent's awareness threshold, which in turn may depend on his motivational state, age, etc., and the signaling intensity of the store or establishment, which is assumed a function of distance and appealing architecture.

Perceptual Field → Activation of the Agent → Completing an Activity

Figure 1. Pedestrian behavioral aspects.

When stores are signaled and become included in agent's perceptual field, the agent has to decide whether or not to act and visit the store. This is called the activation of the agent. We assume that activation is defined and depends among others on agent's personal characteristics, motivation, familiarity with a store, suitability to conduct a visit, and the agent's consideration set.

Estimation results of these behavioral principles are not part of this paper and are described in [11].

III. Engineering Basis of the Simulation Process

This section provides some understanding in the engineering basis of the simulation of pedestrian movement. The principles are rooted in agent-based modeling and simulation, which is currently a fundamental tool for predicting the behavior of complex systems. As mentioned before, we use the principles of Repast Simphony creating the model [12].

The model structure in Repast Simphony is based on contexts and projections. The core data structure is called a context that represents from a modeling perspective, an abstract population: the objects in these populations are referred as agents.

The context provides the main infrastructure to define a population and the interactions of that population. An abstract environment is created in which agents exist at a given point in the simulation. The context also holds its own internal state for maintaining the collection of agents; this state can consist of multiple types of data. That provides agents with information about the world in which they interact. In addition, data fields can be maintained by the context; herein a data field is a n-dimensional field of values with which the agents in a context interact. These data fields can be directly associated with a physical space wherein the field is generic, whereby each value is derived from a set of coordinates.

Projections take the population as defined in a context. They impose a new structure on it, and the structure defines and imposes relationships on the population; therefore an agent population is realized once a projection is applied to it.

A feature of Repast Simphony is the ability to integrate GIS data directly to the simulation; it provides a set of classes that allow shapefiles to be displayed. A shapefile is a storage format for storing geometric and associated attribute information. For example, shapefiles can be provided by QuantumGIS [13]. A GIS contains multiple layers of data; each layer is made up of a number of elements. Each feature in the layer has aspects to it; its geographical coordinates (but it could be also a polygon, a polyline or polypoint) and the data associated with it [14]. GIS store data about layers in database files, with each record in the file referring to a feature in GIS. Actually, integration with GIS means shapefile integration. Agents are created using these data, and the simulation process provides the population by the context creator.

Agents, can be created, recreated and destroyed at each simulation step. They will be created by "Introduce Agents", and the update of all agents ion the environment occurs in the "Agent Loop". Fig. 2 shows the Agent Loop of the context creator.

The interaction with the environment is provided by the shapefile containing GIS data and the other one for the generated network from this GIS data. The context needs this GIS data for the data fields which provides the information from the environment.

In our approach, the environment consists of polygons representing the network of shops and streets. In QuantumGIS, feature data will be connected to cells of the network and layers will be created.

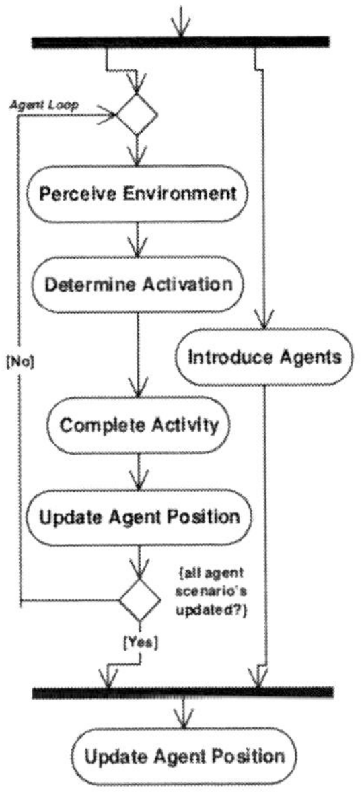

Figure 2. Activity diagram part of the agent loop of the *context* creator.

After that, the GIS database will be provided that can be used in NetLogo for environmental information for pedestrian agents for perceiving this environment.

IV. Simulation of Store Visits

Borgers and Timmermans [15] used Monte Carlo simulation for the incorporation of the numbers of stops and the sequence of planned stops/purposes, because in their opinion the concept of multi-stop, multi-purpose behavior is relevant for understanding pedestrian behavior. According to this line of thought, we assume an activity agenda includes a number of planned and unplanned store visits that can also be considered as a number of non-impulse and impulse store visits.

Every pedestrian agent receives at its introduction in the simulation a pedestrian scenario. This pedestrian scenario includes besides general characteristics like gender, age, companionship, also, familiarity with the city center, motivation, time budget, and activity agenda. After a store visit, the activity agenda will be rescheduled. The number of planned and unplanned store visits is determined by a Monte Carlo simulation.

For this purpose, data from visitors to the city center of Eindhoven are gathered by interviewing them about their motivation and the stores they visited. For this survey about pedestrian behavioral principles, data were collected from 405 respondents. Visitors are also asked about successful visits and which of them were planned and unplanned. Data about their activity agendas were collected from 770 respondents.

These routes provide the collected data. The findings from this collected data of the number of planned and unplanned visit stops show a skewed distribution. The skewed distributions are different depending of gender, age category and motivation. We often need a skewed distribution where probability densities below and above the mean are distributed differently. In this case, we assume, by analogy with multiple stops, a Gamma distribution.

The probability density function of the Gamma distribution is given by:

$$f(x;k,\theta) = x^{k-1}\frac{e^{-x/\theta}}{\theta^k\Gamma(k)} \tag{1}$$

where, k is the shape parameter (k>0) and θ is the scale parameter (θ>0).

Both k and θ will be positive; they are derived from the skewed normal distribution of the number of (planned) stops from their data collection depending on gender, age category and motivation. The shape parameter k is derived from the skewness of the skewed normal distribution and the scale parameter θ is derived from the mean and k. The discussion about the values of the parameters and the related data collection has been described elsewhere [16].

The Gamma inverse function $G(p)$, which is the inverse cumulative distribution function, is given by (2). Given a random number p from a uniform distribution in the interval (0, 1), the value of $G(p)$ has a Gamma distribution with parameters k and θ. That means, given a number p on the x-axis provides the number of stops on the y-axis; where real values are rounded to integer values.

$$G(p) = F^{-1}(p;k,\theta) = \{x: F(x;k,\theta) = p\}$$

where (2)

$$p = F(x;k,\theta) = \frac{1}{\theta^k\Gamma(k)}\int_0^x t^{k-1}e^{-x/\theta}$$

For example, Fig. 3 shows the $G(p)$ distribution for the *goal oriented* orientation with respect to the number of (planned) stops. Also, there is a distinction for gender (male, female) and age (<55, ≥55 years).

The number of unplanned stops can be derived from the calculation of the number of stops minus the number of planned stops.

Time duration is the time spent by a pedestrian in a store. For the simulation run, the time duration is also determined by a Monte Carlo simulation.

The findings from the collected data of the duration of a visit to a store indicate that this duration meets the Weibull distribution, and that this duration is dependent of the store category as well as the priority of the store. Fig. 4 shows the activity diagram of completing an activity in which time duration will be determined.

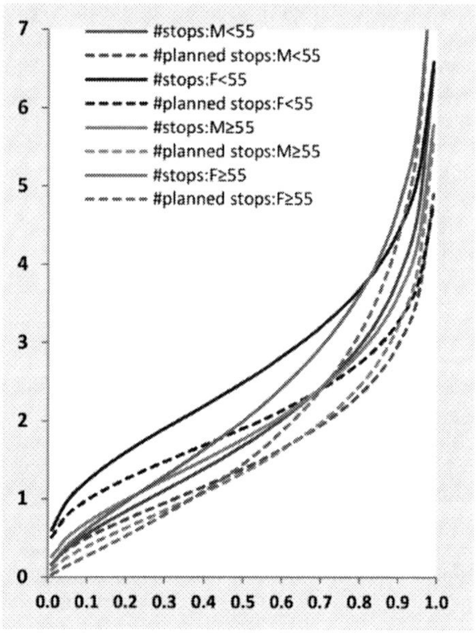

Figure 3. *G(p)* for Goal Oriented motivation, different gender and age category; Number of (planned) Stops vs. Probability.

The Weibull probability function is given by:

$$f(x;k;\lambda;\theta) = \frac{k}{\lambda}\left(\frac{(x-\theta)}{\lambda}\right)^{k-1} e^{-\left(\frac{(x-\theta)}{\lambda}\right)^{k}} \quad (3)$$

where, k is the shape parameter (k>0), λ is the scale parameter, and θ is the location of the distribution.

Table I shows the values of the parameters of the Weibull distribution for the different store categories. The specific store categories include among others, jewelry, bell companies, candy shop, etc. If $\theta = 0$ then we have to do with the 2-Parameter Weibull distribution.

The percent point function $G(p)$, which is the inverse cumulative distribution function, is given by:

$$G(p) = \theta + \lambda(-\ln(1-p))^{1/k} \quad (4)$$

Given a random number p from a uniform distribution in the interval (0,1), the value of $G(p)$ has a Weibull distribution with parameters k, λ, and θ.

TABLE I. WEIBULL PARAMETERS FOR STORE CATEGORIES

Cate-gory	Description	Priority (%)	k	λ	θ
1	Clothes-1	≥1	1.00	1.00	0.46
1	Clothes-2	≥0.5<1	1.22	0.99	0
1	Clothes-3	<0.5	1.80	0.80	0
2	Shoes		1.10	0.62	0
3	Body & health		1.65	0.75	0
4	Department store		1.47	0.83	0
5	Specific-1	<0.7	1.22	0.88	0
5	Specific-2	≥0.7	1.32	0.48	0

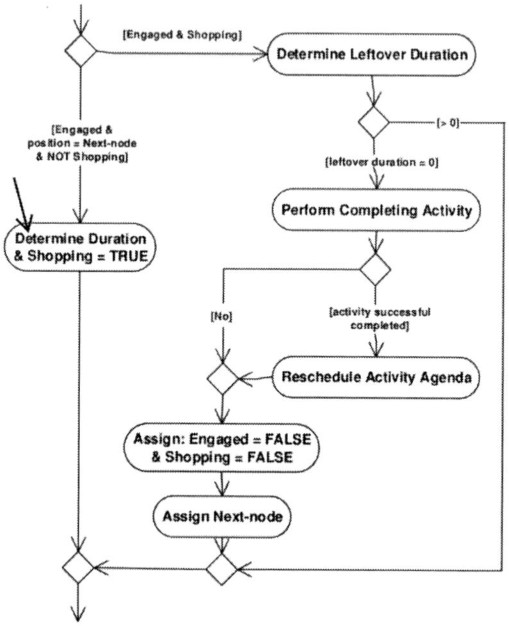

Figure 4. Activity diagram of completing an activity.

That means, a random number drawn from (0,1) provides the probability p which in turn provides the time duration. Fig. 5 shows the percent point function.

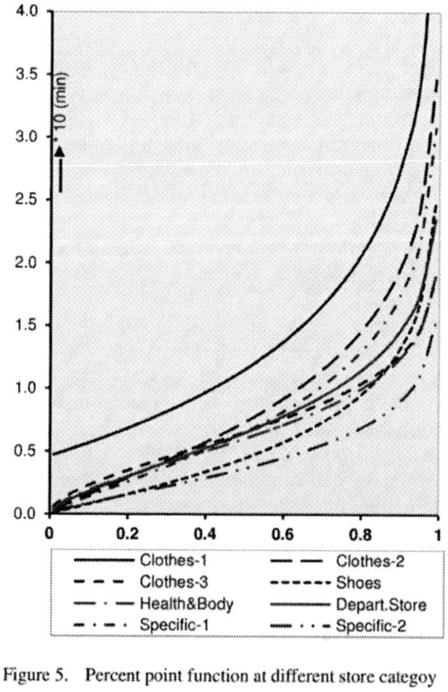

Figure 5. Percent point function at different store categoy

The findings about time duration can be found in [17].

V. SIMULATION PEDESTRIAN DYNAMICS

As mentioned in Section III, the environment consists of polygons representing the network of shops (stores) and streets. Polygons are used to indicate borders, functional areas like walkways. Adjacent cells means that connections are possible, for instance pedestrian agents can move from one cell to an adjacent cell. If cells are not strictly adjacent, no movement from each other is possible.

Each cell in the network has a node. Therefore, the network consists of N nodes and L links. A subset of these N nodes are linked to J shops, and a subset E of these N nodes represents the entry/departure points of the simulation system. The link between a street-cell and a shop-cell will be established by the adjacent part of the polygon representing the shop and the street-cell. Effectively, pedestrian agents are situated in the cells of the network, namely a street-cell or a shop-cell and bounded to a node on the underlying representation, and pedestrian agents can move on the implicit generated network to other nodes if they are linked together. The network is irregular because a clear border between a shop-cell and adjacent cell is desired.

The test ground is the inner-city center of Eindhoven. We will perform the simulation on a segment of a section of this city center. Fig. 6 shows a segment of the city center and the associated full network with their links.

As mentioned before, we use a network of irregular cells. Fig. 6 (right) shows such a network that consists of street-cells, which includes the inner lane and two outer lanes, and shop-cells with one cell for each shop.

In research areas like geo-computation, land-use change, and urban planning, one can find extensions on the traditional formalization of CA to include an irregular spatial structure [18][19][20]. These models are based on uniform CA transition rules.

Tomassini [21] pointed out that standard lattice cellular automata and random Boolean networks can be extended to a

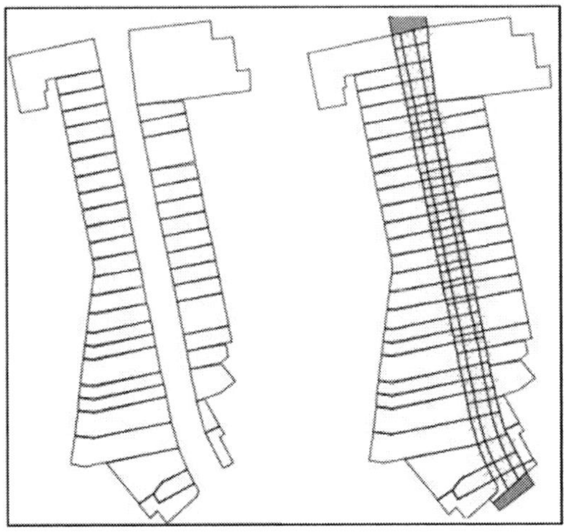

Figure 6. Main street of the city center (left) and the full layers (right).

wider class of generalized automata networks that can be built on any connected graph. In this approach, there is no uniform transition function; the change is in the local transition function.

We have no uniform lattice of cells and no uniform transition rules, because in our approach, a street-cell **i** in the network is bounded to the stay of a maximum number of pedestrian agents related to node **i**.

Pedestrian behavior and pedestrian profile characteristics result in pedestrian activity and choice moments. That results in position change from a current position in cell **i** linked to node **i** to a next position in cell **j** linked to node **j**. Strictly speaking, our approach is not CA-based; nevertheless at each time step there is an update of the network according to 'network rules'.

A pedestrian agent will be introduced in the simulation by setting an entry position, which will be done by Monte Carlo method. Also, a pedestrian agent receives a pedestrian profile including pedestrian characteristics, desired speed, activity agenda, etc. At a certain point of time, the network of shop-cells and street-cells is populated with pedestrian agents. At this point of time, all pedestrian agents have their current-node and according cell position. For each pedestrian agent, the to-node will be derived from the execution of pedestrian's activity. The following 'network characteristics' applies:

Let L consists of a lattice of cells, representing the irregular network of shop-cells and street-cells, with size N which is the number of cells.

The state of cell **i** is determined by its utilization, which depends of the number of pedestrian agents in cell **i** and the maximum possible number of pedestrian agents in cell **i**. Therefore,

the utilization of cell **i** is defined by $u_{i,k_i}^{m_i}$ with i=1,...N,
m_i = maximum of pedestrian agents in cell **i**, $m_i \in \mathbb{N}$, and
k_i = number of pedestrian agents in cell **i**, $k_i \in [0, m_i]$.

A configuration of L at time t is defined as

$Q(t) = (u_{1,k_1}^{m_1}(t), u_{2,k_2}^{m_2}(t), \ldots, u_{N,k_N}^{m_N}(t))$, where

$u_{i,k_i}^{m_i}(t) \in [u_{i,0}^{m_i}, u_{i,m_i}^{m_i}]$ is the state of cell **i** at time t.

The progression of L in time is then given by the network update function, also called the evolution operator, Θ

$$\Theta: Q(t) \rightarrow Q(t+1), t = 0,1, \ldots \quad (5)$$

The network update function contains the *walk-to-node* operation for each pedestrian agent in the network and includes the following rule:

```
If  pedestrian-agent pauses or
 cell linked to to-node is full-occupied
Then wait {to-node ← current-node}
Else walk-to to-node
```

Fig. 7 shows a population of pedestrian agents in the previous mentioned segment of the city center at a certain moment (different colors means opposite direction).

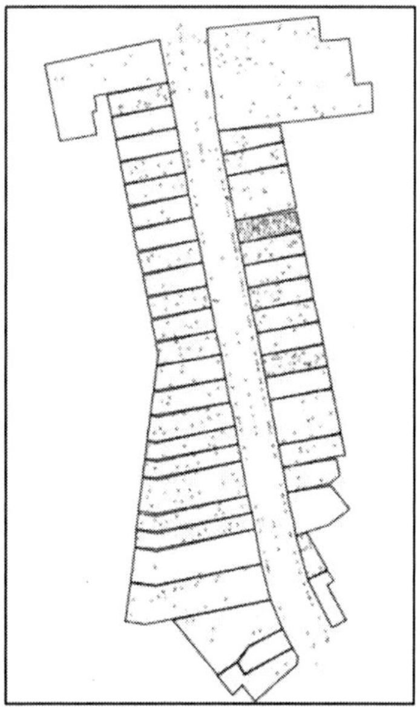

Figure 7. Main street of the city center populated with pedestrian agents.

Striking is the apparent agents overflow at one of the shops. That has to do with the high priority of the shop, and that this shop has a lower floor. This is in contrast to the other shops in this street segment which only have a ground floor.

VI. DISCUSSION AND FUTURE DIRECTIONS

In this paper, we presented a simulation platform for performing pedestrian movement simulation in a shopping environment. Pedestrian movement depends on pedestrian behavior, which depends of behavioral principles like perception, activation and completing an activity. The outcome of pedestrian activation is pedestrian movement on the network of shops and streets. In our approach, pedestrians are represented by agents and the network of shops and streets are represented by a lattice of irregular cells; each represented by their node. Pedestrian agents move from node to node and are situated into the cells related to those nodes. They are situated randomly in those cells, but if the area is occupied they cannot move to that cell. This reduces the complexity of the simulation by ignoring collisions and with that collision detection. This approach makes the simulation feasible because computer power is less binding.

Also, activity agenda's for pedestrian agents could be incorporated, including planned and unplanned shop stops resulting in store visits with time duration of the store visit.

In the next phase, the simulation in a 2D environment must be validated. In first instance we look at face validity, because it appears to be a reasonable imitation of a real-world shopping environment to people who are familiar with the real shopping environment. The validation test will consist of comparing outputs from the system under consideration to model outputs for the same set of input conditions.

Future developments should make the pedestrian agent model suitable for a 3D environment with lifelike virtual persons. In that case, the pedestrian agent movement will be realized from cell point to cell point considering collision detection. Finally, this will result in a virtual environment of a real situation, populated with virtual visitors and a real visitor (user) moving amongst these virtual visitors. In that case, a user can assess an environment that has high reality content. For city managers or designer, it is possible to gain deeper insight into pedestrian activity behavior in city centers, even for those that do not exist yet.

REFERENCES

[1] W. Ali and B. Moulin, "How artificial intelligence agents do shopping in a virtual mall: a 'believable'and 'usable' multi-agent based simulation of customers' shopping behavior in a mall", in Canadian AI, LNAI 4013, L. Lamontagne and M. Marchand, Eds. Berlin: Springer-Verlag, 2006, pp. 73-85.

[2] Y. Shoham and K. Leyton-Brown, "Multiagent Systems: Algorithmic, Game-Theoretic, and Logical Foundations", Cambridge University Press, p. 230, 2008.

[3] The Repast Suite. [Online]. Available from http://repast.sourceforge.net/ 2016.06.13

[4] NetLogo. [Online]. Available from http://ccl.northwestern.edu/netlogo/ 2016.06.13

[5] J. Dijkstra, A. J. Jessurun, and H. J. P. Timmermans, "Simulating pedestrian activity scheduling behavior and movement patterns using a multi-agent cellular automata model", in Proceedings of the Transportation Research Board Conference, Washington, January, 2002.

[6] M. Bierlaire, G. Antonioni, and M. Weber, "Behavioral dynamics for pedestrians", in Moving through Nets: the Physical and Social Dimensions of Travel, K.W. Axhausen Ed. Elsevier Science Ltd., pp. 81-105, 2005.

[7] W. Zhu and H. J. P. Timmermans, "Cut-off models for 'go-home' decision pedestrians in shopping streets", Environment and Planning B: Planning and Design, Vol. 35, No. 2, pp. 248-260, 2008.

[8] R. Najlis and M. J. North, "Repast for GIS", in Proceedings of the Agent 2004 Conference on Social Dynamics: Interaction, Reflexivity and Emergence, C. M. Macal, D. Sallach, and M. J. North, Eds. Chicago, Illinois, pp. 225-260, 2004.

[9] J. Dijkstra, A. J. Jessurun, H. J. P. Timmermans, and B. de Vries, "A framework for processing agent-based pedestrian activity simulations in shopping environments", Cybernetics and Systems, Vol. 42, No. 7, pp. 526-545, 2011.

[10] J. Dijkstra and A. J. Jessurun, "Agent-based pedestrian activity simulation in shopping environments using a choice network approach", in J. Wąs, G. C. Sirakoulis, and B. Bandini, Eds. ACRI2014, LNCS 8751, pp. 680-687, 2014.

[11] J. Dijkstra, H. J. P. Timmermans, and B. de Vries, "Activation of shopping pedestrian agents : empirical estimation results", Applied Spatial Analysis and Policy, No. 6, pp. 255-266, 2013.

[12] T. R. Howe, N. T. Collier, M. J. North, M. T. Parker, and J. R. Vos, "Repast for GIS", in D. Sallach, C. M. Macal, and M. J. North, Eds., Proceedings of the Agent 2006 Conference

on Social Agents: Results and Prospects, Chicago, Illinois, pp. 107-116, 2006.

[13] QGIS Open Source Geographic Information System. [Online]. Avalaible from http://www.qgis.org/ 2016.06.13

[14] R. Najlis and M. J. North, "Repast for GIS", in C. M. Macal, D. Sallach, and M. J. North, Eds., Proceedings of the Agent 2004 Conference on Social Dynamics: Interaction,, Reflexivity and Emergence, Chicago, Illinois, pp. 225-260, 2004.

[15] A. Borgers and H. J. P. Timmermans, "City center entry points, store location patterns and pedestrian route chocie behavior: A micro-level simulation model", Socio-Economic Planning Sciences, Vol. 20, pp. 25-30, 1986.

[16] J. Dijkstra and A. J. Jessurun, "Modeling planned and unplanned store stops for the scenario based simulation of pedestrian activity in city centers", in P. Lorenz and M. Bauer, Eds., Proceedings of the Fifth International Conference on Advances in System Simulation (SIMUL2013), 27 October - 1 November 2013, Venice, Italy, pp. 1-22, 2013.

[17] J. Dijkstra, H. J. P. Timmermans, A. J. Jessurun, and B. de Vries, "Modeling time duration of planned and unplanned store visits in a multi-agent simulation of pedestrian activity in city centers", in U. Weidemann, M. Schreckenberg, and U. Kirsch, Eds., Pedestrian and evacuation dynamics 2012, Berlin: Springer, pp. 815-824, 2014.

[18] D. Stevens and S. Dragićević, "A GIS-based Irregular Cellular Automata Model of Land-use Change", Environment and Planning B: Planning and Design, No. 34, 2007, pp. 708-724.

[19] D. Stevens, S. Dragićević, and K. Rothley, "iCity: A GIS-CA Modeling Tool for Urban Planning and Decision Making", Environmental Modelling & Software, No. 22, pp. 761-773, 2007.

[20] N. N. Pinto and A. P. Antunes, "A Cellular Automata Model Based on Irregular Cells: Application to Small Urban Areas", Environment and Planning B: Planning and Design, No. 37, pp. 1095-114, 2010.

[21] M. Tomassini, "Generalized Automata Networks", in E. Yacoubi, B. Chopard, and S. Bandini, Eds., ACRI 2006, LNCS 4173. Springer-Verlag Berlin Heidelberg, pp. 14-28, 2006.

An Integrated Modelling Approach for Spatial-aware Federated Simulation

Jingquan Xie
Fraunhofer IAIS
Sankt Augustin, Germany
E-Mail: jingquan.xie@iais.fraunhofer.de

Rafal Kozik
University of Science and Technology (UTP), Bydgoszcz, Poland
E-Mail: rkozik@utp.edu.pl

Nikolas Flourentzou
University of Cyprus
Nicosia, Cyprus
E-Mail: flourentzou.nikolas@ucy.ac.cy

Abstract—**Federated simulation provides a powerful means to analyze dynamics of inter-connected large-scale systems like networks of critical infrastructures (CI) including power supply systems, railway systems, telecommunication networks, etc. Building a sound federation model that can be used for federated simulations is however a challenging task, especially when the spatial aspects of the sophisticated networks need to be considered. In this paper, an integrated modelling approach is proposed to reduce the effort in building such spatial models for federated simulation. It aims to automatically produce consistent models that can be accepted by domain-specific simulators like SIEMENS PSS SINCAL and ns-3, in particularly for use cases where federation models evolve frequently. This is a work in progress. The modelling approach itself is general purpose and not limited to certain domains like power or telecommunication systems.**

Keywords-Federated Simulation; Spatial Information System; Integrated Modelling; Dependency Modelling; ns-3; SINCAL; Crisis Management; Training Application; Critical Infrastructure;

I. INTRODUCTION

Large-scale inter-connected systems like networks of critical infrastructures play a central role in our daily life in modern society. It is critical to be able to analyse their behaviours under both normal and stressed situations. Modern simulation technology provides a powerful means to achieve this by combining different domain-specific simulators together - federated simulation [1]. Each simulator is developed by experts in their domain like the electrical energy distribution or IP-based telecommunication systems. A simulation middleware, like the DIESIS [2], is then used to facilitate the federation among the simulators.

One of the challenging tasks in developing and deploying systems based on the federated simulation is building the consistent federation models, especially when the spatial aspects of network elements need to be considered. The root of this challenge lays on the domain-specific simulators, which are in most cases developed independently by different organisations with limited support for modelling spatial information. Moreover, each simulator has its own syntax to describe the models, for example, SINCAL [3] uses relational databases to store the model in a sophisticated schema while ns-3 [4] models can be hard-coded in the source code. The motivation of this work is trying to establish an integrated modelling approach through a unified spatial-aware interface for model developers of different domains. Models that can be accepted by domain-specific simulators can be automatically generated to keep the federation model on a high-level of consistency.

The related research work dealing with federated simulation involves two categories: model generation and runtime environment. Most of the work focuses on the runtime environment to provide an interoperable execution environment for simulator federation. High-Level Architecture (HLA) [5] is a standard for integrating different simulators and it is widely used in the military. The DIESIS federation middleware [2] developed in the EU-funded research project DIESIS focuses on the integration of critical infrastructure simulators with knowledge base support. I2Sim [6] provides a federation mechanism where a common model for all involved domains are needed. To our best knowledge, these systems do not provide sufficient support in spatial-aware dependency modelling out-of-box.

This paper is structured as follows: Section I provides introductory material and motivation of the proposed approach. It is followed by Section II that presents the requirements of the proposed approach for developing spatial-aware federated simulation models. Section III describes the architecture and interfaces of the integrated modelling environment. This is still work-in-progress and the preliminary results are presented in Section IV to help the reader further understand the benefits of the proposed approach. Finally, conclusions are given in Section V.

II. SPATIAL-AWARE FEDERATION MODELLING

In real world, most of the elements in the critical infrastructure networks locate somewhere (e.g., an urban area substation, an antenna for mobile communication). In a well-built model of these systems, they are Geo-referenced - for example, a transformer in the SINCAL [3] model can be assigned with a coordinate in the form of latitude and longitude. Similarly Internet-capable routers used for IP-based communication in ns-3 [4] models also possess spatial information. To our knowledge, domain-specific simulators like SINCAL per se do not have sufficient support for modelling these kinds of geographical information. The reason is that spatial attributes do not affect the simulation results and therefore is irrelevant for most of the simulation tasks. In federated simulation however, spatial information can be used to determine the dependencies between different domain models. For instance, if a cabinet is near a router, it is very likely that the router is powered by the electrical power from that cabinet. The rest of this section discusses the requirements that are essential for developing spatial-aware federation models.

A. Domain Elements as First-class Citizen

In traditional Geographical Information Systems (GIS), primitive spatial features include points, lines and polygons. They are first-class citizens in those systems. Most operations are designed in mind to handle these primitive objects.

For an integrated spatial modelling environment covering federated simulation, the concept is different. First-class citizen objects that need to be managed should be high-level, which again build on top of the traditional primitive objects like points and lines. For instance, instead of dealing with lines directly, the system should provide utilities to manage power lines with additional attributes like power voltage, resistance, etc. For each domain element, a set of attributes should be provided for model developers to manage different physical parameters associated with that element. As an example, a list of elements from the power domain is provided in Table I with the corresponding attributes. It is essential to identify all relevant physical parameters needed by the domain-specific simulators. Model developers are responsible for giving appropriate values during the modelling phase. By design, the provider of the parameters of a given domain is the simulator adapter, which will be elaborated in Section III.B.

TABLE I. THE PHYSICAL PARAMETERS FOR THE POWER SYSTEM ELEMENTS.

	Generation	*Lines*	*Loads*	*Transformer*	*Converter*
ID	Yes	Yes	Yes	Yes	Yes
Category	1	2	3	4	5
Volt rating	Yes	Yes	Yes	Yes × 2	Yes
Resistance	No	Yes	No	Yes	No
Losses	No	Yes	No	Yes	Yes
Dimension	3D	Length	3D	3D	3D
Network	HV	HV, MV, LV	MV, LV	HV, MV	HV, MV
Other	Cooling	Overvoltage	No	Overpower	Cooling

B. Dependency Modelling

Dependency is an essential part of the network of critical infrastructures. It is however a challenging task to model dependencies in federated simulation systems. The reason is twofold:

- Identifying these dependencies between different domain elements is difficult if not impossible. For instance, in a network of CI, a router produces communication services for SCADA systems that remotely control a secondary substation in the power distribution network. In most cases, it is not clear for model developers which router really provides the service due to confidential levels of these kinds of information for CI operators.
- Missing an established methodology with sufficient tool support to facilitate the model developers to map the real dependency into the federation model. During the past years, various approaches have already been proposed to model dependencies [6]-[9]; however, none of them provides enough tool support to really enable the dependency modelling. Furthermore, spatial support is completely missing in these approaches.

In the proposed approach, this issue is addressed by a novel yet pragmatic solution. Dependent domain elements in the federation model will be identified by the model developers. Based on this information, the generated model (see Section II.C) for each domain-specific simulator will contain an instance of the same dependent elements (e.g., if a router provides Internet service for SCADA systems). This router instance will be modelled twice: one in the telecommunication (communication provider) and the other in the electrical distribution model (power energy consumer). Since the targeted domain model is generated automatically and the generation process is automatic, this approach provides a scalable solution for large federation models.

C. Domain Model Generation

Domain-specific simulators are normally developed by different organisations in parallel. Each simulator, both proprietary and open-source, normally provides its own user interface for users to develop models. Subsequently, in most cases, the modelling results are persistent in a proprietary format that can only be correctly handled by the simulator itself. There are some efforts to define standardised ways to represent models for specific domains, like the Common Information Model (CIM) [10] model for power networks. However, we are not aware of any standard for interdomain model representation. To our best knowledge, there is not a unified model representation for multiple domains that can be directly accepted by different domain-specific simulators.

To handle this issue in a pragmatic way, the proposed approach exports separate federation models in a representation that can be accepted by domain-specific simulators directly. For that purpose, simulator adapters (for each domain-specific simulator) are included in the proposed approach. These adapters will be part of the software tool - the integrated modelling environment. The software interfaces between the modelling core and the adapters will be specified and published, so that third parties can also contribute their adapters, e.g., for coupling their own simulators into the modelling system, more details see Section III.B. This feature is of utmost importance to keep the consistency of frequently changing federation models.

III. INTEGRATED FEDERATION MODELLING ENVIRONMENT

The software tool that provides the features mentioned in Section II is called Integrated Federation Modelling Environment (FEMI). In the rest of this section, the system architecture, the software interface specification and the spatial support will be elaborated.

A. Architecture

FEMI is an HTML5 Web application with sophisticated spatial support. The reason to develop FEMI as a Web application instead of traditional Desktop application is twofold:

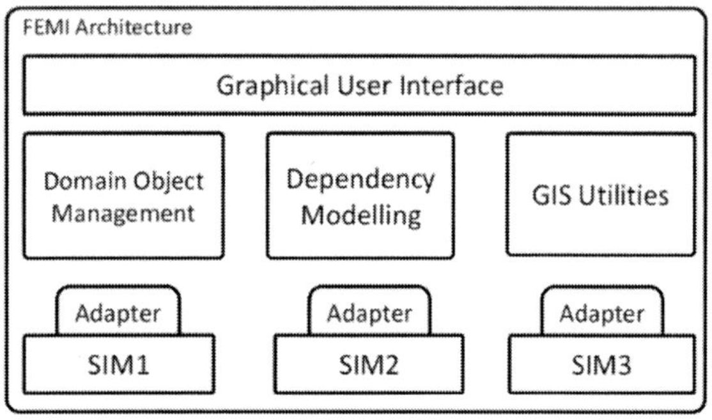

Figure 1. FEMI architecture.

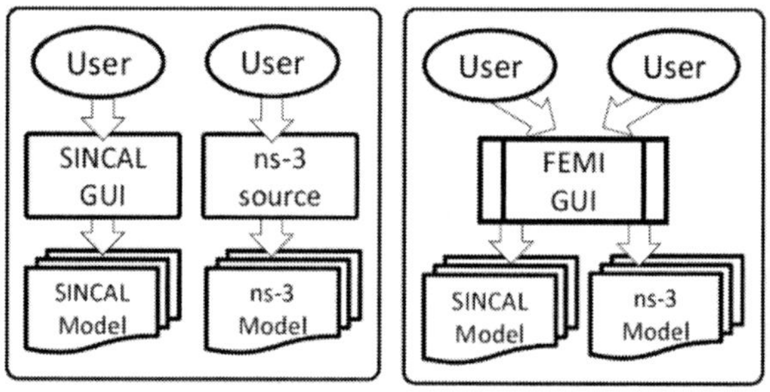

Figure 2. Comparison of the traditional modelling workflow and the FEMI-based workflow.

- Internet provides the most pervasive infrastructure that can be accessed by different users from almost any locations. Browser-based applications that do not require an installation on the native machine greatly reduce the efforts needed to start working with the system.
- Tool support for developing HTML5 applications is evolving extremely fast due to the promotion of large IT companies. Frameworks and libraries like NodeJS [11] and LeafletJS [12] make the development of HTML5 Web applications with spatial support much easier than developing a Desktop application with comparable functionalities.

In general FEMI has three functional layers (see Fig. 1: 1) the Graphical User Interface (GUI) providing easy-to-use interfaces for model developers. FEMI GUI hides all of the low-level technical details of management internal data structures. 2) the management layer that provides support for domain object management, dependency modelling in federated simulations, and the GIS utilities. The domain object management is responsible for handling first-class citizens in FEMI like the power lines, the router, etc. The dependency modelling module is used to manage dependent elements. Finally, the GIS utilities provide sophisticated support for managing primitive spatial features like points and polygons. 3) the simulator layer contains various domain simulators and the adapters. The adapters work like a translator between the FEMI core system and the simulators, which per se do not understand any commands sent by FEMI.

B. Interface Specification

To enable the communication between FEMI core and the domain-specific simulators, a set of software interfaces are needed. On the functional level, these interfaces are the basis for the following:

- Expose the capabilities of the simulators. Capabilities include for instance if the simulator supports stepping functions during the simulation; what kind of physical parameters are needed for a given model element, etc. This interface is normally used during the initial phase before interacting with the simulators.
- Export domain-specific models. Model developers use FEMI GUI to create federation models. The federation model can be converted into multiple domain-specific models for simulation. As aforementioned, this step is necessary because domain-specific simulators normally have their own way of model representation.
- Interact with simulators. At runtime, after the models are generated, it can be loaded into the simulator directly for validation. From FEMI, model developers can control the simulator by starting, pausing and stopping the simulation. The simulation results can be pushed back to FEMI via this interface.

Technically, these services are implemented as RESTful Web Service to cope with the HTML5 Web Application of FEMI. Due to the page limit, the detailed RESTful service specification is omitted.

C. Spatial Support

FEMI has built-in support for spatial objects. Model developers are able to determine the element locations, length, and orientations, etc. via the graphical user interface provided in FEMI. The underlying models will be synchronised automatically if a spatial object is changed.

Dependency recommendation will be performed by analysing the distance between two elements (by taking into account their domains as well). Threshold values can be given by users to automatically trigger the dependency generation. Moreover, areas that model elements can influence (a cabinet is responsible for providing electrical power for a certain area in a city) can also be generated automatically by using methods like the Voronoi diagrams. This provides a convenient way to assess the impacts and consequences of model failures (e.g., how a failure in the power system could potentially influence the operation of a heavily populated area).

IV. Preliminary Results

In order to demonstrate the proposed approach, a training system for crisis management is used. This training system is developed for working with crisis managers by performing What-if Analysis and Consequence Analysis of their decisions [13]. All dynamics of simulated systems are

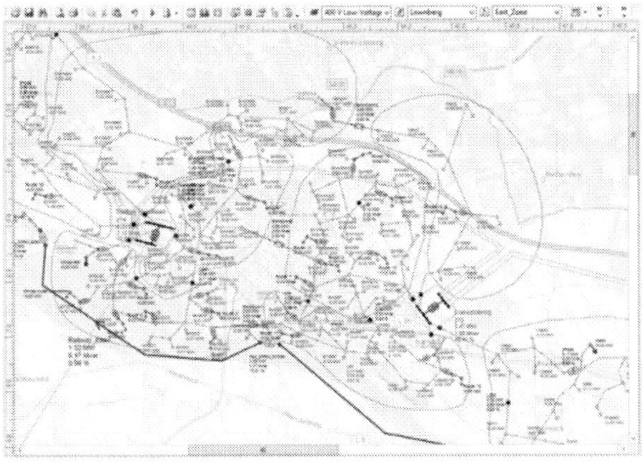

Figure 3. Synthetic electrical distribution network of Emmerich area.

provided by using a spatial-aware federated simulation subsystem.

Two domains are involved in the federated simulation: the power transmission networks and the telecommunication networks. SINCAL is used to perform the power flow calculation and ns-3 is adopted for IP-based Internet traffic analysis. The traditional way to build simulation models is using the tools provided by simulators. For instance, the SINCAL GUI can be used for that purpose and ns-3 models are embedded in the source code of a simulation (see the left part of Fig. 2). Dedicated simulator modules (with limited spatial support) are used to export the destination models. With this approach, the dependencies between models cannot be expressed explicitly. On the right hand side of Fig. 2 is the workflow based on FEMI. Different users, model developers in this case, use the same integrated tool to provide necessary information for building domain-specific models. Dependency modelling is supported out-of-box. Spatial information can be managed by using GIS utilities as explained in Section III.C. With the help of simulator adapters, consistent models can be exported automatically. This is extremely important for federation models that need frequent changes to ensure the model consistency.

The SINCAL model focuses on the distribution network of the given area along with the relevant parameters, as shown in Fig. 3. % (for security reasons we removed the names). The telecommunication routers are included into the SINCAL model as well since they consume electrical power. On the other side, the routers provide the telecommunication services for the given area, which introduce some kind of dependency between the power and the telecommunication systems.

A. Electrical Power System Model

The power system modelled in SINCAL is a synthetic distribution network of the given area. SINCAL is a tool which provides a range of modules for designing, modelling and analysing power models. SINCAL can be used for general load flow analysis, load profile analysis for investigating a daily profile, load development analysis for calculations with load values that vary over time, and

Figure 4. High-level topology of the telecommunication network.

contingency analysis for elements malfunction in individual load flow calculations.

The data required to design the model are the physical parameters and the types of the elements. The main elements along with their types are the following:

- Power generation units: conventional generators, renewable energy systems, representation of transmission line equivalent;
- Power connection lines: transmission in high-voltage (HV), distribution in medium-voltage (MV) and low-voltage (LV), railways in HL and MV;
- Electrical loads (end users): consumers of electricity, power supply of telecommunication system, power supply of water system, electrification of transportation system;
- Power transformers: power stations, sub-stations, distribution cabinets/feeders, boost-transformers;
- Static converters: integration of RES to power system, HVDC stations, FACTS, frequency changer.

The model designed in SINCAL is formed by several power elements. The identified physical parameters are specified in Table I. The SINCAL model of power system elements along with the dependent elements are shown in Fig. 3.

B. Telecommunication Network Model

In order to model and simulate telecommunication aspects, we have used the Network Simulation version 3 tool [4]. It is a discrete-event network simulator, provided as free/open source software under a GNU GPLv2 license. Its purpose is to provide an ``open simulation environment for networking research", including IP-based networks and non-IP based communication networks. In the proposed approach, we used ns-3 for modelling the fixed line and mobile telecommunication net-works of our scenarios. However, since we are lacking the information about the real topology of core telecommunication network in the analyzed geographical area, we have made some conceptual and designing assumption while modelling.

It must be noticed, that in our approach we have chosen some examples of simulators that are recognized by the community. For instance, counterparts for NS3 are tools like OMNet++, OPNET, J-SIM, etc. These tools have different advantages and disadvantages (e.g. openness, community support, etc.). However, there were not any particular reasons for choosing NS3, except the fact that we had some experience with that tool before.

First, we assumed that the broadband network to city is provided by node indicated as ``0'' in Fig. 4. The city center is connected via router indicated as "1", that further connects western (router 7), eastern (router 8) and southern parts (router 2) of modelled area.

In southern part of modelled area, there are redundant paths between routers. For instance, traffic from node 5 to node 1 can be established via node 3 or node 2. However, these paths have different characteristics and the link between node 1 and 3 has 20 ms delay in contrast to link between nodes 1 and 2, which has 2 ms delay. In case of the scenario, where node 2 fails, connection will be established via node 3. Therefore, we will observe the degradation of communication quality. As a result, this will disturb the communication between southern areas of modelled area with remaining elements in the city.

The geographical region with close proximity to node 8 has been indicated as urban area, where schools and households are located. The network elements located in this part of the city will generate significant volume of traffic to other services (e.g., banks, hospitals, etc.).

In the ns-3 tools suite, the topology and the configuration of the simulation are provided either in *.py (python) or in *.cc (c/c++) files. Commonly, these files contain following information:

- ns-3 nodes definition (names, types , positions, etc.),
- Communication links definition (data rates and delays),
- Topology definition,
- IP stack installation,
- IP addresses assignment,
- Routing definition,
- Configuration of the application layer.

In ns-3, the term node is used to name an abstract device connected to a network such as end-users hosts, end-systems, routers, switches, hubs etc. Since ns-3 does not focus on Internet technologies only, it is the responsibility of simulation creator to define nodes properly by adding applications, protocols stack, etc. In ns-3 the concept of application is defined as an element that runs the simulation. It is the basic abstraction of a user program, which generates some network traffic.

Currently, ns-3 does not provide GUI that would support modelling process concerning geospatial aspects. There are some projects that aim to provide environments for network topology prototyping. For instance ns-3 topology generator [14] allows the user to use GUI in order to define nodes, communication channels and applications. However, the generated models are represented as C/C++ code, which in some cases may not compile, due to the fact that ns-3 is still under development and the base code changes between releases. Manual changes of the generated code can fix some compilation errors, but user is required to have some expert skills and the changes need to be applied each time topology is generated. Moreover, there is no functionality that will allow users to specify geographical positions of topology elements. Therefore, we believe that FEMI-based workflow is a good way to address these issues and to facilitate model developers with an abstraction layer that will reduce the modelling effort substantially.

C. *Integrated modelling*

For the crisis management training system, we started the modelling work by using the traditional approach as depicted in Fig. 2. Soon we noticed that it does not scale and is very time-consuming to maintain the model consistency with different tools.

With the proposed approach, for dependent elements like routers that exist in both domain-specific models, only one instance needs to be managed. By specifying the corresponding domains, separate instances will be generated automatically in the target model. This feature substantially reduces the efforts to improve the model consistency. For instance, it happens quite often in preparing federation models for training that the name of a router in the ns-3 model is changed while the reference in the SINCAL model still has the old name. This causes unexpected runtime behaviours of the federated simulation system and it can be avoided with the proposed approach. Unfortunately, since FEMI is still under development and the GUI part is still not complete, we will show screenshots in the forthcoming publications. In addition, formal ontology is also considered as a common vocabulary between different domains to facilitate a consistent modelling. However, at this stage of our development cycle we still rely on consistent naming convention when connecting the same elements in different simulators. Also some specific mapping between FEMI core system and the simulators (e.g. bandwidth or delay of telecommunication links) are still hardcoded into adapters logic.

V. CONCLUSION

This paper briefly presented the motivation, ideas and benefits of using an integrated modelling environment for spatial-aware federated simulations. The motivation of this work laid mainly in the extremely high overhead in maintaining model consistency in traditional federated simulation modelling workflow. Moreover, limited GIS support makes it difficult, if not impossible, to facilitate modelling and visualising spatial objects and dependency. Based on this consideration, the FEMI system was illustrated. The software architecture, the interface specification and the spatial support were elaborated to provide a high-level overview of this system. It is still a work in progress and currently under development. One of the core parts of FEMI is the simulator adapter. Implementing such an adapter is a challenging task, because the developers need to know the technical details of communication interface provided by FEMI and simulators. This is one of the drawbacks of the proposed approach. Due to the heterogeneity of different domain specific simulators, this can be an effort-intensive task.

In the future, we plan to accelerate the development work of FEMI and make it publicly available as a cloud platform for modelling federated simulations. Collaborative modelling is also one of the features that we want to address in FEMI so that different model developers can work together within one Web-based platform. Formal ontologies will be adopted as common vocabularies to facilitate a consistent modelling process. Finally, the envisioned European Scenario Database [15] can be connected with FEMI to provide an end-to-end solution for generating and reusing federation models.

ACKNOWLEDGMENT

This research leading to these results was funded by the European Commission within the Seventh Framework Programme project CIPRNet (grant agreement N° 312450) and PREDICT (grant agreement N° 607697). The authors thank all of the project partners for many constructive discussions and useful suggestions.

REFERENCES

[1] E. Rome, P. Langeslag, and A. Usov, "Federated modelling and simulation for critical infrastructure protection," in Networks of Networks: The Last Frontier of Complexity. Springer, 2014, pp. 225–253.

[2] A. Usov, C. Beyel, E. Rome, U. Beyer, E. Castorini, P. Palazzari, and A. Tofani, "The DIESIS Approach to Semantically Interoperable Federated Critical Infrastructure Simulation," in Advances in System Simulation (SIMUL), 2010. IEEE, 2010, pp. 121–128.

[3] SimTec, "PSS SINCAL," 2015. [Online]. Available: http://www.simtec.cc/sites/sincal.asp

[4] NS-3 Consortium, "NS-3 Network Simulator," 2015. [Online]. Available: http://www.nsnam.org

[5] IEEE, "IEEE 1516-2010 - Standard for Modeling and Simulation (M&S) High Level Architecture (HLA) – Framework and Rules," IEEE, Tech. Rep., 2010.

[6] J. Mart'ı, C. Ventura, J. Hollman, K. Srivastava, and H. Juarez, "I2sim modelling and simulation framework for scenario development, training, and real-time decision support of multiple interdependent critical infrastructures during large emergencies," in NATO (OTAN) MSG-060 Symposium on How is Modelling and Simulation Meeting the Defence Challenges out to, vol. 2015, 2008.

[7] S. Rinaldi, J. Peerenboom, and T. Kelly, "Identifying, understanding, and analyzing critical infrastructure interdependencies," Control Systems, IEEE, vol. 21, no. 6, 2001, pp. 11–25.

[8] A. Nieuwenhuijs, E. Luiijf, and M. Klaver, "Modeling dependencies in critical infrastructures," in Critical Infrastructure Protection II. Springer, 2008, pp. 205–213.

[9] A. D. Giorgio and F. Liberati, "A bayesian network-based approach to the critical infrastructure interdependencies analysis," Systems Journal, IEEE, vol. 6, no. 3, 2012, pp. 510–519.

[10] IEC, "IEC 61970-301 Energy management system application program interface – Common Information Model base," International Electrotechnical Commission, Geneva, Switzerland, ISO 27019-2013, 2013.

[11] S. Tilkov and S. Vinoski, "Node.js: Using javascript to build high-highperformance network programs," IEEE Internet Computing, vol. 14, no. 6, 2010, pp. 80.

[12] P. Crickard III, Leaflet.js Essentials. Packt Publishing Ltd, 2014.

[13] CIPRNet, "The EU CIPRNet Research Project," 2013. [Online]. Available: http://www.ciprnet.eu

[14] University of Strasbourg, "Topology Generator Project," 2016. [Online]. Available: https://www.nsnam.org/wiki/Topology%5FGenerator.

[15] J. Xie, M. Theocharidou, and Y. Barbarin, "Knowledge-driven scenario development for critical infrastructure protection," in Critical Information Infrastructures Security - 10th International Workshop, CRITIS 2015, Berlin, Germany, October 5-7, 2015, ser. Lecture Notes in Computer Science. Springer, 2015, pp. 91-102.

Agent-Based Model to Simulate Outpatient Consultations at the "Hospital de Clínicas"

Work-in-Progress Paper

Ramona Galeano, Cynthia Villalba
Facultad Politécnica
Universidad Nacional de Asunción (UNA)
San Lorenzo, Paraguay.
e-mail: eligal0930@pol.una.py, cvillalba@pol.una.py

Dolores Rexachs, Emilio Luque
Computer Architecture and Operating Systems Department
Universitat Autónoma de Barcelona (UAB)
Barcelona, Spain
e-mail: dolores.rexachs@uab.es, emilio.luque@uab.es

Abstract—**The "Hospital de Clínicas" is one of the busiest hospitals in Paraguay, with an average of 1150 outpatient per day. Usually, patients have to wait a very long time to be treated, causing anger and discomfort. This paper presents an agent-based model of the process of outpatient consultation for the Department of Internal Medicine. The goal is to have a better understanding of the process and evaluating different solutions to reduce the patient waiting time.**

Keywords- ***agent-based model; Simulation; consultations; patient flow; outpatient.***

I. INTRODUCTION

Patient waiting time is a significant topic in medical institutions, and has considerable effects on patient's satisfaction. In special, long waiting times and long queues of patients are the most prominent problems [1].

These problems also affect the Paraguayan "Hospital de Clínicas" (CH). The CH has more than 45 medical specialties; and it is one of the largest, complex, and busiest hospitals of Paraguay. The Statistics Department from the Hospital reported that 17,270 attentions were recorded for outpatient in the first half of January 2016. These numbers imply an average of 1,150 visits per day [2].

During a survey it was found that patients in the outpatient area must wait several hours before being treated. Patients line up in two different places: cash register and admission.

In order to understand the process of outpatient consultation and evaluate different solutions aimed at reducing patient waiting time, we proposed to simulate that process. This paper presents an agent-based model (ABM) for the process for the outpatient consultation at the Department of Internal Medicine of the CH.

ABM is an approach to model systems comprised of individual, autonomous, interacting "agents". Agent-based modeling offers ways to more easily model individual behaviors and also how these behaviors affect others [3]. ABM offers some advantages such as: an increased detail in experiments based in simulation, a transparent learning process, and the ability to control and easily modify individual behaviors [4].

ABM has seen a tremendous growth in many areas over 15 years and more recently in hospital and healthcare settings. One of the primary applications of ABM to hospital environments examines patient flow in Emergency Departments (ED)[5][6].

An evolving literature exists regarding applying ABM, alone or together with other technique, to the operations of ED. In general, this literature addresses system-level performance dynamics, quantified in terms of patient safety [7], economic indicators [7][8], staff workload and scheduling [5][9], and patient flows.

More recently, other works have modeled improvements to patient flow using an ABM running on High Performance Computing resources [10]. The ABM was built with NetLogo. More extensive considerations of ABMs for patient flow in EDs were developed by the same researchers [11][12], including the use of an ABM within a decision support system for EDs [4].

For the topic of outpatient consultations, we found works that use the discrete event simulation models, which implies that the status of the system only changes due to certain events, such as a request for a consultation or completing a consultation [13]. One of the most popular softwares used is Arena, which is used to develop the simulation model in order to examine the patient flow, especially the waiting time [14].

The rest of the paper is organized as it follows. In Section II, we explain the process performed by a patient to make an appointment at the CH. Section III presents the method to be used for the model. Section IV describes the simulation model proposed and Section V presents the conclusion of this project.

II. CURRENT SYSTEM IN OUTPATIENTS CONSULTATION

In this section we will describe the current process to request an appointment with the Internal Medicine doctor, which is shown in Fig. 1:

1) Request a service: At the beginning of the day, box officials receive the schedule established for the doctors at seven o'clock a.m., which contains the number of patients to be treated in each deparment. Patients line up to request a service (waiting time to request a service: t_{wrs}) and pay when it is necessary. The officials proceed to register and give the return receipt for the payment (Time for register a required service: t_{rs}).

proceed to call patients (health care Time: t_m). If it is the First Consultation, doctors fill data about patients, such as treatment forms, prescriptions, and other sheets. Doctors may requiere patients a next appointment or discharge them. Doctors inform nurses next appointments. Once all the patients have been served, doctors return health records to nursing. Officers pick up records and leave them in the Central Record.

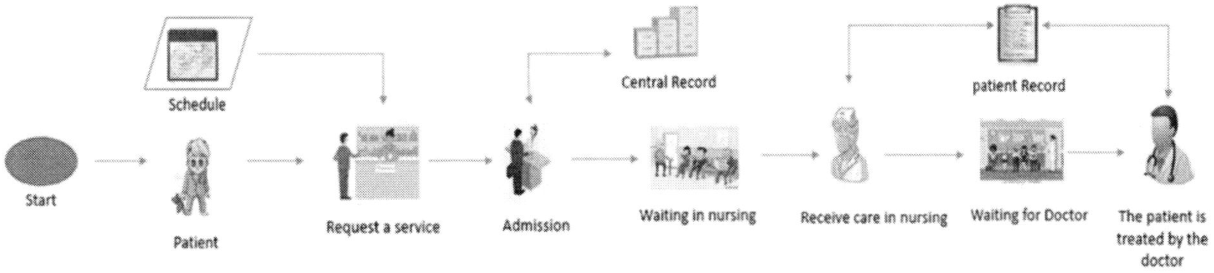

Figure 1. Process to request an appointment for Internal Medicine

2) Admission: After request a service, patients go to admission office and line up again to signing (waiting time in admission or signing: t_{wa}). Here, patients present their identity card or passport and the receipt obtained in the cash register. Officials ask what type of consultation patients need: First Consultation, Control, Interconsultation (First consultation time: t_{af}; Control Time: t_{ac}, Interconsultation time: t_{ai}). In the First Consultation, officials fill the header of the patient record with name, surname, identity card number and other extra information. If it is not the First Consultation, patients give their record number. This number is recorded in the receipt (time to sign a patient: t_a). When a certain amount of record numbers are collected, the official goes to the Central Record to collect the records and take them to the nursing. The last process is repeated until they have engaged all patients.

3) Waiting in nursing: After signing, patients go to nursing and wait for the nurse call (Waiting time in nursing: t_{wn}).

4) Receive care in nursing: Here nurse registers the patient physical data (weight, height) and vital signs (blood pressure) (time nursing care: t_e). Then, patient is assigned to a doctor. After this, patient waits for the medical consultation (medical consultation standby time: T_{wmc}). In case a patient with previous appointment arrives, nurse checks the appointment and give him a certificate of his appointment. Then, this patient goes to the cash register and admission in order to confirm his appointment.

5) Waiting for Doctor: After received care in nursing, in the waiting room, patients wait to be called by the doctor.

6) The patient is treated by the doctor: Doctors first go to the waiting room and take the records of patients assigned for that day. Then, they go to their consulting room and

III. METHOD

Agent-based simulation (ABS), or agent-based modeling (ABM), is a modeling and computational framework for simulating dynamic processes that involves autonomous agents [4].

Agent-based modeling offers ways of easily modeling individual behaviors and how behaviors affect others in ways that have not been available before. There is much interest in developing agent-based model for many application problem domains. Applications range from modeling agent behavior the spread of epidemics, to project the future needs of the healthcare system. Progress in the area suggests that ABS promises to have far-reaching effects on the way that businesses use computers to support decision-making and researchers use agent-based models as electronic laboratories to help in discovery [3].

Agent-based simulation (ABS) is an approach to model systems comprised of individual, autonomous, interacting "agents". The interaction is a key characteristic since the smallest element defines the functionality of the system. Such interaction data has incredible potential to address complex features and dynamics of the objective system. Agent-based modeling offers ways to model individual behaviors more easily and to see how behaviors affect others in ways that have not been available before [3]. Furthermore, in the micro-level, the spatial agent-based simulator is not a design for any specific application. Instead, it is just a general behavioral simulator to simulate interaction among the smallest components of the Internal Medicine health system.

The reasons why ABS was selected to model a department of Internal Medicine of the HC in this study are: (1) In a department Internal Medicine system, agents have dynamic relationships with other agents. For example, patients have dynamic relationships with nurses, preceptors, doctors and patients. These dynamic relationships are important to consider and, by their nature, well suited to be modeled as part of agent-based model. (2) The agents have a spatial component to their behaviors and interactions, i.e., most of the agents in outpatient consultation need to move around and the spatial location is one of the key states which determines their potential interacting object and state transferring. (3) A large number of agents, agent interactions and agent states are important for information extraction. In a department of outpatient consultation, services are provided via multiple interactions, patients pass through a department of Internal Medicine. These interactions can deeply reflect the functionality of the target system. (4) Model reusability.

The first step of the job is to make a conceptual model of system operation, from which the computer model is capable of simulating the system. We are planning to use the simulation environment and high-level platform called Netlogo.

IV. OUTPATIENT CONSULTATION MODEL

A collection of information that is presented in this paper proposes a working model that aims to reduce waiting times for patients attending the CH.

1) Active agents: During the collection of information they are the active agents representing individuals and entities acting on their own initiative.

- Box official: administrative staff to which the patient comes to get a receipt.
- Admission official: administrative staff to which the patient comes for a slot, update their personal data and request the opening or searching for the medical record.
- Nurse: health personnel which is called by the patient to carry out pre-outpatient activities.
- Doctor: the doctor fills data about the patient, such as treatment forms, prescriptions, and other sheets. The doctor may assign the patient to a medical appointment, discharge the patient, or ask her to return after a certain period of time.
- Central recorder officer: administrative staff in charge of saving the medical records of patients.
- Patient: person who comes for treatment.

2) State variables: Agents move from one place to another interacting with other agents. During this time as a result of interactions each agent changes its state. This behavior is perfectly represented by a state machine, so we have chosen a state machine to model all agents. Specifically, the agents are represented by a Moore machine.

An initial set of state variables defined through the round of interviews with doctors is based on the minimum amount of information necessary to model each patient and staff. Such initial set of state variables is shown in Table 1.

TABLE I. INITIAL SELECTION OF STATE VARIABLES AND THEIR VALUES.

Variables	Values
Name / identifier <id>	Unique per agent
Location <location>	Admission; consultancy room; waiting room; nursing; central file; patient records.
Action	Idle; requesting information from; giving information to; searching; moving to.
Physical condition	Hemodynamic-constant; Bartel index.
Symptoms	Healthy; cardiac/respiratory arrest; severe/moderate trauma; headache.
Communication skills	Low: medium: high
Level of exprerience (Staff)	Low: medium: high.

3) Inputs: The entries represent all the ways that an agent can accumulate information. In the case of a person, this represents everything that the person sees, hears, smells, tastes, or feels, but really most entries represent vision or sounds, those entries are communication received by the agent. The next state of an agent depends on the current state.

4) Outputs: the agents are represented by Moore machines, each state can only have a different output. Some of the outputs where used of the simulator wants to analyze are waiting time of each stage (e.g waiting time for service request: T_{wrs}, time service record: t_{rs}, time of admission: t_a, waiting time in admission or signing: t_{wa}, first: t_{af}, control: t_{ac}, interconsultation: t_{ai}, waiting time in nursing: t_{wn}, time nursing care t_{we}, medical consultation standby time: T_{wmc}, while health care: t_{wm} and others).

5) State transitions: At each time step the state machine moves to the next state. This may be another state or the same before the transition. The next state the machine takes is dependent on the input during that state. The input may be more accurately described as an input vector (I) that contains a number of input variables, each one may take a number of different values. As this is a Moore machine, the output depends only on the state, so each state has its own output, although various states may have outputs that are identical. Again, the output is more accurately described as an output vector (O), a collection of output variables, each with a number of defined possible values. Transitions between states are dependent on the current state at time t (S_t) and the input at time t (I_t) [4].

6) Passive agents: Passive individuals do not act alone, but react to the actions of the active individuals. These liabilities agents do not have the same complexity as the active agents, as they are not entities that move by the department. An example of a passive agente is a computer system.

7) Environment: Without the environment there is no place where agents can interact with each other. In this model the environment is the outpatient department of Internal Medicine. The operation of outpatient hospital is based on processes consisting of different stages or phases in which each patient is passing from its admission into service.

A generic outline of a department outpatient Internal Medicine is shown in Fig. 2. The areas represented in boxes were explained above.

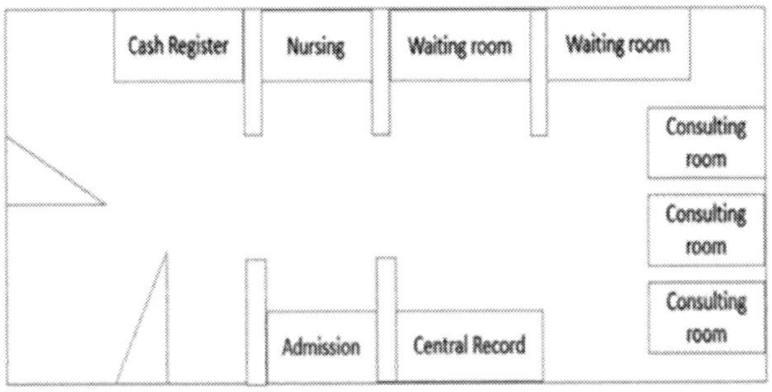

Figure 2. Representation of the environment of an outpatient department.

V. SIMULATION

The simulation provides a safer and more efficient way to try new techniques and processes with the goal of improving the efficiency of the outpatient management. A sufficiently complete model can be used to test and ensure real system changes without compromising real people. In addition, a simulation can be used to test a much too large sample set to study in a department consultation, and also can be done in a much smaller amount of time.

The advantages of using simulation is that it allows the automatic search for scenarios that provide the best solutions to a set of constraints and future states.

As the basis of a support system decision to reduce waiting time for patients is to develop a simulator that will have to run multiple simulations with combinations of different parameter values, each combination of values representing a different scenario simulation. There are a large number of combinations of values that constitutes the parameter space. In equation (1) the parameters that can generate a large number of different scenarios observed.

$$n_{scenarios} = n_{number\_admissions} * n_{time\_admissions} * n_{number\_signings} * n_{time\_signings} * n_{number\_nursing} * n_{time\_nursing} * n_{number\_doctor} * n_{time\_doctor} \quad (1)$$

With the simple model used in the simulator, there is a very large number of combinations of parameter values, large enough so that there is the possibility of launching each one manually. Therefore, parametric simulations, a way in which the simulator launch a set of simulations, with all combinations of values of the different parameters are required.

In general, the time to compute a time interval of a simulation based on agents is the product of time it takes to simulate the actions of an agent within the world of simulation in this step. In the model described agents in the simulation are the hospital staff and patients.

The simulator will be conducted by time. Time is divided into discrete, identical intervals and period each time step the agents operating system.

Each time step is divided into two phases. Assuming that the simulator this at time t, the phases are:

First, each agent processes the inputs of the last phase, (I_{t-1}) and according to that input and the state as it was during the last step (S_{t-1}) and changes to its new state S_t. Second, each agent emits its output to its current state, O_t. This output is input using receivers to switch to the next state.

At each time step, each agent changes state. It may change to the same state it was in the previous state, but there is nonetheless a change.

The metrics that are to be used for each state input I_t and output O_t are: waiting time to request a service: t_{wrs}, Time for register a required service: t_{rs}, time admission: t_a, waiting time in admission or signing: t_{wa}, First consultation time: t_{af}, Control Time: t_{ac}, Interconsultation time: t_{ai}, waiting time in nursing: t_{wn}, time nursing care: t_e, medical consultation Standby time: T_{wmc}, health care Time: t_m

The machine simulation has been chosen as the basis for when the simulator is implemented because NetLogo has all the features needed to implement a model of this type. NetLogo is a simulation environment agent-based model. NetLogo provides a basis for machine simulation agent-based system.

There are no preliminary results available yet, but we want to implement the simulator to verify the proposed model, obtain the different scenarios to see which one is the best to reduce the waiting time of patients.

The run time of a simulation step, in an agent based model simulation, is the product of the time it takes to simulate the actions of an agent and the number of agents in the simulation world in this step. In the model described, agents in the simulation are the hospital staff and patients. During simulation, the hospital staff is fixed, does not enter or exit the simulation. On the other hand, patients are constantly in and out of the simulation. This changes the load of each time slot simulation basing on the equation (2) that calculates the running time T_i in step i, with the number of hospital staff h, the number patients in the simulation in step i and the runtime of a t_{agente} agent.

$$T_i = (h + p_i)T_{agente} \quad (2)$$

We assume that the runtime of an agent is a fixed value. In different simulations, the number of hospital staff can change, but during one simulation, the number of hospital staff is maintained. Concerning the number of patients, this can change from one simulation step to the other because there are patients in and out, but within each simulation step, this number is constant. For a simulation that takes n steps, equation (3) shows the formula.

$$T = (h_n + \sum_{k=1}^{n} p_k)\, T_{agente.} \quad (3)$$

A good configuration made with the aim of reducing the waiting time for patients will also come with a shorter execution.

In order to generalize the process of all patients, the next status will be decided by probability distribution during simulation. The distribution model of the probability was based on the statistical data from the department outpatient Internal Medicine. Figure 1 indicates the general process-transfer strategy during the patients stay in department outpatient Internal Medicine, P1(%), P2(%), P3(%) and P_n (%) represent the probability of the next state transition separately. All of the probabilities follow some probability distributions. The probability density function of the distribution is decided by several key parameters based on the statistical analysis of doctor's decision and patient's behavior, the value of these parameters are estimated by a tuning process from real historical data of the specified department outpatient Internal Medicine. The uniform forms of the density functions are:

$$P_i = f\,(LoS, age, level) \quad (4)$$

$$\sum_{i=1}^{n} P_i = 100\ \% \quad (5)$$

$$P' = f'\,(ToT, age, level) \quad (6)$$

$$\sum_{i=1}^{n} P'_i = 100\ \% \quad (7)$$

where LoS is the patient's length of stay and age is the age of the patient, which also has big influence to the probability of status transition. Level is the acuity level of the patient and ToT is the type of test service or diagnosis by doctor. The functions f and f' are the probability density function.

These functions will be implemented by analyzing real historical data in tuning process. As the simulator is implementing the general model of the departments of outpatient Internal Medicine, the tuning/calibration process must be carried out for each one of them, in order to adjust its simulation parameters to the specific characteristics of each department (e.g., experience of the specific department staff).Therefore, combined with (1) - (10), every patient will show different behavior during the execution of the model because of the probability distribution and their own differences in body condition. But the statistical property of agents will reflect their common behavior.

VI. CONCLUSION AND FUTURE WORD

An agent-based simulation model of the process of outpatient's consultation in the Department of Internal Medicine of the CH was presented. With the development of this model we will be able to study the process of outpatient consultations and then propose a model aimed in reducing the waiting time in different stages of the process.

The simulation can be used as an important component of a system of decision support to help hospital administrators and the people responsible of the outpatient department of Internal Medicine, aimed to achieve efficient and better patient care cycle.

This work will help reduce the patient waiting time and provide additional knowledge on programming admission of patients and doctors. It will also help to optimize resources, among other situations.

Our future work is to implement the simulator with the Netlogo tool, examine, analyze and validate the data produced by the simulator. Then, we will examine the different scenarios in the department of Internal Medicine to improve waiting times for patients.

The first step of future work should be creating the computational model of the object; the next step of future work should be creating design of experiment, experiment execution and statistical analysis of simulation results. In order to validate the simulator, performing some real simulations of department of Internal Medicine is mandatory. Therefore, the future work should be validation. Some real historical data of department of Internal Medicine will be needed in order to perform the tuning process. This is due to the great number of parameters for the model, and the large number of agents and interactions between them. To increase the number of studied scenarios and reduce execution time as well, the use of high performance computing will be mandatory.

ACKNOWLEDGMENT

This research has been funded through the projects "Formació y recerca en l'Àmbit de la gestió i eficient Segura d'hospitals" by the "Fundació Autònoma Solidària", Universidad Autónoma de Barcelona, UAB, Spain by the Facultad Politécnica of the Universidad Nacional de Asunción, UNA, Paraguay; and "Sistema Integral de Gestión Hospitalaria – fase 3" by the Facultad Politécnica and by the Facultad de Ciencias Médicas de la Universidad Nacional de Asunción, UNA, Paraguay and supported by the MINECO (MICINN) Spain, under contract TIN2014-53172-P

REFERENCES

[1] Özer, Özlem; Kar Ahmet; Songur Cuma; Sonmez, Volcan; Sahin, Ismet. A Simulation Modelling Study: The Case of Department of Gynaecology and Obstetrics of A University Hospital, Turkey/Bir Üniversite Hastanesinin Kadin Hastaliklari ve Dogum Bölümü'nde Simülasyon Modelleme Çalismasi. Ege Akademik Bakis, 2014, vol. 14, no 4, p. 531

[2] http://www.sanlorenzopy.com/34958/

[3] C. Macal, and North M. 2014. "Introductory Tutorial: Agent Based Modeling and Simulation". In Proceedings of the Winter Simulation Conference 2014, 6–20.

[4] M. Taboada; E. Cabrera; M. L. Iglesias; F. Epelde and E. Luque. An Agent-Based Decision Support System for Hospitals Emergency Departments Procedia Computer Science, Elsevier, 2011, 4, 1870-1879

[5] S. S. Jones and R. S. Evans, ''An agent based simulation tool for scheduling emergency department physicians,'' in Proc. AMIA Annu. Symp., 2008, pp. 338–342.

[6] M. R. Friesen, and R. D. McLeod. A Survey of Agent-Based Modeling of Hospital Environments Access, IEEE, IEEE, 2014, 2, 227-233

[7] A. K. Kanagarajah, P. A. Lindsay, A. M. Miller, and D. W. Parker, ''An exploration into the uses of agent-based modeling to improve quality of health care,'' in Proc. Int. Conf. Complex Syst., Boston, MA, USA, Jun. 2006, pp. 1–10.

[8] D. Blachowicz, J. H. Christiansen, A. Ranginani, and K. L. Simunich, ''Future EHR ROI: Agent-based modeling and simulation offers a new alternative to traditional techniques,'' J. Healthc Inf. Manag., vol. 22, no. 1, pp. 39–45, 2008.

[9] C. W. Spry and M. A. Lawley, ''Evaluating hospital pharmacy staffing and work scheduling using simulation,'' in Proc. Winter Simul. Conf., Dec. 2005, pp. 4–7.

[10] M. Taboada, E. Cabrera, F. Epelde, M. L. Iglesias, and E. Luque, ''Using an agent-based simulation for predicting the effects of patients derivation policies in emergency departments,'' Proc. Comput. Sci., vol. 18, no. 1, pp. 641–650, 2013.

[11] E Cabrera, M Taboada, Ma L Iglesias, F Epelde, E Luque. Optimization of Healthcare Emergency Departments by Agent-Based Simulation. ICCS 2011: 1880-1889.

[12] E. Cabrera, E. Luque, M. Taboada, F. Epelde, and M. L. Iglesias, ''ABMS optimization for emergency departments,'' in Proc. Winter Simul. Conf., 2012, p. 89.

[13] S. G. Elkhuizen, S. F. Das, P. J. M. Bakker, & J. A. M. Hontelez. Using computer simulation to reduce access time for outpatient departments. Quality and Safety in Health Care, 16(5), 2007, 382-386.

[14] A. F. Najmuddin, I. M. Ibrahim, S. R. Ismail, A simulation approach: improving patient waiting time for multiphase patient flow of obstetrics and gynecology department (O\&G Department) in local specialist centre. WSEAS transactions on mathematics, 2010, 778-790.

Simulation of Device Behavior for InAlAs/InGaAs HEMT under Optical Illumination

Pritam Sharma, Jyotika Jogi
Microelectronics Research Laboratory
Department of Electronic Science, A.R.S.D College,
University Of Delhi, South Campus
New Delhi-110021, India.
email: jogijyotika@rediffmail.com

R.S Gupta
Dept. of Electronics and Communication Engineering
Maharaja Agrasen Institute of Technology
New Delhi-110085, India.

***Abstract*—This paper presents simulation of optical effects on the DC parameters of 100 nm single gate InAlAs/InGaAs High Electron Mobility Transistor (HEMT). The advantage of this model is that it provides us the flexibility to study the effects of optical illumination on the device parameters by specifying a user defined photo-generation rate as a constant or as a function of position in the device. The current–voltage characteristics of the device under dark and illuminated conditions have been simulated using luminous module (Silvaco Device Simulator) and recalling C-Interpreter function F.RADIATE to specify a constant photo generation rate. Significant increase in the drain to source current has been observed, suggesting future possible applications as optoelectronic device.**

Keywords- Heterostructure; HEMT; Optical-illumination; Photo-generation; Simulation.

I. Introduction

The concept of Internet of things (IOT) promises to connect anything with everything. The vision of IOT emphasizes on connecting physical things with the real world. This certainly requires a new revolution in the field of wireless and optical communication technology which further imposes the need for modern devices with ability to operate at higher frequencies and with reduced noise. With the advancements in the fabrication techniques, Compound semiconductor based heterostructure devices are replacing the conventional devices to operate at higher frequencies and low noise. Among various such devices, HEMT has emerged as a potential device to be able to operate effectively at higher frequencies and low noise.

HEMT, demonstrated in 1980 [1], exploits the superior carrier transport properties of modulation doped heterojunction. HEMT is now a well established technology and we can find its wide application in micro and millimeter wave frequency range [2]-[4]. HEMT technology has already reached a level where we have reduced the device dimensions to improve its performance in terms of noise and speed. Further reduction in gate length is limited by the short channel effects. HEMTs with a current–gain cut-off frequency of 562 GHz and with maximum frequency of oscillation of 330 GHz have been reported for 25 nm gate length [5]. In order to improve the further performance of the device, optical illumination seems to be a potential technique.

The material used for the fabrication of HEMT has evolved from the first generation lattice matched AlGaAs/GaAs HEMTs to AlGaAs/InGaAs/GaAs psuedomorphic HEMTs (pHEMTs). AlGaAs/InGaAs/GaAs pHEMTs suffer from dislocations due to high lattice constant mismatch between InGaAs and GaAs substrate. InAlAs and InGaAs lattice matched to InP substrate have emerged as suitable high band gap and low band gap materials respectively for HEMT structures. Compared to GaAs the InGaAs channel has higher mobility. Further, InAlAs does not suffer from the problem of Deep Levels (DX centers) as AlGaAs does [6]. Also the higher conduction band offset in InAlAs/InGaAs HEMT results in higher 2-DEG density as compared to AlGaAs/GaAs HEMT.

The study of the performance of high speed microwave semiconductor devices under optical illumination is an area of growing interest due to their potential application in fiber-optical communication and optical integration [7]. In context of optical applications, HEMT is emerging as an important optoelectronic device for high speed photo-detection, amplifier gain control, frequency tuning oscillators, and in phase shifters [8]-[15].

In the recent past, several authors carried out the simulation of optically illuminated MOSFETs and MODFETS [16][17]. Fallahnejad et.al [18] simulated the noise characteristics of AlGaN/GaN HEMT on SIC substrate for low noise applications using silvaco device simulator. None of these authors have used C –Interpreter function to specify the photo-generation rate. This paper simulates the effect of optical illumination on the performance of 100 nm InAlAs/InGaAs single gate HEMT using Atlas device simulator where C-Interpreter function F.RADIATE has been used.

The device structure and the simulation model for optical illumination are described in Section II. The simulation results thus obtained are reported and discussed in Section III. Finally the conclusion is presented in Section IV.

II. Device Structure And Model

The schematic of the 100 nm InAlAs/InGaAs SG HEMT is presented in Fig. 1, with dimensions tabulated in Table I. The structure is fabricated and reported by Wichmann [19].

The gate is illuminated by a laser source in a perpendicular direction. ATLAS device simulator has been used to simulate the device behavior. ATLAS simulator uses luminous module, a general purpose light propagation and absorption program integrated into the atlas framework for optical illumination. This module includes various physical models for light propagation. Ray tracing model has been used here, which is a general method for light propagation in 2D and 3D non-planar geometries and completely ignores coherence and diffraction effects.

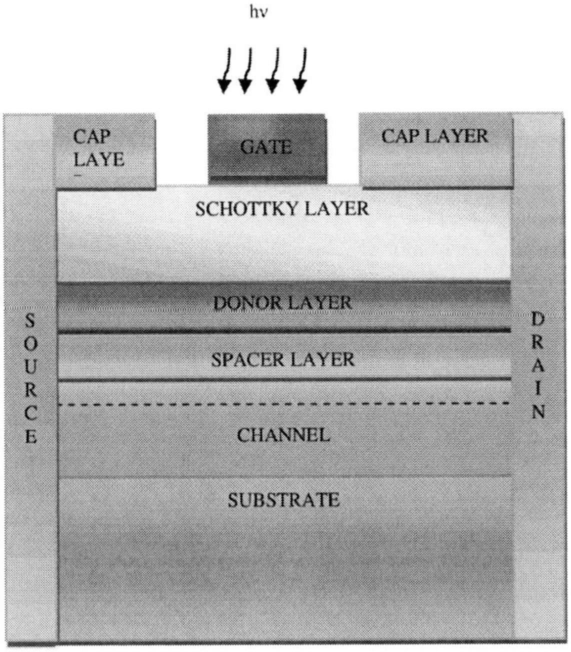

Figure 1. Simulated structure of InAlAs/InGaAs HEMT under illumination.

TABLE I. DEVICE DIMENSIONS

Layer	Dimension	Doping Concentration
Schottky(InAlAs)	12 nm	nid
Donor (InAlAs)	5 nm	10^{25} per m^3
Spacer(InAlAs)	5 nm	nid
Channel(InGaAs)	20 nm	nid
Buffer (InAlAs)	200 nm	nid

The device is physically modeled by using Shockley-Read-Hall (SRH), Concentration dependent mobility (CONMOB) and parallel electric field dependence mobility (FLDMOB) models. The SRH is a recombination mode that uses fixed minority carrier lifetimes. CONMOB uses simple power law temperature dependent mobility and FLDMOB is required to model any type of velocity saturation effect. Gummel Newton Iteration scheme has been used to obtain the numerical solution. Drift diffusion model is employed to evaluate potential, electron and hole concentration with appropriate assumptions and hence, calculate the drain to source current [20].

Ray tracing uses the real part of the refractive index to calculate the optical intensity at each grid point and imaginary part to calculate the carrier concentration due to photo generation at each grid point. Ray tracing models the source current due to photo generation as [20]:

$$I_s = \frac{qB_n\lambda W_t}{hc} \quad (1)$$

q is the electronic charge. B_n is the intensity of the beam number n defined in the SOLVE statement. λ is the source wavelength specified by the wavelength parameter in the BEAM statement which is used to model the effect of optical illumination on the device behavior. h is the Planck 's constant. c is the speed of light in vacuum. W_t is the width of the incident beam.

The source current available to the device including the losses due to reflection and transmission is modeled as available photo-current:

$$I_A = \frac{qB_n\lambda}{hc}\sum_{i=1}^{N_r} W_R \int_0^{y_i} P_i\alpha_i e^{-\alpha y} dy \quad (2)$$

q is the electronic charge, B_n is the intensity of the beam number n, λ is the wavelength of the incident radiation specified in the BEAM statement, h is the Planck's constant and c is the speed of light, W_R is the width assosciated with the ray. P_i accounts for the attenuation the incident ray suffers due to non unity transmission coefficients and absorption. y is the distance traced by the ray in the device. The limits of integration extend from the origin of the ray to the depth that the ray traces in the device. α_i is the absorption coefficient in the material that the ray is traversing which depends on the imaginary part of the optical index of refraction of the material and is given as:

$$\alpha_i = \frac{4\pi k}{\lambda} \quad (3)$$

k is the imaginary part of the optical refractive index.

Photo-generation rate accounts for the number of electron hole pairs generated in the channel due to illumination. C-interpreter function F.RADIATE is used to specify a constant photo-generation rate. BEAM statement is used to specify the C-interpreter function using F.RADIATE [20] parameter in the input deck. It calls the radiate function that defines a constant photo-generation rate of 10^{25} carriers per cubic centimeter. Optical Source and available currents thus produced are calculated using equations (1) and (2). The photo-generated carrier increases the overall drain to source current of the device.

Maximum optical efficiency of the device is obtained by assuming the gate metal and the subsequent layers of the device to be transparent. In such case the optical source current is equal to the available photo-current.

III. RESULTS AND DISCUSSION

Device behavior of 100 nm InAlAs/InGaAs SG HEMT has been investigated under optical exposure and dark condition. Optical Source current and available photo current in the channel are evaluated for a constant photo-generation rate specified using F.RADIATE C-interpreter function in the luminous module of Atlas 2-D device simulator.

Fig. 2 presents the simulated drain to source current (I_D-V_{DS}) characteristics under dark and illuminated conditions at a constant photo generation rate of 10^{25}per cubic centimeters. For low values of drain to source bias, current proportional to drain to source bias flows from drain to source along the electron gas channel. As the drain to source bias is increased, the electron velocity and the channel current saturate.

As the device is exposed to optical illumination, the drain to source current increases. This is because the photo-generated carriers produce a source photo-current. Under the assumptions made, the source current is equal to the available photo-current. This available photo-generated current is added to the dark drain to source current and hence, increases the overall drain to source current of the device under optical illumination.

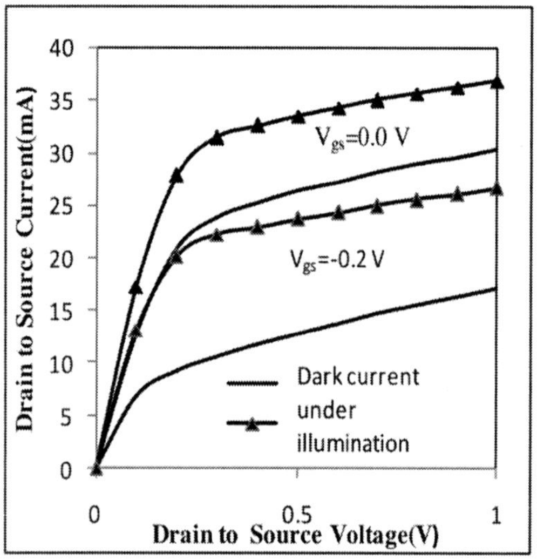

Figure 2. Variation of drain to source current with drain to source voltage under illumination and dark condition for a 100 nm InAlAs/InGaAs HEMT (λ=0.623 um and P_{op}=10 Watt/cm^2).

Fig. 3 shows the variation of drain to source current (I_{ds}) with gate to source voltage (V_{gs}) under dark and exposure conditions. Under exposure the threshold voltage of the InAlAs/InGaAs HEMT shifts turning the device on at a lower gate to source voltage. This suggests an increase in the transconductance of the device and hence the frequency of operation.

Fig. 4 depicts the drain (I_D-V_{DS}) characteristics of the device for varying optical power density. With increasing optical power density the available photo-current in the channel increases thus, increasing the drain to source current.

Table II represents the simulated source current (Eqn.1) generated at varying optical power density. It shows that as we increase the optical power density, the optical source current increases.

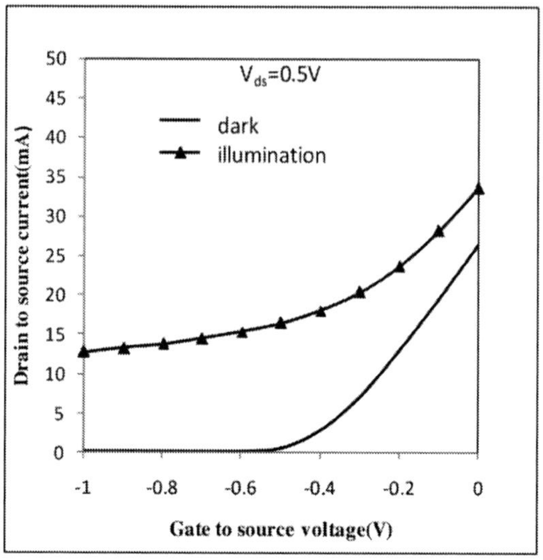

Figure 3. Variation of drain current with gate to source voltage under illumination and dark condition for a 100 nm InAlAs/InGaAs HEMT. (λ=0.623 um and P_{op}=10 Watt/cm^2).

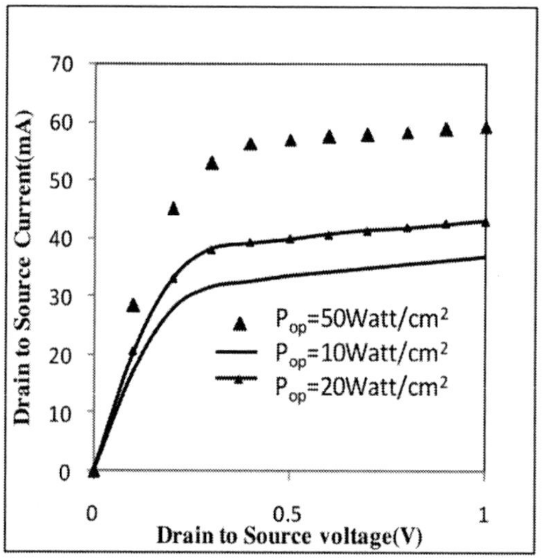

Figure 4. Variation of drain to source current with drain to source voltage for different optical power density for 100 nm InAlAs/InGaAs HEMT.

TABLE II. SOURCE CURRENT AT DIFFERENT OPTICAL POWER DENSITY

Optical Power Density (Watt/cm^2)	10	20	50
Optical Source current(mA)	0.415	0.830	2.075

IV. CONCLUSION

I-V characteristics of InAlAs/InGaAs HEMT under illumination has been studied using luminous module in

Atlas device simulator. Under exposure, the drain to source current is found to increase maximum by 7.6 mA for gate to source voltage ($V_{gs}=0$ V) and drain to source voltage ($V_{ds}=0.3$ V) at an optical power density of 10 Watt/cm^2. A significant shift in the threshold voltage is observed. At a voltage corresponding to the dark threshold voltage (-0.6 V) the device offers a higher drain current of 15.3 mA under illumination. Thus, optical illumination is seen to enhance the performance of the device. The simulation technique used gives us freedom to utilize any source. This would be helpful in studying both photovoltaic and photoconductive effects. This model provides us the flexibility to study the effects of optical illumination on the device parameters by specifying a user defined photo-generation rate. The accuracy of the model can be further improved by incorporating losses due to reflections at the interface. The photo-generation rate defined in the model is taken as a constant by the user. This work can be further extended by defining the photo-generation rate as a function of position in the device.

ACKNOWLEDGMENT

The authors acknowledge University Grants Commission for providing financial support for this work.

REFERENCES

[1] T. Mimura, S. Hiyamizu, T. Fujii and K. Nanbu, "A New Field Effect Ttransistor with Selectively Doped GaAs /N-$Al_xGa_{1-X}As$ Heterojunctions", Japanese Journal of Applied Physics, vol. 19, no 5, pp. 225-227, 1980.

[2] M. Bhattacharya, J. jogi, R.S Gupta and M. Gupta "Scattering Parameter based Modeling and Simulation of Symmetric Tied Gate InAlAs/InGaAs Double-gate High Electron MobilityTransistor for Millimeter-Wave Applications", vol.63, no.1, pp.149-153, September 2011.

[3] S.K. Jain, A. Kumar, R. Chakarbarty and D.K. Singh," Ka-band low noise amplifier sub-system module for communication satellite payload", International Microwave and Rf conference, IEEE, 2014 Bangalore .

[4] P. Parveen, N. Verma, M. Bhattacharya and J. Jogi, "Modeling of InAlAs/InGaAs/InAlAs DG-HEMT Mixer for Microwave Application", IOSR Journal of Electronics and Communication Engineering (IOSR-JECE), vol 10, pp.21-27, 2015.

[5] Y. Yamashita, A. Endoh, K. Shinohara, K. Hikosaka, T. Matsui, S. Hiyamizu, and T. Mimura, "Pseudomorphic InAlAs/InGaAs HEMTs with an ultrahigh frequency of 562 GHz," IEEE Electron Device Lett., vol. 23, no. 10, pp. 573–575, Oct. 2002.

[6] M. Golio and J. Golio, "RF and Microwave Passive and Active Technologies", RF and Microwave handbook, CRC Press, 2008.

[7] H. Mitra, B.B. Pal, S. Singh, and R.U. Khan, "Optical Effect In InAlAs/InGaAs/InP MODFET", IEEE Transactions on Electron Devices, vol.45, no 1, January 1998.

[8] M.S. Reid, "Low Noise Systems in Deep Space Network", Deep Space Communication and Navigation Series, DESCANSO Book Series, Jet Propulsion Laboratory California Institute of Technology, 2008.

[9] R.N. Simons and K.B. Bhasin,"Analysis of Optically Controlled Microwave/Millimeter-Wave Device Structures," IEEE Transaction on Microwave Theory and Techniques, vol. MIT-34, no 12, December 1986.

[10] R.N. Simons,"Microwave Performance of an Optically Controlled AlGaAs/GaAs HEMT and GaAs MESFET,"IEEE Transactions on Microwave Theory and Techniques, vol MTT-35, no-12, December 1987.

[11] Y. Takanashi and Y. Muramato,"Characterstics of InAlAs/InGaAs High Electron Mobility Transistors under Illumination with Modulated Light", IEEE Transactions on Electron Devices, vol.46, no 12, December1999.

[12] Y. Takanashi and Y. Muramato,"Characterstics of InAlAs/InGaAs High Electron Mobility Transistors under 1.3μm Laser Illumination ", IEEE Transactions on Electron Devices, vol.46, no 12, December1999.

[13] A.A De Salles and M.A. Romero, "$Al_{0.3}Ga_{0.7}As$/GaAs HEMT Under Optical Illumination", IEEE Transactions on Electron Devices, vol. 39, no. 12, December1991.

[14] G.J Chaturvedi, R.K. Purohit and B.L. Sharma, "Optical Effect On GaAs Mesfets, "Infrared Phys, vol.23, no 2, pp 65-68, 1983.

[15] Yajian and A. Alphones, "Frequency Dependent Behavior of .Optically Illuminated HEMT, "Microwave and Optical Technology letters / vol.30, no.2 , July20,2001.

[16] R. Gautam, M. Saxena, R.S. Gupta and M. Gupta,"Analytical Model Of Double Gate MOSFET For High Sensitivity Low Power Photosensor", Journal of Semiconductor Technology and Science, vol.13, no 5, October 2013.

[17] P. Jain and B.K. Mishra, "Evaluation Of Optically Illuminated MOSFET Characterstics by TCAD Simulation", International Journal of VLSI design & Communication Systems, vol. 4, no.2, April 2013.

[18] M. Fallahnejad , A. Kashaniniya and M. Vadizadeh ," Design and Simulation Noise Characteristics of AlGaN/GaN HEMT on SIC Substrate for Low Noise Applications", IOSR Journal of Electrical and Electronics Engineering (IOSR-JEEE), vol.15, pp 31-37, 2015.

[19] N. Wichmann, I. Duszynski, X. Wallart, S. Bollaert, and A. Cappy," Fabrication and Characterization of 100-nm $In_{0.52}Al_{0.48}As/In_{0.53}Ga_{0.47}As$ Double-Gate HEMTs with Two Separate Gate Controls", IEEE Electron Device Letters, vol. 26, no 9, 2006.

[20] ATLAS Device Simulator User's Manual, Silvaco International, Santa Clara, U.S.A, 2010.

UrMo Accessibility Computer

A tool for computing contour accessibility measures

Daniel Krajzewicz and Dirk Heinrichs
Institute of Transport Research
German Aerospace Center
Berlin, Germany
email: daniel.krajzewicz@dlr.de, dirk.heinrichs@dlr.de

Abstract— **Contour accessibility measures are a set of performance indicators used to value a location by the amount of accessible activities, places, or space within certain time or distance limits. They are used for evaluating a region's activity offers taking the connectivity to its surrounding into regard and act as input data for land use planning models and traffic demand models. With the availability of disaggregated data and sufficient computer power, accessibility measures can be computed at a very fine-grained level of single buildings, points of interest or areas. This report describes a tool that realizes this purpose.**

Keywords-Accessibility measures; performance indicators; intermodality.

I. Introduction

With a raising awareness about (road) traffic's impacts on the environment and the quality of life, especially in urban areas [1], measures and incentives for supporting sustainable modes of transport become increasingly important. Of course, proper performance indicators for determining areas that need improvements as well as for measuring the results of planned or already performed measures are needed. One class of performance indicators for valuing a given area or location are so-called accessibility measures [2]. They describe how well a location is connected to the surrounding activity locations. Accessibility is used for a large number of different applications in the field of transportation and land-use planning.

"Accessibility" is not a single, well-defined function, but rather a set of concepts. One common understanding is that accessibility is a compound measure that describes how many locations can be approached within a given time from a given starting point. Compound, as accessibility consists of two parts. The first is the space that can be reached within the limits. The second one is the existence of locations of the investigated type within this accessible space. But this describes only a subset of known accessibility measures. [2] gives a summary of accessibility measures' classes and distinguishes between "spatial separation measures", "contour measures", "gravity measures", "competition measures", "time-space measures", "utility measures", and "network measures".

The different variations of accessibility measures are not the scope of the presented research. Rather, a tool for computing contour accessibility measures at a fine-grained level of detail of buildings and the transportation network will be described. Often, accessibility measures are used at the level of so-called "traffic analysis zones" (TAZ). TAZs usually divide a region such as a city or a bigger area into cells with a most possible homogenous travel behavior. So-called macroscopic demand models compute the amount of traffic between such TAZs and macroscopic land-use models describe the attributes of locations at this level for computing the development of cities or regions. Increasingly, macroscopic approaches are replaced by microscopic models where every single entity – household, person or vehicle in transportation context – is modelled and simulated individually. Accordingly, "microscopic" approaches for computing accessibility are attempted. A fine-grained accessibility computation makes use of available disaggregated data, should be more exact than macroscopic approaches and may come along with the inclusion of further information, such as elevators, stairs or other hindrances.

The remainder is structured as following. In Section II, the context of work and the requirements that yield in designing the application described herein are given. The application's design and workflow is presented afterwards in Section III. Then, in Section IV, some usage examples are given, focusing on visualization. The report ends with a summary and outlook in Section V.

II. Requirements from the Projects

The described tool was developed in the scope of the project "Urbane Mobilität" (UrMo) [3][4] of the German Aerospace Center (DLR) [5]. The major topic of this project is intermodality – travelling using different modes of transport (e.g. walking, using the public transport, and cycling) along a single journey. Three simulation models are used within this project: the microscopic demand model "Travel Activity PAttern Simulator" (TAPAS) [6][7], the microscopic traffic flow simulation "Simulation of Urban MObility" (SUMO) [8][9], and the location choice model "SimulAting Location Demand and Supply in Urban Agglomerations" (SALSA) [10]. Supporting SALSA with data about a location's value was the major reason for developing an accessibility computation tool.

SALSA is macroscopic – locations are grouped into areas at the level of "Teilverkehrszellen" (TVZ, English: sub traffic assignment zone). Berlin's 1223 TVZs are shown in Fig. 1. SALSA uses a large number of different measures for describing different aspects of the locations within a given TVZ. Besides attributes such as the average price, size, or construction year, different accessibility measures can be found among them.

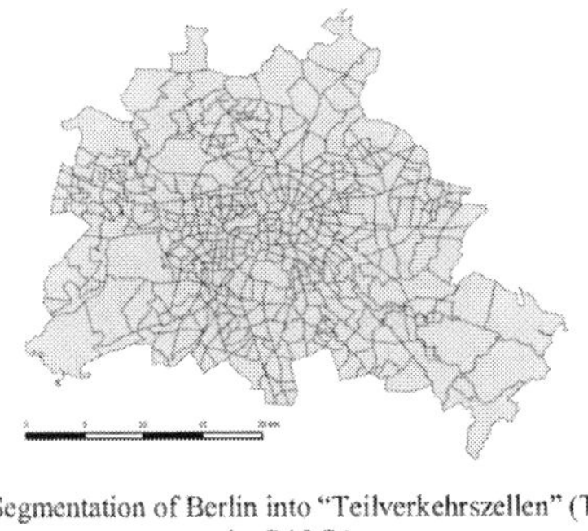

Figure 1. Segmentation of Berlin into "Teilverkehrszellen" (TVZ) as used by SALSA.

The large variety of accessibility measures used by SALSA is not only a result of using different types of sources and sinks like dwellings, job locations, shops, or parks. Instead, one may as well find different rules for limiting the investigated area, different types of aggregation, or an optional collection of a variable that is attached to the accessible sinks. Some examples of accessibility measures used by SALSA are:

- average travel time to other zones;
- average distance to other zones;
- travel time to nearest commercial center;
- travel time to nearest railway station;
- travel time to closest grocery store (>= 200m^2);
- travel time to closest small park (>= 10000m^2);
- grocery retail floor space within 10min travel time;
- green space area within 30min travel time;
- number of jobs within 30min travel time;
- travel time to closest large park (>= 50000m^2).

Much of the underlying data used in the UrMo project is available in a disaggregate manner. This includes the positions of dwellings, shops and job offers. In conjunction with an intermodal transport network, it makes sense to use these disaggregated data for computing the needed accessibility measures directly, without any kind of preprocessing and/or aggregation.

III. Application Implementation

The tool was written in the Java programing language. Currently, it is a command line application, what means that no graphical user interface is provided. Before describing the different processing steps, it should be noted that within a single call of the application only one transport mode or mode combination is regarded. The application currently supports the modes "walking", "bicycling", "motorized individual traffic", and "public transport", the latter in combination with walking or bicycling. When determining accessibility measures for public transport, a starting time must be given for choosing according public transport rides. Within the scope of the UrMo project, the peak hour at 8:00 am is used.

Albeit the used methods – mainly routing using the Dijkstra algorithm [11] – are not neither novel or complex, the overall tool is very flexible, realized by some simple features. They include filtering, variable limits, or weighting the sources and will be emphasized in the following subsections.

A. Input data

For a regarded region, the application reads the sources' and sinks' positions from a database, as well as a road network. Different disaggregated data are used for sinks and sources, including dwellings, bus stops, job locations, shops, parks, etc. Fig. 2 shows the first two ones of the named as a visual example. While some of the locations are represented as their footprints using polygons, the tool currently uses the centroids of them only. This is surely an approximation that introduces an error. But the error is assumed to be small and better models of the access/egress to the road network could only be achieved if the positions of the dwellings' entrances would be known what is not the case.

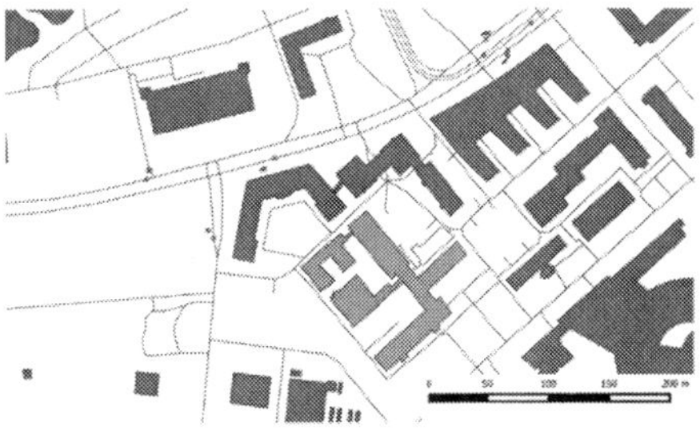

Figure 2. Examples for sources and sinks – dwellings (grey polygons) and bus stop positions (red dots) around the DLR in Berlin (light grey).

When reading sources/sinks a simple filter realized as a SQL WHERE-clause can be given. For bigger datasets – e.g. the locations of all shops in a city – this can be used to select a subset only, e.g., only groceries or only shops that are bigger than a given threshold.

Both, sources and sinks can hold a numerical value. For sources, this value is used for weighting the individual source's influence when aggregating. A possible application is weighting dwellings by the number of persons inhabiting them. For sinks, the value's semantics are kept abstract and the values can be summed up for the accessible sinks after computing the accessed space. Usual applications are counting the number of jobs accessible from a location or, as a more abstract measure – determining the selling areas of groceries in a specific range.

Currently, road networks obtained from the OpenStreetMap database (OSM) [12] are used, which were preprocessed and stored into the database. The preprocessing mainly includes a) the determination of intersections by selecting nodes used by more than one way, b) consolidation of access and one-way information for obtaining a unidirectional network with access information for different transport modes. After these steps, the road network is written into the database. For the city of Berlin, the road network consists of 709713 edges (roads) and 269604 nodes (junctions). The network's edges include the information about the maximum speed allowed for motorized individual traffic and about the allowed modes of transport.

Optionally, the tool additionally reads a public transport network using a database representation of a General Transit Feed Specification (GTFS) [13] data set. The database uses the original GTFS format.

B. *Preprocessing data after reading*

In a first step, the objects read from the database to route between are allocated on the road network. For every centroid representing a source/sink, the nearest road is determined that allows the investigated mode of transport. A direct, shortest access to this road is assumed, being a line normal to the road's shape at the point that is nearest to the object. A spatial index, namely the RTree [14] implementation from the Java Spatial Index library [15], is used during this process for increasing the computation speed by searching for roads in the objects' vicinities only. It should be noted that because the RTree structure stores the roads via their bounding box, obtaining the closest bounding box for a given point is not sufficient as the road may be located at the opposite site of the bounding box than the point.

A second issue to solve when allocating objects to roads is to find the road's correct direction. In OSM, as well as in many other road network formats, bidirectional roads are represented by straight lines with no geometrical distinction between both directions. Thereby, both directions have the same distance to the source's/sink's position and an arbitrary one of them would be chosen. This ambiguity is solved by determining the road direction and mapping it onto the direction the halt is located right to. Fig. 3 shows the connections between sources/sinks and the road network.

Figure 3. Attaching sources/sinks to the road network; buildings (grey polygons) and public transport stations (black points) are connected to the road network (grey lines) via access paths (black lines).

Optionally read halting positions of public transport have to be assigned to the previously read road graph as well. Again, for each halting position, the nearest road is determined and the halt is mapped onto it. Albeit OSM partially includes detailed information about paths across a station or a hub, stations are allocated at the road network via their centroids only, as already done for sources and sinks. To avoid splitting edges at the positions of mapped stations, new edges are introduced that connect the starting and the end node of the edge the station is located at with the station itself. Whether this is more or less performant than splitting edges has not yet been evaluated.

C. *Processing*

The process of computing accessibility measures is very straightforward. The application iterates along the read sources. For each, the road network is scanned using the plain Dijkstra algorithm regarding whether the used mode of travel is allowed at a visited edge or not. In dependence to the regarded mode, the travel speed used for determining the travel time to pass an edge is chosen as shown in Table I.

TABLE I. SPEEDS OF THE MODELLED MODES.

Mode	Speed
Walking	5km/h
Bicycling	12km/h
motorized individual traffic	minimum of 200km/h and the road's speed limit
public transport	time schedule (from GTFS)

It should be noted that using the road network as the only factor that limits space accessibility is not correct. Additional travel time delays posed by traffic lights and other traffic participants are neglected when doing so. This issue can be solved by additionally reading travel times or time lines of these. For a given demand, such travel times can be obtained from traffic flow simulations such as SUMO. As well, humans do not walk along edges and cross roads at intersections only. Some approaches for routing across empty – vacant and accessible – space are under development [16] and could be used for extending the application.

When encountering a public transport stop, the available connections to next stations are regarded, using the arrival times as given in GTFS instead of the usually used travel time along the road network's edges.

The process ends as soon as one of the following limits is reached:

- *maximum travel time*: stops as soon as the given travel time is exceeded;
- *maximum distance*: stops as soon as all objects in the given distance have been visited;
- *maximum number*: stops as soon as the given number of sinks has been visited;
- *maximum variable sum*: stops as soon as the sum of the variable attached to the sinks values' is above the given number;
- *shortest*: stop as soon the first sink is reached.

For each source, the result of this routing consists of the seen edges with attached sinks and their values, as well as the used transport modes or lines. The travel time and the distance are given as well. Of course, a measure used for limiting the accessible space is fixed in the output. The obtained outputs may be aggregated as described in the next section.

D. *Aggregation and Output Generation*

One of the tool's major features is the capability to perform different kinds of aggregation. For both, the sources and the sinks, additional aggregation areas (e.g. TVZ) can be read from the database. If given, the measures collected by routing from individual sources are aggregated by averaging them. When being applied to the sinks, the values of all sinks within a given aggregation area that are accessible in the given limits will be joined and averaged. Additionally, an "aggregate all" option is available, which joins all found sinks. Currently, no other statistical characteristics are generated, mainly because the averaging is optional. When needed, such characteristics can be computed from not aggregated results.

As shown in Table II by example, the different aggregation possibilities, in conjunction with flexible limits, allow for the computation of different accessibility measures.

TABLE II. EXAMPLES FOR AGGREGATION IN COMBINATION WITH OTHER OPTIONS (PER TAZ).

Description	Sources agg.	Sinks agg.	Additional parameters
average travel time to other zones	TAZ	all	
travel time to nearest railway station	TAZ		shortest
number of jobs within 30min travel time	TAZ	all	variable=employee; max-tt=30min

IV. EXAMPLE RESULTS AND VISUALISATION

Isochrones are a very simple form of accessibility measures and their visualization. They neglect any kinds of destination locations and regard a single source only. Following [2], isochrones belong to the category of spatial separation measures. Fig. 4 shows isochrones for comparing the space accessible by individual motorized traffic (top) and public transport in combination with walking (bottom).

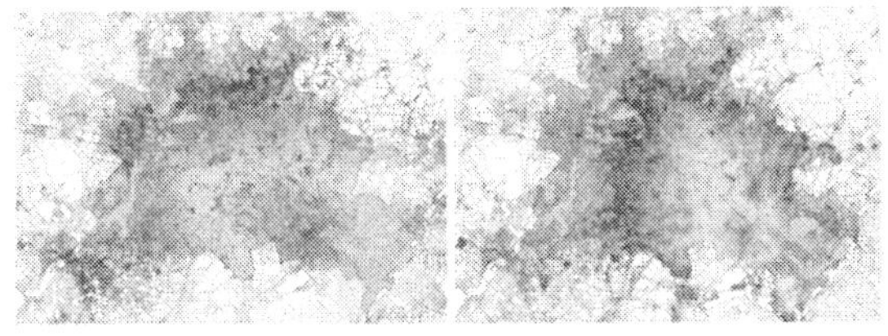

Figure 4. Comparison of isochrones for different transport modes (starting point: DLR center in Berlin); top: motorised individual traffic, bottom: public transport (and walking).

When visualizing the results, one may note that showing disaggregated data (e.g. dwellings) within a bigger area and coloring them is not meaningful, because they vanish due to their small size in comparison to the region and the vacant land. Indeed, an aggregation should be performed when visualizing accessibility measures. Fig. 5 demonstrates this by showing the travel times to the next metro or city rail station for every dwelling individually and aggregated into TVZs.

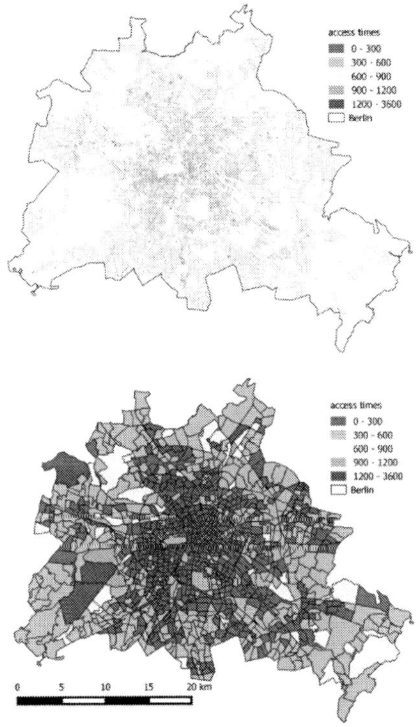

Figure 5. Not aggregated vs. aggregated visualisation of accessibility measures (here: travel time to the next metro or city rail station).

As a final example, the influence of weighting sources is given. Fig. 6 shows the difference between aggregated travel times from dwellings to the respectively next city rail or metro station, once weighted by the households living in each building, once not. As visible, neglecting the households yields in significant deviations.

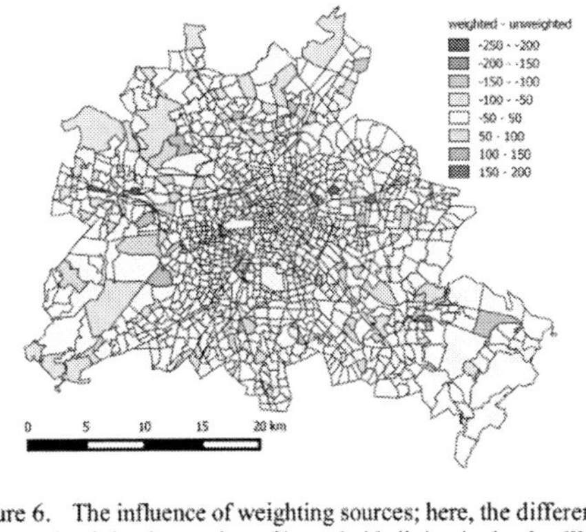

Figure 6. The influence of weighting sources; here, the difference between weighted (by the number of households living in the dwelling) and unweighted accesss to the next city rail/metro station is shown.

The figures were generated using Quantum GIS (QGIS) [17].

V. SUMMARY AND OUTLOOK

This report presents a tool for computing accessibility measures as used for benchmarking areas and as used within land use planning models and traffic demand models. The tool follows a fine-grained attempt to compute accessibility measures by routing between individual sources and sinks, mainly dwellings, shops, bus halt positions and other man-made objects.

Albeit contour accessibility measures come in many different variations, only some simple methods seem to be sufficient for enabling the tool to compute a large amount of them, fulfilling the requirements put by the UrMo project. One important feature are flexible limits, including a maximum travel time, distance, or the possibility to abort the search when a first sink was seen. Another one is the possibility to aggregate the individual sources' accessibility values into averages for bigger areas, including a variable weighting of the individual sources. Reading sources and sinks from a database and supporting a pre-filtering when doing so has proved to be valuable as well. Finally, attaching values to the sinks is required for computing some of the needed accessibility measures and was accordingly implemented.

Some microscopic approaches choose subsets of sources and sinks for estimating accessibility. But the experiences with the tool described herein do not prove the necessity for reducing the amount of data to process. In all cases, the complete sets could be processed.

While being usable as-is, some improvements to the tool and the data it uses seem to have the capacity to improve the results and enable investigations of further research questions. As mentioned, the currently used representation of sources and sinks via their centroids introduces an error in the paths between the respective source/sink and the road network. Using the nearest position to the road network from a given source's/sink's polygon would be possible. Still, this does not regard the positions of a building's doors or entrances.

The used road networks should be reinvestigated as well. While OpenStreetMap has a usable quality in most parts of Europe and the USA, other parts of the world are only badly covered. Thereby, other digital traffic maps should be investigated. Inclusion of new networks is very simple, because of the low requirements of the tool.

Routing itself should be extended by proper travel times for motorized individual traffic which may be obtained from traffic flow simulations, such as SUMO. As well, approaches for a more realistic person routing could be integrated.

Summarizing, it is surprising how much flexibility can be achieved within a very small and simple application.

REFERENCES

[1] UN Habitat, "Planning and Design for Sustainable Urban Mobility: Global Report on Human Settlements 2013", Global Report on Human Settlements Series, 978-92-1-132568-3, 2013.

[2] J. Scheurer, C. Curtis, "Accessibility Measures: Overview and Practical Applications", urbane WORKING PAPER No. 4, Curtin University of Technology, 2007.

[3] L. Gebhardt et al., „Intermodal urban mobility: users, uses, and use cases", in: Transport Research Arena, Elsevier Ltd. Selection and peer-review. Transport Research Arena (TRA), Warsaw, Poland, 2016.

[4] DLR, "Urbane Mobilität" project web pages, http://www.urmo.info/, 2016, last visited on 23rd of April 2016.

[5] DLR, DLR web site, http://www.dlr.de, last visited on 24th of April 2016.

[6] A. Justen, R. Cyganski, "Decision-making by microscopic demand modeling: a case study", in: Transportation decision making: issues, tools, models and case studies, Venice, 2016, ISBN 9-78-88-96049-06-8.

[7] DLR, TAPAS web page, http://www.dlr.de/vf/en/desktopdefault.aspx/tabid-2974/1445_read-29381/, 2016, last visited on 23rd of April 2016.

[8] D. Krajzewicz, J. Erdmann, M. Behrisch, and L. Bieker, "Recent Development and Applications of SUMO - Simulation of Urban Mobility". In: International Journal On Advances in Systems and Measurements, 5 (3&4), pp. 128-138, 2012, ISSN 1942-261x.

[9] DLR, SUMO web pages, http://sumo.dlr.de/, 2016, last visited on 23rd of April 2016.

[10] B. Heldt, K. Gade, and D. Heinrichsm "Challenges of Data Requirements for Modelling Residential Location Choice: the Case of Berlin, Germany", European Transport Conference 2014, 2014.

[11] E. W. Dijkstra, "A note on two problems in connexion with graphs", In: Numerische Mathematik 1, pp. 269–271. 1959, doi:10.1007/BF01386390.

[12] OpenStreetMap contributors, OpenStreetMap project pages, http://www.openstreetmap.org/, 2016, last visited on 23rd of April 2016.

[13] Google, General Transit Feed Specification pages, https://developers.google.com/transit/gtfs/, 2016, last visited on 25th of April 2016.

[14] A. Guttman, "R-Trees: A Dynamic Index Structure for Spatial Searching", In: Proc. ACM SIGMOD International Conference on Management of Data, pp. 47-57, 1984, doi:10.1145/602259.602266

[15] JSI contributors, JSI (Java Spatial Index) RTree Library web pages, http://jsi.sourceforge.net/, 2016, last visited on 25th of April 2016.

[16] S. Andreev, J. Dibbelt, M. Nöllenburg, T. Pajor, and D. Wagner, "Towards Realistic Pedestrian Route Planning", In: Proceedings of the 15th Workshop on Algorithmic Approaches for Transportation Modeling, Optimization, and Systems (ATMOS'15), volume 48 of OpenAccess Series in Informatics (OASIcs), pages 1-15. Schloss Dagstuhl - Leibniz-Zentrum fuer Informatik, September 2015.

[17] QGIS Development Team, QGIS Geographic Information System, Open Source Geospatial Foundation Project. http://qgis.osgeo.org, 2016, last visited on 29th of April 2016.

Simulation of the Influence of Curb-Parking on the Efficiency of Designated Curb Bus Lanes

Marek Bauer
Department of Transportation Systems
Cracow University of Technology (PK)
Cracow, Poland
e-mail: mbauer@pk.edu.pl

***Abstract*—This paper discusses the influence of curb parking on speeds of buses on designated bus lanes. This is a universal practical problem, its solution would aid the running of buses in many cities. This is also an important issue from the point of view of the construction of the simulation models used in the planning of transportation systems. It often happens that in the planning and design process, overly optimistic values of bus speeds are often adopted, and these can be very difficult to achieve after implementation of the planned solutions. The main tool in this discussion is the author's own probabilistic model of conflict between running buses and parking cars. This model states the part of comprehensive bus lane studies in Polish cities, leading to develop a scientific method of traffic organization within the right curb bus lanes. The model is based on the real measurement of the results of bus running times and parking facilities. The paper presents the results of the duration of parallel parking maneuvers by buses and cars within designated bus lane space and the time of occupying the potential conflict area in the separated lane. In this analysis, inter alia – bus driver's decision time and the time required for safe bus stopping are considered. The presented model can be used in simulations of the effects of curb-parking on bus speeds, in relation to different frequencies of parking maneuvers.**

Keywords-urban transport; bus lane; curb-parking.

I. Introduction

Designated lanes for bus public transport are an effective tool of transport policies, the objective of which is to increase the share of trips effected by public transport, as described in [1]. Thus, they form part of the group of highly relevant issues for managing mobility in cities. Dedicated lanes provide far more advantageous conditions for bus transit than lanes used by the generality of vehicles. They enable buses to reach high speed, contribute to an increasing punctuality and regularity of service. In Polish conditions (including Cracow), mostly right curb bus lanes have been introduced. Their greatest advantage is the ease of locating bus stops on the pavement, i.e., directly by the lane [2]. They are, however, susceptible to disturbances largely resulting from traffic signaling systems, the movement of vehicles turning right involving bus lane usage and due to maneuvers related to the service of buildings located in the immediate vicinity of the bus lane, including sidewalk parking [3]. These factors are characterized by substantial randomness of impact and the impossibility of their mutual separation. An illustration of these problems is shown in Figure 1.

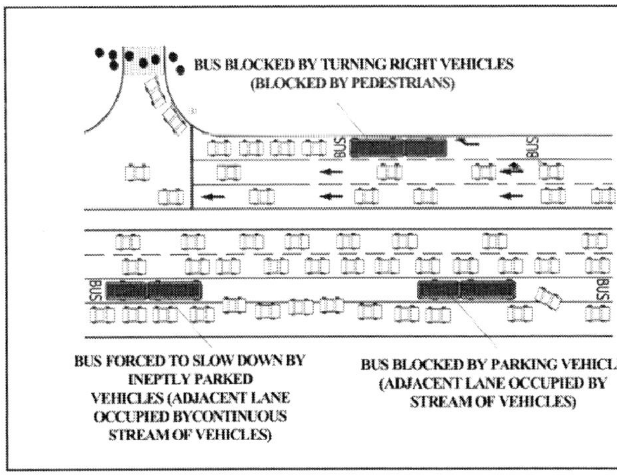

Figure 1. Disadvantages of right curb bus lanes (own work).

The negative impact of vehicles parking on the sidewalk results directly from the necessity for parking cars to use the bus lane, and also from bus drivers' apprehension to drive faster in conditions of limited visibility. In current research in Cracow (unpublished own research), it has been established that the average speed of buses on sections with bus lanes where sidewalk parking is permitted is on average 2.3-4.3 [km/h] (section lengths: 0.3 – 0.7 [km]) lower than where it is not allowed. This means a significant decrease in average speed, amounting to between 13 and even up to 22 [%]. Yet, the fact cannot be ignored that sidewalk parking is regarded as being particularly convenient for car users due to its relatively short parking operation time and quick access to journey destinations located in the immediate vicinity of the parking spaces. In this context, it is crucial to determine the scale of the difficulty of sidewalk parking for bus traffic. This is of even greater importance, because increasingly frequently paid parking areas are being introduced in Polish cities, which is an highly efficient method of restricting car traffic in central city districts.

In Section 2, the probability model of conflict between running bus and parking car is presented. Section 3 includes the results of the duration of parking maneuvers, whilst in

Section 4, the time of occupying the potential conflict area on a separated bus lane is analyzed. Section 5 presents a practical application of the model. Finally, Section 6 presents the conclusion of the paper.

II. The Model of Conflict: Running Bus Versus Parking Vehicle

Various possible solutions to the given problem, including the queueing theory, were taken into account. However, at the stage of the construction of the model, it was found that to describe the influence of sidewalk parking maneuvers on bus running time on a dedicated bus lane, reliability theory [4] is most useful. In this fully individual approach, the reliability structure of a system presents the manner of mutual connections of components, determining the dependency of system failures on failures of its elements. In the case of a section with sidewalk parking allowed right next to the bus lane, the system elements are the subsequent points on the bus lane, where a running bus and parking vehicle can meet [5]. This is an approach used in models of discrete events. However, the case here is not the probability of physical collision but specification of the probability of disturbances in bus running as a result of a parking vehicle [6]. This was defined as the probability of conflict between a running bus and a parking vehicle. The system will be unreliable if a bus driver, traveling along a dedicated bus lane is not be able to continue at the chosen speed as a result of a parking maneuver. When seeing a vehicle being parked (or a vehicle preparing for such a maneuver), the driver has three possibilities: he can slow down or change the lane or even stop the bus on the separated lane. All of these options are a waste time for passengers [7]. Since conventional parking spaces are located sequentially along the bus lane, it can be stated that the system has a serial reliability structure in which inefficiency of any component causes inefficiency of the entire system. In other words, a maneuver related to parking on one of the parking lots impacts on the reaction of a bus driver, even if the distance from the potential conflict place is significant. In general, the system unreliability function describing the probability of the conflict between a running bus and parking vehicle has the following form:

$$\Lambda_s(t) = \sum_{i=1}^{n} \lambda_i(t) \quad (1)$$

where:
$\Lambda_s(t)$ – function of failure intensity of the system, which is a function of intensity of potential disturbances of running time on the analyzed section (as a result of parking vehicles);
$\Lambda_i(t)$ – function of failure intensity of i-th component of the system, as a result of a parking vehicle at parking position number i.

Most often, the peak hour (morning or afternoon) is adopted as the reference point, because of the increased number of parking maneuvers. The model can be simplified by applying average values of intensity of potential running time disturbances; i.e., the same for each parking space, regardless of its location on a section. Then, the average intensity of disturbances in the bus lane area, right next to one parking space – can be multiplied by the number of parking positions:

$$\overline{\Lambda}_s = n \cdot P(C) \cdot P(A) \quad (2)$$

where:
Λ_s [No. of maneuvers/h] – average intensity of potential disturbances of running time on the analyzed section, during one hour of analysis;
n [-] – number of effective parking positions at the analyzed section, assuming that in case of unspecified parking positions – one position is on average 6.0 [m] long;
$P(C)$ – probability that a parking car enters the bus lane (taking position or leaving parking position), right next to one parking space, during 1 hour;
$P(A)$ – probability of bus entries into the analyzed section, during 1 hour.

In the proposed approach, the intensity of section running time disturbances is modeled as the product of the probability of a meeting between a parking vehicle and an approaching bus, at the same time and place. These probabilities can be determined, including the time of occupying the separated lane by buses and maneuvering cars, attributable to one parking position.

The time of occupying the potential conflict area on the separated bus lane can be divided into two parts: the bus driver's decision time and the time required for eventual (if needed) safe bus stopping before a maneuvering vehicle. Decision time $t_{A,d}$ is defined as the time when a bus driver, having diagnosed the possibility of a parking maneuver (taking or leaving a parking position), makes the decision to slow down, stop the bus or change the lane. While the time required for safe stopping $t_{A,s}$ is defined as the time anticipated by the driver for potential slowing down at a deceleration acceptable for the passengers (Figure 2).

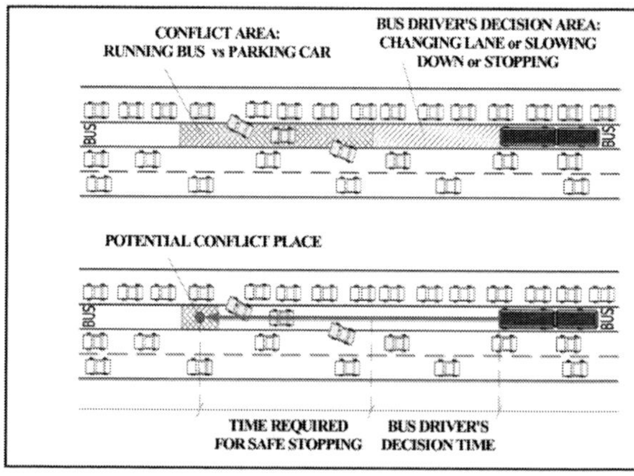

Figure 2. Bus driver's decision time and the time required for safe stopping before a maneuvering vehicle (own work).

Finally, the average intensity of section running time disturbances has the form:

$$\overline{\Lambda}_s = n \cdot \left(\frac{a \cdot \overline{\lambda}_{tp} \cdot \overline{t}_{C,tp}}{3600} + \frac{b \cdot \overline{\lambda}_{lp} \cdot \overline{t}_{C,lp}}{3600} \right) \cdot \left(\frac{c \cdot Q_A \cdot (\overline{t}_{A,d} + \overline{t}_{A,s})}{3600} \right) \quad (3)$$

where:

Λ_{tp}, Λ_{lp} [veh/h] – average intensity of car maneuvers related to one typical parking position, in the case of – respectively: taking a parking position and leaving a parking position;

$t_{C,tp}$, $t_{C,lp}$ [s] – average time of typical parking maneuver – respectively: taking or leaving a parking position;

Q_A [veh/h] – bus traffic volume;

$t_{A,d}$ [s] – average bus driver's decision time;

$t_{A,s}$ [s] – average time required for safe bus stopping;

a, b [-] – disturbance factor for – respectively: taking a parking position and leaving a parking position by a single car – values can be estimated on the calibration stage;

c [-] – coefficient of other traffic on bus lane;

all remaining variables – according to equation (2).

This is the classic approach used in traffic engineering, where calculations are often based on the average durations of the traffic processes. However, it should be noted that the choice of a mathematical formula and the choice of model variables are the result of the work of the author.

III. The Duration of Parking Maneuvers

The characteristics of parking maneuvers are similar in European cities. In Polish conditions, the duration of parallel parking maneuvers was measured by Gaca, Suchorzewski and Tracz [8]. They have established that the average full duration of typical parallel parking manoeuver is 30 [s]. To confirm these values, my own measurements were carried out on one typical street section with a bus lane and parking places located at the sidewalk, right next to bus lane. During a 12-hour video registration, not only was the duration of maneuvers while taking or leaving parking positions taken into consideration, but also the time spent by the parking vehicle on the bus lane, looking for a free space as well as leaving bus lane and taking the general access lane was measured. In a situation when after leaving the parking space a vehicle continued driving on the bus lane, the moment of leaving the entire section was regarded as the time of leaving the lane. The duration of maneuvering only on the sidewalk area was not included, unless its effects could impact the bus traffic on the dedicated lane. Characteristics of maneuvers are shown in Table I.

TABLE I. CHARACTERISTICS OF PARALLEL PARKING MANEUVERS WITH BUS LANE USAGE

Kind of maneuver		**Time [s]**			
		Minimum	***Maximum***	***Average***	***Standard deviation***
Entry to the position	Time spent on the bus lane	2	19	**8**	4
	Taking parking position	7	59	**20**	13
Departure from the position	Leaving parking position	2	26	**10**	8
	Time spent on the bus lane	4	31	**13**	8

The results provide a good insight into the time of taking and leaving a parking position located on the sidewalk right next to a bus lane. The more important values are those concerning the time taken to park and then leave positions – these are on average 20 and 10 [s]. However, the additional time spent by a car on the bus lane is also significant. In the case of leaving a parking position – this is on average 13 [s].

The differences in times are caused by the differential characteristics of maneuvers. Drivers taking position are looking for a free space from a distance. In general, they continue driving along the general access lane and change lane only when they see a free parking place. These maneuvers are done under time pressure. In the case of leaving a parking position, drivers must wait for a gap on the bus lane. A maneuver without time pressure is easier to do. Total average time of taking position is 28 [s], but the time of leaving a parking position is 23 [s]. These results are very similar to the general findings from publications presented at the beginning of this Section. So, they can be used in further analysis. Of course, such research should be conducted on a much broader scale, in order to obtain more reliable variables for the conflict model.

On the basis of the above measurement results, it would be difficult to conduct a reliable analysis including the randomness of parking duration caused by different spaces between already parked vehicles and the sizes of vehicles being parked. This should be the next level of studies. Therefore, at the present stage of analysis it has been decided that the study will have a deterministic character. Cases of unlawful car movement on the bus lane were also recorded. These will not be considered in the current analysis.

IV. Time of Occupying the Potential Conflict Area on the Separated Lane

The model presented in Section 2 can be applied to analyze the increase in probability of conflict between the buses driving on a dedicated bus lane and the cars performing maneuvers related to parking.

A. Bus driver's decision time

Firstly, the study focused on the period of time when a bus driver upon seeing a vehicle maneuvering can diagnose the situation and make a decision either to potentially slow down (or stop, or change the lane), or to continue driving at the current speed. The point here, however, is not emergency braking (which can also occur in exceptional situations), but any decrease in speed resulting in longer running time. In the case of a decision to continue driving, without visible danger, more time is required. This is the reason why values from the interval 3-7 [s] were taken into account. A comparison of distances covered during 3-7 [s] are presented in Figure 3.

For example, during 5 [s] a bus driving at a speed of 30 [km/h] covers the distance of 42 [m]. Due to the fact that buses on dedicated lanes often move at a speed of 40 [km/h] and faster, it was decided not to include longer decision times.

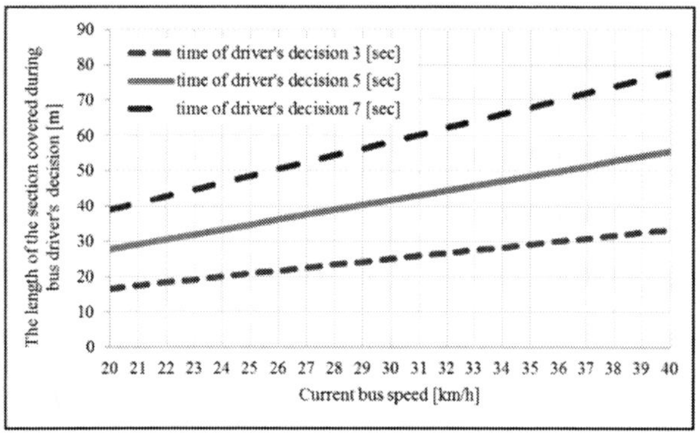

Figure 3. Comparison of distances covered by buses during bus drivers' decisions in relation to current speed of vehicle (own work).

B. Time required for safe bus stopping

Furthermore, the study also covered the time in which the bus reaches the potential conflict. Decelerations from 0.8 [m/s^2] to as much as the exceptionally acceptable for passengers value of 1.6 [m/s^2] were taken into account. Assuming that a bus running at a speed of 30 [km/h] brakes with a smooth deceleration of 0.8 [m/s^2], the breaking distance can be as long as 43 [m]. In the case of 1.6 [m/s^2], which is generally inconvenient for passengers – this distance is only 22 [m]. Both cases seem unlikely, therefore in Figure 4, braking distances only for decelerations from 1.0 to 1.4 [m/s^2], depending on the current bus speed, are presented.

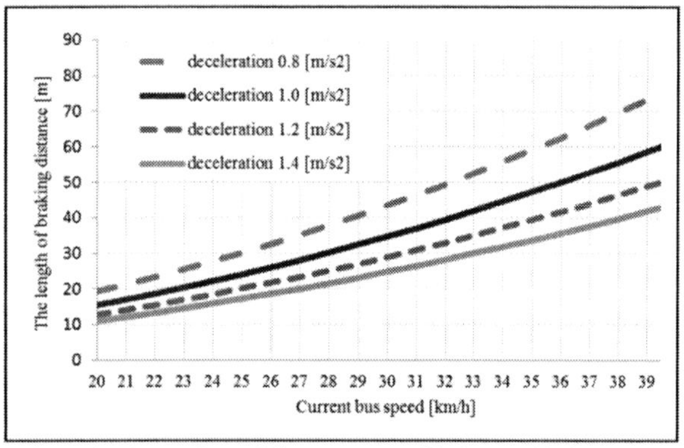

Figure 4. Comparison of distances covered by buses with time required for safe stopping (own work).

Current speed has a very significant influence on braking distances. Due to the fact that buses on dedicated lanes often move at a speed of 40 [km/h] and faster, even distant parking maneuvers can lead to bus (and passenger) time losses.

C. Total time of occupying the potential conflict area

On the basis of the length of the section covered during the driver's decision about potentially slowing down and of the length of the section covered during safe braking, the time in which the bus reaches the point of potential conflict with a parking vehicle was established. These times are presented in Figure 5.

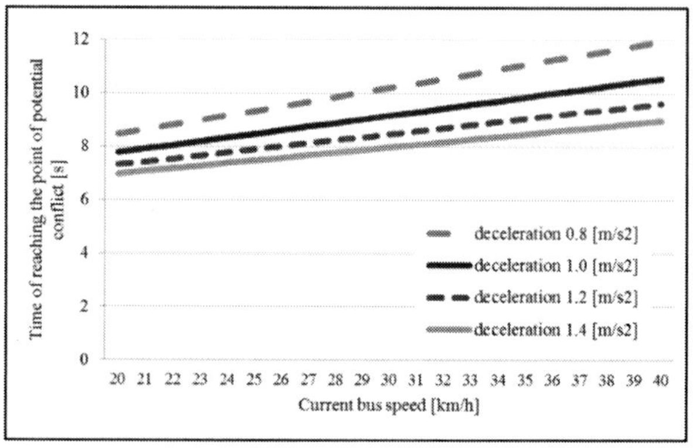

Figure 5. Comparison of times of reaching the point of potential conflict with a parking vehicle (own work).

V. Application of the Model of the Conflict: Running Bus Versus Parking Vehicle

Analyses of potential conflicts on the designated bus lanes were conducted on the basis of results of measurements carried out along a section of Trzech Wieszczow Avenue in Krakow (Figure 6).

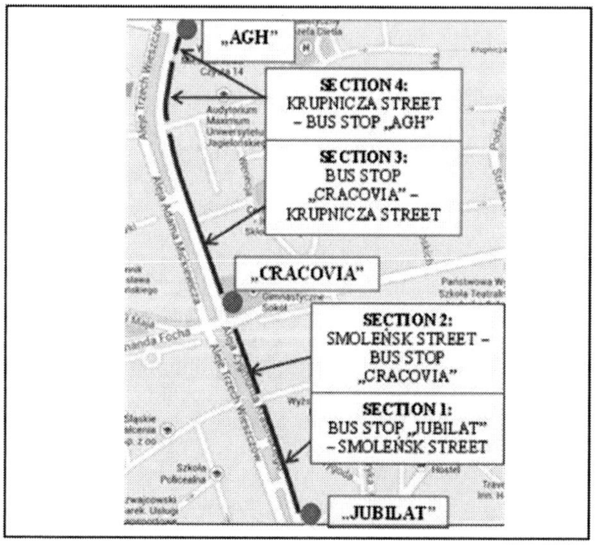

Figure 6. Analyzed sections along Trzech Wieszczow Avenue in Cracow.

From a bus public transport perspective, this is one of the key transport corridors in the city. It has been provided with right curb bus lanes which can be used by all public transport vehicles, taxis and vehicles from municipal services (police and municipal guard) and additionally at intersection entries – by all vehicles, turning right. This part of the transport corridor has a typical urban character with intersections controlled by traffic signals, without priorities for buses. The analysis covers a section starting from the "Jubilat" bus stop to the stop "AGH". Taking into account distances between stops, the studied section amounts in total to 920 [m]. If one was to accept that parking takes place only in the allowed areas there would be 425 [m] at drivers' disposal for parking.

As parking positions have not been designated, drivers occupy them according to their needs, habits and skills, not infrequently against the regulations. In order to determine the potential number of available parking spaces, it was assumed that the length of one parallel parking position is 6.0 [m]. Having assumed this, only 68 parking positions in total have been made available in the studied section. In practice, only intersection zones, pedestrian crossings and bus stop areas are free from parking. The numbers of parking positions are presented in Table II.

TABLE II. NUMBER OF PARKING POSTIONS AT THE ANALYZED SECTIONS

No.	Section	Total length of the section [m]	Length of the section (with legal and illegal) parking spaces [m]	Approximate number of parking positions [-]
1	"Jubilat" stop – Smoleńsk street	197	176	29
2	Smoleńsk street – „Cracovia" stop	203	108	18
3	„Cracovia" stop – Krupnicza street	261	236	39
4	Krupnicza street – „AGH" stop	259	75	12

A. *The number and intensity of maneuvers related to parking on the sidewalk right next to the bus lane*

From the perspective of potential conflicts between buses driving on a dedicated lane and the vehicles parking on a sidewalk and thus using the bus lane, the number of all maneuvers related to parking positions appears to be of great importance.

Studies were conducted using the patrol measurements method, by registration of vehicle numbers on individual positions. These were logged during subsequent measurement cycles – in morning (6:00 – 10:00) and afternoon (14:00 – 18:00) time periods. In order to describe the impact of parking vehicles on bus traffic, average intensities of entries and leavings were established for individual peak hours. Here it was assumed that in relatively homogenous peak periods the numbers of maneuvers can be divided evenly into single hours of study. It needs to be taken into account that the relatively long hourly measurement cycle could result in some maneuvers not being logged. Therefore, it can be acknowledged that the actual maneuver intensities will not be lower than those given in Table III.

In the current state, the number of maneuvers related to a single parking position in the analyzed section varies greatly – ranging between 0.028 and 0.291 maneuvers. In some cases, this ratio exceeds 0.2. Therefore, the number of parking positions at the analyzed sections will be crucial.

TABLE III. NUMBER OF PARKING MANEUVERS AT THE ANALYZED SECTIONS (PER 1H)

Section	Average intensity of entries per 1h [-]		Average intensity of leavings per 1h [-]	
	Morning peak hour	Afternoon peak hour	Morning peak hour	Afternoon peak hour
"Jubilat" stop – Smoleńsk street	**0.207**	0.126	0.057	**0.218**
Smoleńsk street – „Cracovia" stop	0.148	0.148	0.074	0.167
„Cracovia" stop – Krupnicza street	**0.291**	0.179	0.034	0.171
Krupnicza street – „AGH" stop	**0.222**	0.111	0.028	0.194

B. *Running times of buses*

There are 40 urban transport (municipal) buses and additionally 80 microbuses from private companies during each peak hour along Aleje Trzech Wieszczow. The measurements of running time were conducted using GPS receivers in selected buses. These were collated after 37 (morning peak hour) and 40 (afternoon peak hour) running times of two analyzed stop-to-stop sections. Average values of running times and running speeds are shown in Table IV.

TABLE IV. AVERAGE BUS RUNNING TIMES AND SPEEDS

Section	Average running time [min]		Average running speed [km/h]	
	Morning peak hour	Afternoon peak hour	Morning peak hour	Afternoon peak hour
"Jubilat" stop – "Cracovia" stop	1.20	1.21	20.3	20.1
„Cracovia" stop – "AGH" stop	1.25	1.29	24.7	24.0

The running times of buses are very similar in both the peak periods. Unfortunately, in both sections, the running speeds of buses are not very high, which may be partly the result of curb-parking. Average time loss per bus is 15 [s], so in total, this is a significant problem for public transport passengers.

C. *Probability of the conflict: running bus vs parking car*

The impact of parking maneuvers on bus traffic, calculated using the model described in Section 2, is the greatest in the longest section where the number of potential conflicts is the lowest (Table V). On average, in existing situation, every fourth public transport bus is blocked by a parking vehicle. It should be noted that the process of taking and leaving a parking position includes the behavior of car drivers towards approaching buses. It was established that, in the case of entries, drivers generally do not take bus traffic into consideration as they need to occupy the bus lane earlier and when driving on the bus lane they need to find a free parking space. The situation in the case of leaving a parking position is different. In the majority of cases, drivers wait for the possibility to leave as long as there are no buses within a well seen distance. A problem arises when visibility is limited and a bus is running fast.

TABLE V. PROBABILITY OF CONFLICT BETWEEN RUNNING BUS AND PARKING VEHICLE IN CURRENT SITUATION

Section	Probability of conflict [-]	
	Morning peak hour	*Afternoon peak hour*
"Jubilat" stop – Smoleńsk street	0.038	0.032
Smoleńsk street – „Cracovia" stop	0.018	0.020
„Cracovia" stop – Krupnicza street	0.072	0.056
Krupnicza street – „AGH" stop	0.018	0.014

Therefore, after the model calibration process, it was proposed to adopt the following values of disturbance factors (equation (3)): 0.9 and 0.5 [-], for – respectively: taking and leaving a parking position by a single car.

D. *Scenarios of increase of rotation on parking positions and the simulation results*

In this analysis, the influence of the elimination of curb-parking and a potential increase in rotation at the parking positions along the bus lane is taken into account. There following four scenarios are included:

- Scenario S0: current state;
- Scenario S1: elimination of curb-parking along the bus lanes;
- Scenario S2: implementation of a paid parking zone, parking rotation rate = 0.50 [veh/h];
- Scenario S3: implementation of a paid parking zone, rotation rate = 1.00 [veh/h].

In the interest of simplification it was assumed that the rotation rates will remain the same at positions located in all four parts of the analyzed transport corridor. Simulation of probability of conflict between a running bus and a vehicle performing a parking maneuver was carried out for all scenarios using formula (3). The results of the simulation are presented in Table VI.

TABLE VI. PROBABILITY OF CONFLICT (ALL SCENARIOS, AFTERNOON PEAK HOUR)

Section	Probability of conflict [-]				Running time of buses [min]			
	S0	*S1*	*S2*	*S3*	*S0*	*S1*	*S2*	*S3*
"Jubilat" – Smoleńsk	0.016	0.000	0.017	0.032	1.21	1.18	1.21	1.24
Smoleńsk – „Cracovia"	0.010	0.000	0.010	0.019	1.21	1.18	1.21	1.24
„Cracovia" – Krupnicza	0.028	0.000	0.035	0.068	1.29	1.26	1.30	1.34
Krupnicza – „AGH"	0.007	0.000	0.007	0.014	1.29	1.26	1.30	1.34

Liquidation of parking along the bus lane will shorten running times of buses by an average of only 4 [s], while increasing the rotation to 1 [veh/h] will result in an extension of 3-6 [s], depending on the section. This is a relatively small effect, but it affects many passengers. If we assume that the section in the afternoon rush hour is traveled along by 3,000 passengers, this total can be achieved in close to 3.5 hours. However, one can conclude that the possible introduction of paid parking zones will not cause a serious loss of time for passengers. Another problem is a slower ride on buses resulting from reduced visibility - in this case, the profit would have been much larger.

VI. CONCLUSIONS

Parking vehicles have a relatively slight influence on running speeds of buses along the designated bus lanes. Also, it will not be easy to find an efficient solution to the problem resulting from the growth of parking rotation on sidewalks located right next to bus lanes. One immediate solution, i.e., to create a maneuver lane between the bus lane and the sidewalk, cannot be applied in every case due to a lack of space. Therefore, it is worthwhile considering the removal of sidewalk parking from those transport corridors with separated bus lanes. This could have positive results, in the form of shortening the bus running times. This action could have yet another positive aspect. The area retrieved in this way could be used to improve conditions for pedestrian traffic, or it could be dedicated to the needs of bike traffic. It is true that even the least efficient bus lanes are better than general access lanes in increased traffic conditions, yet this should not be a reference point. Instead, the maximum functional possibilities, especially high speed of running, should be the reference. Studies on the efficiency of bus lanes, including the impact of sidewalk parking, will be continued, also with the use of stochastic methods.

REFERENCES

[1] G. Marsden, K.T. Frick, A.D. Maya and E. Deakin, "How do cities approach policy innovation and policy learning? A study of 30 policies in Northern Europe and North America," Transport Policy, 18, 3, 501–512, 2011,

[2] J. Młyńczak, "Analysis of Intelligent Transport Systems (ITS) in Public Transport of Upper Silesia," Modern Transport Telematics Communications in Computer and Information Science 239, 164 – 171, 2011,

[3] M. Bauer, "Model of Running Time Disturbances for Buses Using Designated Lanes on Approaches to Junctions Equipped with Traffic Signals," In Proceedings of The Sixth International Conference on Advances in System Simulation SIMUL2014, (Nice, France, October 12 - 16, 2014,

[4] I. Bazovsky, "Reliability Theory and Practice," Englewoods Cliffs, NJ, Prentice-Hall, 1961,

[5] K.Ch. Keong Goh, G. Currie, M. Sarvi and D. Logan, "Bus accident analysis of routes with/without bus priority," Elsevier: Accident Analysis and Prevention 65, 18-27, 2014,

[6] A.E. Wåhlberg, "Characteristics of low speed accidents with buses in public transport: part II," Accident Analysis and Prevention 36, pp. 63–71, 2004,

[7] H. Guo, Z. Gao, X. Yang, X. Zhao and W. Wang, "Modeling Travel Time under the Influence of On-Street Parking," J. Transp. Eng., 138(2), 229–235, 2012,

[8] S. Gaca S, W. Suchorzewski and M. Tracz, „Inżynieria ruchu (in English: Traffic engineering)," Warsaw, 2008,

[9] Z.P. Sándor and C. Csiszár, "Role of Integrated Parking Information System in Traffic Management," Periodica Polytechnica. Civil Engineering 59.3 (2015): 327.

Design and Control of a Mechatronic Vehicle Dynamics Simulator Pitch and Roll Dynamics

Jorge de-J. Lozoya-Santos
Julio Salinas
Evaristo Mendez
Gerardo Gonzalez
Juan C. Tudon-Martinez

Universidad de Monterrey
San Pedro Garza Garcia, Nuevo Leon 66238
Mexico
Email: jorge.lozoya@udem.edu
julio.salinas@udem.edu, evaristo.mendez@udem.edu
gerardo.gonzalez@udem.edu, juan.tudon@udem.edu

Ricardo A. Ramirez-Mendoza

School of Engineering
Tecnologico de Monterrey
Monterrey, Nuevo Leon 64000
Mexico
Email: ricardo.ramirez@itesm.mx

Abstract—**A pitch-roll simulator platform has been designed and built for the validation and analysis of control systems algorithms in vehicle dynamics. The system consists of a real time industrial computer, and an instrumented three degrees of freedom platform. A motion cueing algorithm has the function of translating the movement of a vehicle to the platform, moving three rotary actuators, while satisfying all boundaries. A set of encoders feeds back the actuators angle. Two control strategies has been designed and tested through simulation and experiments. Results show that a simple control scheme allows the driver assess the pitch and roll, however, a better control scheme is needed for vehicle design purposes.**

Keywords–vehicle dynamics, simulation, platform, simulation, motion cueing

I. Introduction

Driving simulators are found in several areas of application: entertainment, research and advanced training. These simulators deliver motion cues to the driver. The fidelity of the cues depends on the degrees of freedom. These systems are called also motion cueing systems. Motion cueing systems in driving simulators join the physical motion of the simulated vehicle with the real-time image generation system. It allows the drivers to perceive and control their vehicle motion [1] as if he were inside the vehicle. Motion simulators have been a topic of great interest in last years [1]-[9]. The applications of interest are to test Advanced Driver Assistance Systems (*ADAS*), In-Vehicle Information Systems (*IVIS*), and the effects of noise and vibrations on driver performance [6].

The automotive industry in Mexico has a boom in manufacturing and investment [10]. However, important challenges remain for the future, such as the development of more research and development centers, local design and validation for automotive components [10][11]. Some efforts are being done between universities and automotive industry [12][13]. This research is under the goal of having better capabilities for the development of new technology in partnership between mexican universities and companies.

TABLE I. Nomenclature.

Variable	*Units*	*Description*
$\ddot{x}$	$\frac{m}{s^2}$	Longitudinal acceleration
$\ddot{y}$	$\frac{m}{s^2}$	Lateral acceleration
$\tilde{\theta}$		Washout pitch angle
$\tilde{\phi}$		Washout roll angle
$\hat{\theta}$		Estimated pitch angle
$\hat{\phi}$		Estimated roll angle
θ_d		Desired pitch angle
ϕ_d		Desired roll angle
u_θ	v	Command for θ_d
u_ϕ	v	Command for ϕ_d
$M_{1,2,3}$	-	Electric motor 1, 2 and 3
$c_{1,2,3}$	v	Step sequence from electric motor encoders
$u_{x,y,z}$	v	Output from gyroscope
ω_{M_1,M_2,M_3}	$\frac{-}{s}$	Mechanical angular speed
$a_{x,y,z}$	$\frac{m}{s^2}$	Measured angular speed by gyroscope axis
$p_{1,2,3}$	-	Generated pulses according to motor shaft, $M_{1,2,3}$

In this paper, a driving simulator of three degrees of freedom is presented and its control system for vehicle dynamics pitch and roll variables. The nomenclature used in the elaboration of this paper it is in Table I. The goal of this simulator is to validate *ADAS* including the biometrics systems and autonomous vehicle assessment, as well as the transportation of finish goods. The paper consists of VII sections. Key concepts are described in Section II. Section III describes vehicle dynamics simulator and the hardware platform. The proposed control algorithms are described in Section IV. Section V enumerates the process of design and validation of the control system. The results and discussion are shown in Section VI. Conclusion ends this paper in Section VII.

II. Literature Review

The key parts of a motion cueing system are the driving simulator and the control algorithm.

Motion cueing allows the simulator driver to *feel* inside a vehicle in motion. The realism of simulation depends strongly on the fidelity of the motion platform and the motion perception by the human driver [3]. The human vestibular system located in head is found to be dominant in human motion sensation. It senses the rotational and linear motions, more details on [14]. Rendering vehicle motion cues in a driving simulator is possible within a small displacement envelope. Its physical validity is limited to the mid-frequency range, but its perceptual validity may be extended in the low frequencies by tilt coordination techniques [1].

A driving simulator typically consists of a seat, a vehicle dynamics model interacting with a driver through a steering wheel and pedals with haptic feedback, a sound feedback, a set of screens with a visual engine reproducing the vehicle dynamics results of the simulator's driver manoeuvre, and, in some cases, translational and rotational actuators for the motion cueing system. The driving simulators are mainly classified by the fidelity of the simulation level and its application. The simulation fidelity cllassification corresponds to low-level, mid-level and high-level fidelity. At a low-level simulator, the driver sits in a car seat, which is fixed to the ground. The driver looks at a screen, which is fixed to the ground too. The screen is designed such that the view angle is as large as possible. The driver manipulates a set of driving controls such accelerating, braking and steering wheel in order to receive visual cues corresponding to the actual driving situation. In some types of applications, it is desirable to provide a motion and haptic restitution to improve the simulation fidelity. Therefore, the driving simulators use a moving platform to restitute, in a limited and constrained workspace, a sufficient sensation of movement as closely as the one sensed in a real vehicle [1][2][15][16]. Low level simulators can include longitudinal axis motion in one axis while the mid and high level simulators include more motion axis, a detailed state of the art can be found in [9]. The main applications are Entertainment (*E*), Training (*T*) and Research (*R*). Table II shows a complementary summary.

TABLE II. DRIVING SIMULATORS COMPLEXITY, THE OBJECTIVES OF SIMULATION CAN BE ENTERTAINMENT (*E*), TRAINING (*T*), AND RESEARCH (*T*).

Level	*Components*	*Feedback*	*Degrees of freedom*	*Objective*
Low	Large screens, steering wheel, pedals, one linear actuator	Force Sound Longitudinal motion	0, 1 (x, y, or z axis)	E T
Mid	plus at least one linear actuator	Force Sound Longitudinal and rotational motions	2 or 3	E T R
High	plus at least four more linear actuator	Same as mid	6	T Advanced research

A three Degree of Freedom system is designed to have a rotation about the x, y, and z axes and it allows to simulate main vehicle dynamics variables. This system causes the sensation of acceleration through rotation around these three axes, maintaining a tilt angle (typically to a 45 degrees angle) and it uses the gravity. The tilt limitation in this system prevents to create an acceleration sensation over 0.707gs [9]. This research is focused in a *3DoF* driving simulator.

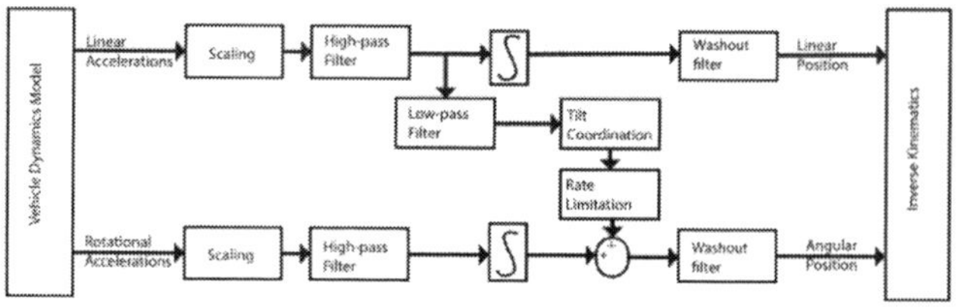

Figure 1. Washout filtering approach for motion cueing systems.

The control algorithm for motion cueing systems is called washout filtering with classical, optimal and predictive approaches [1][14], proportional-integral-derivative washout filtering [2], and optimal and model predictive control [4][8] among others. However, the classical washout filtering is the most common because of it is implementation simplicity and fair simulation results [9], Figure 1. The classical washout filtering consists of a combination of high-pass and low-pass filters. Commonly, the parameters of these filters are empirically determined. Its inputs are vehicle-specific longitudinal accelerations and angular rate and expressed in vehicle-body-fixed frame. Acceleration (angular rate) is high-pass filtered, and yields the simulator translations (rotations). To simulate the motion platform tilt, a tilt coordination algorithm supplies the low-frequency component of acceleration for rotation calculation.

III. VEHICLE DYNAMICS SIMULATOR

The *Vehicle Dynamics Simulator (VDS)* consists of a real time vehicle dynamics model system interacting with a driver through a steering wheel, acceleration, brake and clutch pedals, speed control, a set of three flat screens and a set of speakers.

The real time vehicle dynamics model simulation system consists of the *Dynacar* system [17], which is a low level driving simulator, and a three Degrees of Freedom (*3DoF*) platform, Figure 2.

a) Back view of VDS.

a) Lateral view of VDS.

Figure 2. Vehicle dynamics simulator in Automotive Engineering Lab, Universidad de Monterrey.

The full scheme of the *VDS* shows all the components and describes the interactions between the *Dynacar* and the *3DoF* platform, Figure 3.

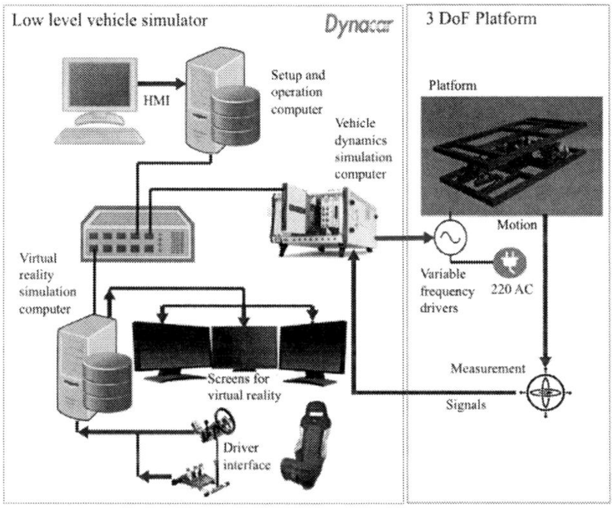

Figure 3. Experimental system: hardware in vehicle dynamics simulator.

The *3DoF* platform consists of two mechanical frameworks (lower an upper base) separated by an active suspension. The upper base holds the driver cabin, and the lower base holds three crank shaft mechanisms conforming the active suspension as well as a vertical sliding guide, Figure 4.

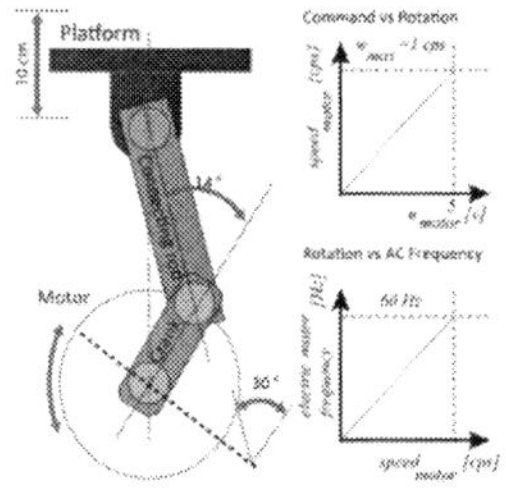

Figure 4. Crank shaft mechanism and input-output signals.

A set of actuators and sensors acts and measures the platform dynamics, Figure 5. Each crankshaft mechanism is governed by an actuator and a sensor. This consists of an alternate current induction electric motor and its electric drive. The motor shaft holds an absolute encoder allowing the angle measurement of the crank. The upper base has one sensor: a gyroscope. It is located under the driver seat. A Real Time (*RT*) computer (same as for the *Dynacar* system) reads the gyroscope and encoder signals. A set of reference signals is delivered from the selected vehicle dynamics model and compared with the measurements. The control algorithm computes in the *RT* computer the commands for each electric drive.

IV. *VDS* CONTROL ALGORITHMS

The *VDS* control system consists of: vehicle dynamics model (Dynacar), control algorithm, signal conditioning, power driving and platform. The control system considers

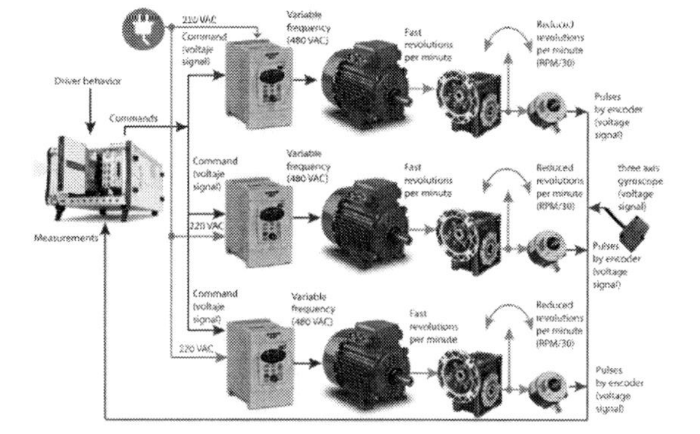

Figure 5. Actuators and sensors for platform.

two control algorithm modes: (a) conditional control, and (b) washout filtering with feedback, Figure 6.

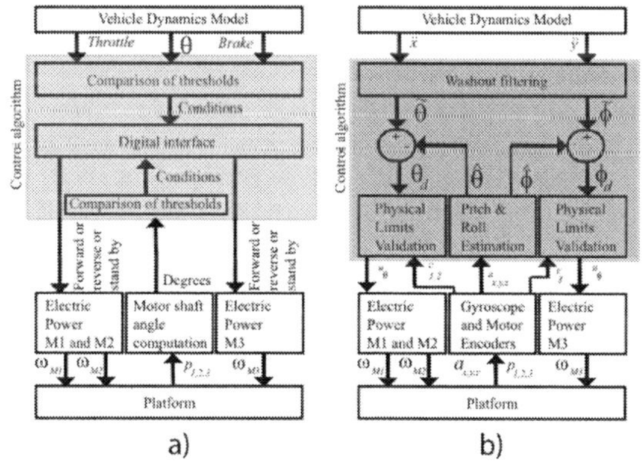

Figure 6. Control system proposal: a) physical-limits-based, b) washout filters.

The *conditional control* is a physical-limits-based control using a continuous comparison of signals with a priori defined thresholds. The Revolution Per Minute (*RPM*) of each *AC* motor is constant. The signal conditioning consists of: a) processing of sensor signals in order to obtain crankshaft angles, b) acquisition from *Dynacar* of roll and proportional values of throttle and brake pedals, and c) digital outputs activation according to controller output. The controller inputs are roll, proportional brake, proportional throttle, and degrees of each motor shaft. The controller outputs are sixteen digital outputs whose control three motor conditions in the *AC* drive are: move forward, move reverse and stand by. When the driver accelerates/brakes the vehicle, the front motor ups/down the platform. The control system emulates proportionally the pitch motion. Regarding to the roll platform emulation, when the simulated roll (reference) from *Dynacar* is between a priori interval, the platform moves in a direction according to the sign of the reference until a threshold is reached. Then the platform stops and the control system waits until the change of sign in the reference signal. This sequence is repeated during all *VDS* driving operation. For a higher speed platform motion, the *RPM* in each motor must be set according to the driver assessment.

The *washout filtering with feedback control* consists of

a physical limits validation including backslash exclusion, a classical washout filtering algorithm, Figure 1, an estimation algorithm of pitch and roll, and a proportional gain. The physical limits validation is continuous in each sample time, however the algorithm adds an offset to the controller output voltage in order to avoid the inertia under two system conditions: stand by and low speed of the motor. The controller computes the *RPM* of each *AC* motor and the sense of rotation around the zero angle. The signal conditioning consists of: a) processing of sensor signals in order to obtain crankshaft angles, b) acquisition from *Dynacar* of longitudinal and lateral accelerations, c) conversion from pulses to angle for each motor shaft, and d) conditioning of controller output in order to obtain the *AC* motor drive input voltage (proportional to the revolution per minute of the *AC* motor). The controller inputs are longitudinal and lateral accelerations from *Dynacar*, angular speeds for x, y, and z from gyroscope, and each motor shaft angle obtained from encoders. The outputs of the controller are three: voltage command for each *AC* motor drive. The command has a range with an offset. The magnitude of this signal indicates *RPMs* of the *AC* motor. Over the offset the voltage indicates forward direction, below the offset it indicates reverse direction. The control system emulates both movements: the pitch and the roll. The estimated pitch ($\hat{\theta}$) is subtracted from the simulated pitch (output of washout filtering, $\tilde{\theta}$) conforming a pitch error signal (θ_d). Then θ_d is validated through a physical limits algorithm and multiplied by a gain (P controller) and it becomes controller output u_θ as the command voltage to the *AC* motor drive. The same control sequence applies for roll control.

The power driving (using any control algorithm) converts the controller outputs in mechanical motion.

V. Methodology

The design and validation of the control system in the *VDS* consist of open loop and closed loop tests. The computation of parameters and the programming of the control algorithm are done with *Matlab*®. The methodology consists of:

A. Design of Experiments

The main goal is to define the frequency response of the platform from the manipulation variable to the pitch and roll motions in open loop. A set of experiments is applied to the platform in order to analyze the input-output relationship. There are two experiments: (a) driver test under random scenario, and (b) sinusoidal test for actuator characterization.

1) *The driver test under random scenario* consists of using the Dynacar system with an specific driver, track and vehicle in order to get the frequency response of the simulated roll and pitch of the given vehicle model. The experiment considers ten replicates. The peak value of the roll (ϕ_{max}) and pitch (θ_{max}) as well as the cut-off frequency $f_{cut\ off}$ for each one are the experiment outputs computed with the Fast Fourier Transform, Figure 7.
2) *The sinusoidal test for actuator characterization* explores the frequency response according to the bandwidth and magnitudes obtained from the first experiment. Each experiment consists of a sinusoidal excitation of the electric drive manipulation in order to observe the encoders and the pitch (roll) responses with a constant frequency and amplitude. The amplitude remains constant and at least five cycles are completed ending the experiment. Then the frequency is incremented and the experiment repeated. This *DoE* ends when the cut-off frequency is reached. The magnitude of roll and pitch at the given frequency of each experiment allows to build a pseudo-bode diagram. This *DoE* consists of a total of three replicates, Figure 8. The function of this experiment is to obtain the frequency response of the motor under controlled inputs in the operation domain according to the vehicle model. The control algorithms will take into account this information for its design and to consider these parameters for a safety operation.

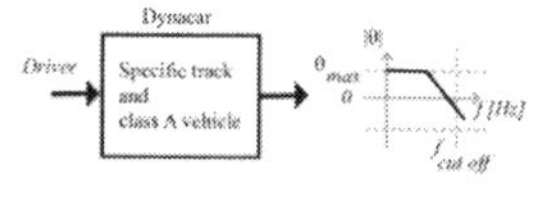

Figure 7. Input to output relationship in the driver test under random scenario.

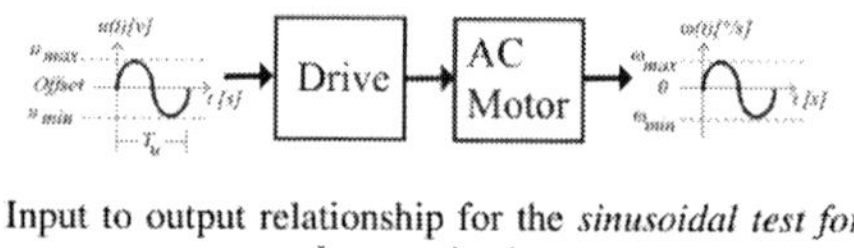

Figure 8. Input to output relationship for the *sinusoidal test for actuator characterization*.

B. Domain Operation and Design of Control Algorithms

The results of the *DoE* will allow to specify domain operation of the *VDS* as well as the parameters for the control algorithm. The domain operation consists of the electrical and mechanical thresholds of the *3DoF* platform . The electrical thresholds consider the maximum frequency and amplitude to be applied as input to the *AC* motor drive, The mechanical thresholds consist of the initial motor shaft positions as well as the angle intervals of safe motion for each crankshaft mechanism.

C. Control Algorithms Performance

The driver test under random scenario is repeated with the *VDS*: Dynacar and the *3DoF* platform simulating the pitch and roll vehicle motion. The goal is to evaluate the closed loop performance under the two control modes. The assessment of the driver and qualitative plots are the results of this test.

VI. Results

The results of the control algorithm implementation are presented.

The driver test under random scenario shows the frequency domain to explore is 0.5-2.0 Hz according to the pitch and roll frequency content. This bandwidth has been obtained from data analysis from DynaCar simulated variables. The ranges of the simulated pitch and roll are $\tilde{\theta} = \{-5, 5\}$ degrees and $\tilde{\phi} = \{-8, 8\}$ degrees.

The sinusoidal test for actuator characterization shows a linear relation between shaft speed and drive command, Figure

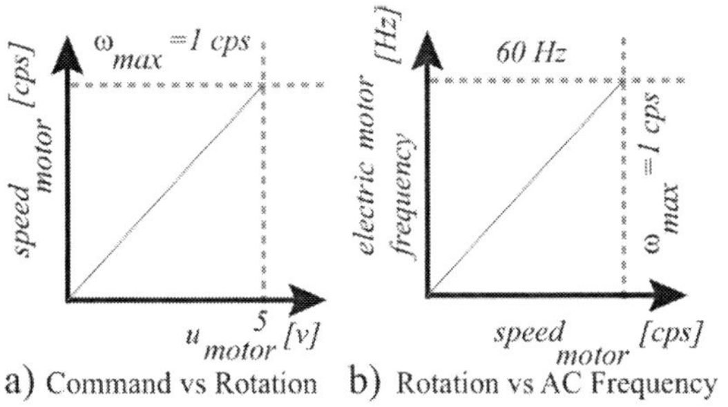

Figure 9. Experimental relation between *AC* motor drive command and shaft speed.

9. The maximum voltage command allows until 1 cycles per second for each motor shaft, Figure 9a. One *cps* is proportional to 60 Hz of *AC* voltage frequency in the *AC* drive. So, this is the maximum speed.

A comparison of the command voltage versus motor angular speed versus initial angle in the motor shaft shows non linearities on the speed regarding low command voltage, Figure 10. There is an offset in the voltage since the drive requires 5 V in order to stop motor. Any voltage over/below 5 V moves the motor shaft in the forward/reverse direction. Moreover, the motor do not respond in the range $5 \pm (0.5, 1)$

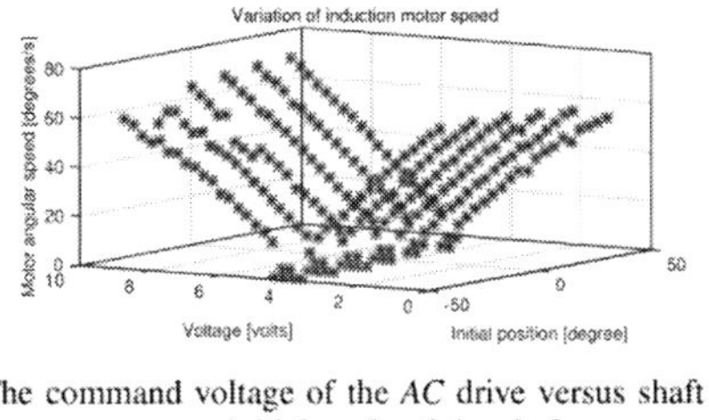

Figure 10. The command voltage of the *AC* drive versus shaft angle speed versus initial angle of the shaft.

V. When the command is over $\sim \pm 6$ V the motor starts the motion. Regarding to the initial angle position, the angular speed remains the same response, Figure 11.

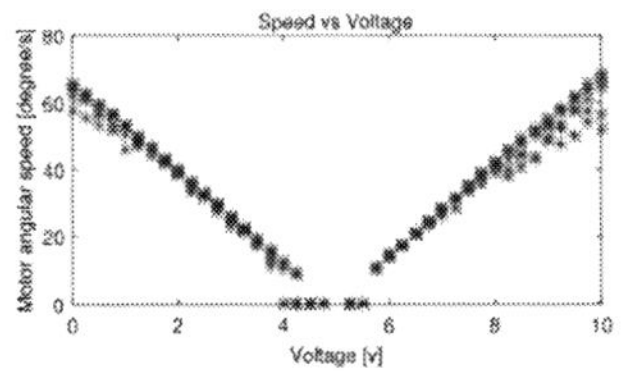

Figure 11. Command voltage versus shaft angular speed.

The design of the *conditional control* algorithm utilizes thresholds for roll from *Dynacar*, two absolute encoders, and throttle and brake pedals. Pitch and roll functional values are between defined parameters, greater than 0.8 or less than -0.8 in the case of the roll. In the case of the pitch, it was established the minimum of acceleration greater than 0.5 and the brake greater than 0.4. In the case of pitch, it has to be in the limit of 10 degrees and in the case of roll, the limit is between 0-5 degrees.

The design of the washout filtering with feedback control considers the design of low and high pass digital filters using *Matlab*, Figure 12. The output of this algorithm is the simulated variables pitch and roll. Classically these signals will be converted to voltage and then feed to the *AC* motor drives. However, this control system considers the feedback of *measured* pitch and roll. In order to translate the rotational

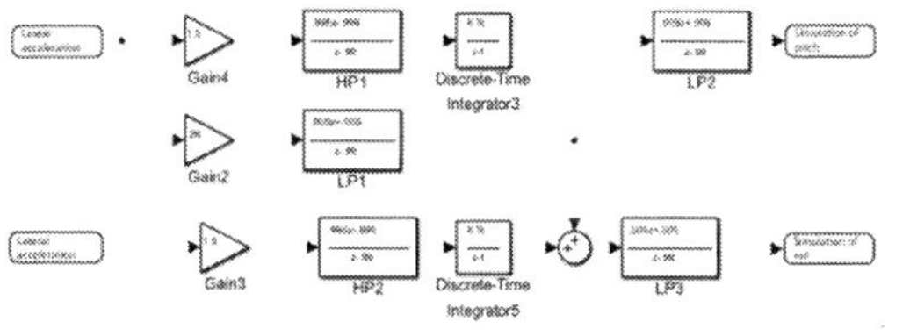

Figure 12. Washout filter algorithm: final parametrization.

angle of each motor shaft to the upper base plane, a set of trigonometric operations is done. Then the result is transformed to an estimation of pitch and roll signals based on the angular speeds delivered for gyroscope using the proposal from [18]. An offset of ± 0.7 is added to each controller output in order to avoid the dead zone of the command versus the shaft speed response. The proportional control gain multiplies the controller output. The complete scheme shows the computation blocks, Figure 11.

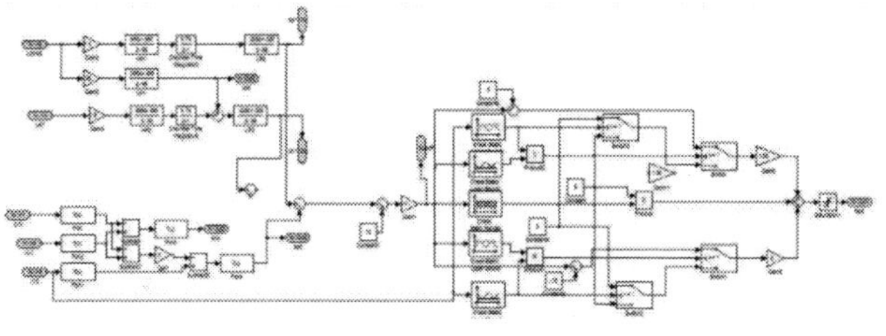

Figure 13. Design of control algorithm.

The results of closed loop test show the advantages of both control algorithms proposals, Figure 14.

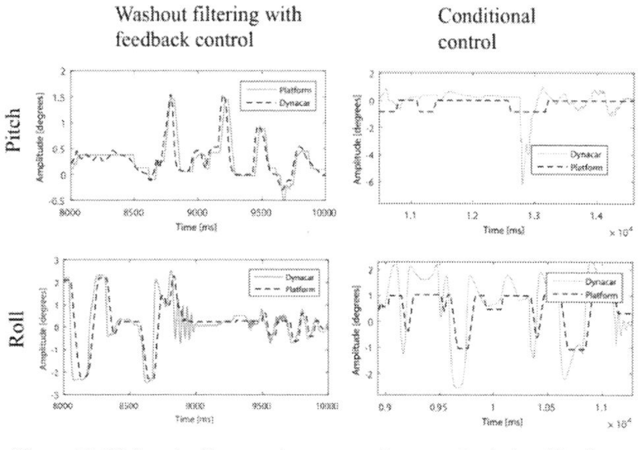

Figure 14. Pitch and roll comparison versus *Dynacar* simulation. The first and second row shows the pitch and roll variables. The columns defines the results for washout filtering and conditional control respectively.

Both approaches move the platform in the right direction. The frequency response is limited by the frequency response of the AC motors and its manipulation. The conditional control performs an inertial control where the motion is felt by the user. However, the final application of this control can not be training due to the lack of fidelity of the pitch and roll platform simulation. The delay of this algorithm is enough to be notice by the user. However, its simplicity allows to tune the control system with thresholds under constant motor speed, see second column of Figure 14.

Regarding to the washout filtering with feedback control it can be seen a high fidelity in the platform motion regarding the simulation in Dynacar. The control is continuous and tracks the reference delivered by the washout filtering algorithm. The user experiences a real time motion synchronized with the visual engine of Dynacar. This experience is a added value that allows to use this control mode for training and for evaluation other vehicle systems in the full user experience. The delay is considerably small when compared with the one of the conditional control, see first column of Figure 14.

VII. Conclusion

The control system of a VDS with three degrees of freedom motion platform has been developed. It uses the positions of each motor shaft and the angular speeds of a gyroscope. The variables of interest are the pitch and roll and simulated in real time according to the DynaCar software. Two control schemes have been validated. Despite the configuration of hardware is commercially available by several companies, the control algorithms always are the challenge. This platform has a low cost in the hardware because the use of AC motors and it can be integrated to another vehicle model simulation using the proposed algorithms. The results show it is possible to use this AC motors for motion control in this application.

References

[1] G. Reymond and A. Kemeny, "Motion cueing in the renault driving simulator," Vehicle System Dynamics, vol. 34, no. 4, 2000, pp. 249–259. [Online]. Available: http://www.tandfonline.com/doi/abs/10.1076/vesd.34.4.249.2059

[2] C. J. Gutridge, "Three degree-of-freedom simulator motion cueing using classical washout filters and acceleration feedback," Ph.D. dissertation, Citeseer, 2004.

[3] C. Weiß, "Control of a dynamic driving simulator: Time-variant motion cueing algorithms and prepositioning," Ph.D. dissertation, Universität Stuttgart, DLR, 2006.

[4] L. Nehaoua, H. Mohellebi, A. Amouri, H. Arioui, S. Espie, and A. Kheddar, "Design and control of a small-clearance driving simulator," IEEE Transactions on Vehicular Technology, vol. 57, no. 2, March 2008, pp. 736–746.

[5] D. R. Berger, J. Schulte-Pelkum, and H. H. Bülthoff, "Simulating believable forward accelerations on a stewart motion platform," ACM Transactions on Applied Perception (TAP), vol. 7, no. 1, 2010, p. 5.

[6] J. J. Slob, "State-of-the-art driving simulators, a literature survey," DCT Report, vol. 107, 2008.

[7] C. D. Larsen, "Comparison of three degree of freedom and six degree of freedom motion bases utilizing classical washout algorithms," Ph.D. dissertation, Iowa State University, 2011.

[8] H. Arioui, S. Hima, L. Nehaoua, R. J. V. Bertin, and S. Espi, "From design to experiments of a 2-dof vehicle driving simulator," IEEE Transactions on Vehicular Technology, vol. 60, no. 2, Feb 2011, pp. 357–368.

[9] N. Mohajer, H. Abdi, K. Nelson, and S. Nahavandi, "Vehicle motion simulators, a key step towards road vehicle dynamics improvement," Vehicle System Dynamics, vol. 53, no. 8, 2015, pp. 1204–1226. [Online]. Available: http://dx.doi.org/10.1080/00423114.2015.1039551

[10] R. Berger, "Being prepared for the next mexican automotive boom," Roland Berger, 2016.

[11] Promexico, Ed., The Mexican Automotive Industry: Leading the World, Promexico, 2015 2015. [Online]. Available: https://www.promexico.gob.mx/documentos/revista-negocios/pdf/abr-2015.pdf

[12] Cluster automotriz de nuevo leon. CLAUT. [Online]. Available: http://www.claut.com.mx/

[13] J. Reyes-Alvarez, "La estrategia de localización de actividades i+d de audi: Un referente para el caso de san jose chiapa, puebla mexico," Tecsistecatl, vol. 2016, no. 19, April 2016.

[14] R. J. Telban, W. Wu, F. M. Cardullo, and J. A. Houck, "Motion cueing algorithm development: Initial investigation and redesign of the algorithms," NASA, Tech. Rep., 2000.

[15] L. Nehaoua, H. Arioui, S. Espie, and H. Mohellebi, "Motion cueing algorithms for small driving simulator," in Proceedings 2006 IEEE International Conference on Robotics and Automation, 2006. ICRA 2006., May 2006, pp. 3189–3194.

[16] H. Arioui, S. Hima, and L. Nehaoua, "2 dof low cost platform for driving simulator: Modeling and control," in 2009 IEEE/ASME International Conference on Advanced Intelligent Mechatronics, July 2009, pp. 1206–1211.

[17] A. Peña, I. Iglesias, J. J. Valera, and A. Martin, "Development and Validation of Dynacar RT Software, A New Integrated Solution for Design of Electric and Hybrid Vehicles," in Proceedings of International Battery, Hybrid and Fuel Cell Electric Vehicle Symposium (EVS 26), Los Angeles, USA, 2012, pp. 13–16.

[18] M. Pedley, "Tilt sensing using a three-axis accelerometer," Freescale Semiconductor Application Note, 2013, pp. 2012–2013.

Developing an Interface between ANSYS and Abaqus to Simulate Blast Effects on High Security Vehicles

Enrico Hansen, Nicole Ehlers, Arash Ramezani, Hendrik Rothe

Helmut-Schmidt-University
Holstenhofweg 85
22043 Hamburg
Germany
Email: {e.hansen, ehlersn, ramezani, hr}@hsu-hh.de

***Abstract*—The present time is shaped by a variety of religious, political and military conflicts. In times of asymmetric warfare and constantly changing sources of danger from terrorist attacks and other violence based crimes, the personal need for protection continues to rise. Aside from military applications there is a large area for the use of high security vehicles. Outwardly almost indistinguishable from the basic vehicles, security vehicles are used for protecting heads of state as well as individuals. To remain state of the art it is necessary for security vehicles to permanently continue to develop protection against modern weapons and ammunition types. It is enormously cost intensive to check any new technology by firing or blasting of real vehicles. Therefore, more and more calculations of new security concepts and materials are carried out by numerical computer simulations. However, product simulation is often being performed by engineering groups using niche simulation tools from different vendors to simulate various design attributes. The use of multiple vendor software products creates inefficiencies and increases costs. This paper will present the analysis and development of an interface between the most common computer-aided engineering applications ANSYS Autodyn and Abaqus to exploit the advantages of both systems for the simulation of blast effects.**

Keywords*–*CFD-FEM coupling methods; fully automatic structure analyses; high-performance computing techniques; blast loading; vehicle structures.

I. Introduction

In the security sector, the partly insufficient safety of people and equipment due to failure of industrial components are ongoing problems that cause great concern. Since computers and software have spread into all fields of industry, extensive efforts are currently being made in order to improve the safety by applying certain computer-based solutions. To deal with problems involving the release of a large amount of energy over a very short period of time, e.g., explosions and impacts, there are three approaches, which are discussed in [1].

As the problems are highly non-linear and require information regarding material behavior at ultra-high loading rates, which is generally not available, most of the work is experimental and may cause tremendous expenses. Analytical approaches are possible if the geometries involved are relatively simple and if the loading can be described through boundary conditions, initial conditions, or a combination of the two. Numerical solutions are far more general in scope and remove any difficulties associated with geometry [2].

For structures under shock and impact loading, numerical simulations have proven to be extremely useful. They provide a rapid and less expensive way to evaluate new design ideas. Numerical simulations can supply quantitative and accurate details of stress, strain, and deformation fields that would be very costly or difficult to reproduce experimentally. In these numerical simulations, the partial differential equations governing the basic physic principles of conservation of mass, momentum, and energy are employed. The equations to be solved are time-dependent and nonlinear in nature. These equations, together with constitutive models describing material behavior and a set of initial and boundary conditions, define the complete system for shock and impact simulations.

The governing partial differential equations need to be solved in both time and space domains. The solution over the time domain can be achieved by an explicit method. In the explicit method, the solution at a given point in time is expressed as a function of the system variables and parameters, with no requirements for stiffness and mass matrices. Thus, the computing time at each time step is low but may require numerous time steps for a complete solution. The solution for the space domain can be obtained utilizing different spatial discretisations, such as Lagrange [3], Euler [4], Arbitrary Lagrange Euler (ALE) [5], or mesh free methods [6]. Each of these techniques has its unique capabilities, but also limitations. Usually, there is not a single technique that can cope with all the regimes of a problem [7]. Fig. 1 gives a short overview of the solver technologies mentioned above. The crucial factor is the grid that causes different outcomes.

Due to the fact that all engineering simulations are based on geometry to represent the design, the target and all its components are simulated as CAD models. Real-world engineering commonly involves the analysis and design of complicated geometry. These types of analysis depend critically on having a modeling tool with a robust geometry import capability in conjunction with advanced, easy-to-use mesh generation algorithms [8]. It is often necessary to combine different simulation and modeling techniques from various CAE applications. However, this fact can lead to major difficulties, especially in terms of data loss and computational effort. Particularly the leading software providers prevent an interaction of their tools with competing products. But, to analyze blast loading and its effects on vehicle structures, different CAE tools are needed. Therefore, it is important that an interface is provided that

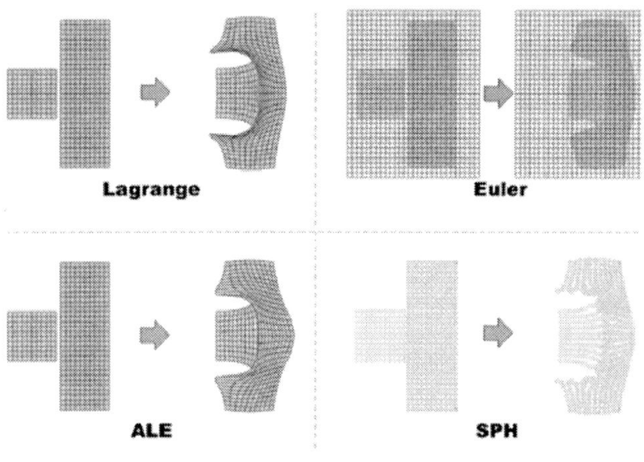

Figure 1. Examples of Lagrange, Euler, ALE, and SPH simulations on an impact problem [1].

allows a robust interaction between various applications. Using a CAD neutral environment that supports direct, bidirectional and associative interfaces with CAE systems, the geometry can be optimized successively and analysis can be performed without loss of data.

This work will present an interface between ANSYS and Abaqus, both leading software suites for finite element analysis and computer-aided engineering. The goal is to develop and demonstrate an efficient FEA/CFD coupling technique for vehicle structures under high-pressure shock compression. The coupling is achieved by an iterative procedure between FEA and CFD calculations using CATIA, ANSYS Autodyn, and Abaqus. ANSYS Autodyn provides shock compression data and the knowledge of shock-wave properties. Abaqus and CATIA (both developed by Dassault Systmes) implement the numerical models with all relevant information. Here, the major challenge is to establish a continuous and fully automatic transfer of blast loadings with high-variation rates from ANSYS Autodyn to Abaqus.

After a brief introduction with a description of the different methods of space discretization in Section I, there is a short section about the concept of this work. Section III describes the experimental set-up and the implementation of our interface. The paper ends with an outlook in Section IV and a concluding paragraph.

II. Concept

Real-world engineering commonly involves the analysis and design of complicated geometry. These types of analysis depend critically on having a modeling tool with a robust geometry import capability in conjunction with advanced, easy-to-use mesh generation algorithms [8]. It is often necessary to combine different simulation and modeling techniques from various CAE applications. However, this fact can lead to major difficulties, especially in terms of data loss and computational effort. Particularly the leading software providers prevent an interaction of their tools with competing products. But to analyze blast loading and its effects on vehicle structures, different CAE tools are needed. Therefore, it is important that an interface is provided that allows a robust interaction between various applications. Using a computer-aided design (CAD) neutral environment that supports direct, bidirectional and associative interfaces with CAE systems, the geometry can be optimized successively and analysis can be performed without loss of data.

This work will present an interface between ANSYS and Abaqus, both leading software suites for finite element analysis and computer-aided engineering. The goal is to develop and demonstrate an efficient finite element analysis/computational fluid dynamics (FEA/CFD) coupling technique for vehicle structures under high-pressure shock compression. The coupling is achieved by an iterative procedure between FEA and CFD calculations using CATIA, ANSYS Autodyn, and Abaqus. ANSYS Autodyn provides shock compression data and the knowledge of shock-wave properties. Abaqus and CATIA (both developed by Dassault Systmes) implement the numerical models with all relevant information. Here, the major challenge is to establish a continuous and fully automatic transfer of blast loadings with high-variation rates from ANSYS Autodyn to Abaqus.

III. Experimental Section

In computing, an interface is a shared boundary across which two separate components of a computer system exchange information. The exchange can be between software, computer hardware, peripheral devices, humans and combinations of these. Some computer hardware devices such as a touchscreen can both send and receive data through the interface, while others such as a mouse, microphone or joystick operate one way only [9].

Coupled FEA/CFD analysis is an alternative technique, where separate FEA and CFD codes are used for solid and fluid regions, respectively, with a smooth exchange of information between the two codes to ensure continuity of blast loading data. The main merit of the approach is to enable users to take full advantages of both CFD and FEA capabilities.

The objective of this work is to develop an interface between ANSYS Autodyn and Abaqus. The software ANSYS is used to solve linear and non-linear problems of structural mechanics, computational fluid dynamics, acoustics and various other engineering sciences [10]. Here, ANSYS will provide data from the simulation of blast effects. The capability to couple Eulerian and Lagrangian frames in ANSYS is helpful in blast field modeling. The Eulerian frame is best suited for representing explosive detonations, because the material flows through a geometrically constant grid that can easily handle the large deformations associated with gas and fluid flow. The structure is modeled with the Lagrangian frame in Abaqus. Abaqus supports familiar interactive computer-aided engineering concepts such as feature-based, parametric modeling, interactive and scripted operation, and GUI customization [11]. First, every possibility of transferring the data from ANSYS outputs to Abaqus inputs has to be detected (see Fig. 2).

ANSYS will provide the data by generating a data set for the blast loading (see Figure 3). This data set will include snapshots of given points in time. At this stage there is a data set of five points in time, between 0.0291s and 0.0475s (after detonation). Related to the points in time this data set includes the pressure values with Cartesian coordinates based on the

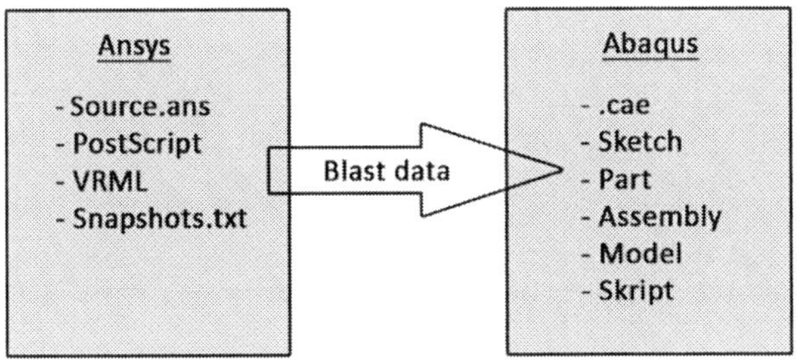

Figure 2. Inputs and outputs for an interface.

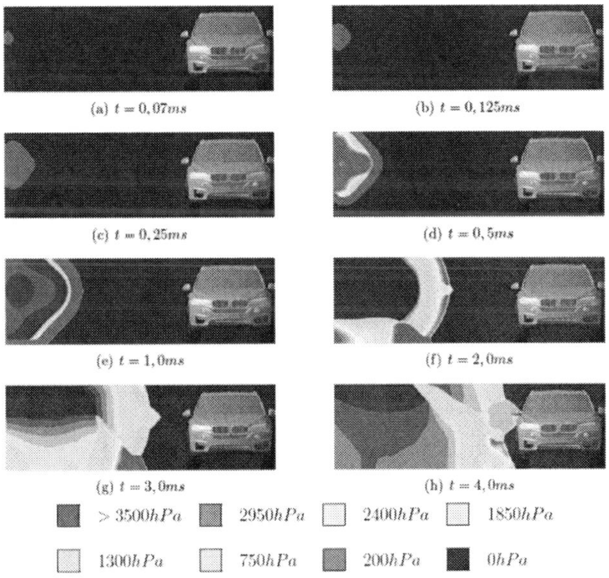

Figure 3. Expansion of blast in ANSYS Autodyn.

simulation of the spread of explosive materials. A script is coded to read the blast loading data in Abaqus. This script, coded in Python, uses the line interface in Abaqus directly. First, a blast loading data is generated in ANSYS and saved as a normal text file in .txt format. The data set will be splitted to separate the different types of information. After that, a list will be created to save the data and connect the related time points to the coordinates and pressure values. At this point, there is a possibility to use linear interpolation between the five time points to generate a larger data base. After reading and saving the data set, the script will load the model used for impact tests in Abaqus. A surface of the model must be selected to project the blast data on it.

The goal is to investigate the impact of the blast data on a full vehicle model in Abaqus. This work (in progress) starts with a less complex model to validate the function of the script and the interface itself. The first model was a basic rectangle to be strained by the pressure data. Afterwards, two more complex models were tested successfully. This approach will lead to a surface similar to the silhouette of high security vehicles (see Figure 4). The coupling is realized through an iterative loop between the FEA and CFD simulations, with

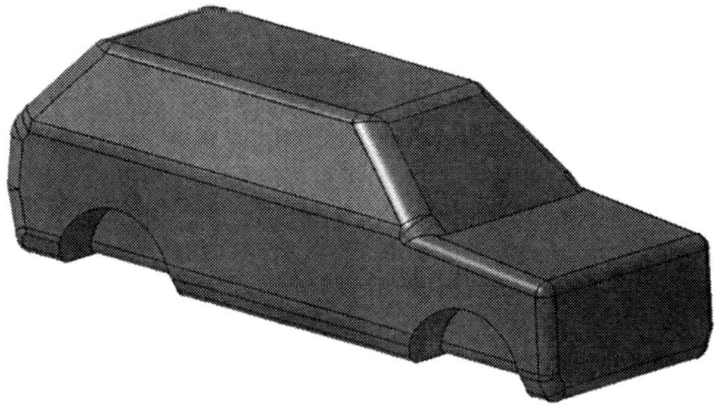

Figure 4. Testing structure in Abaqus.

communications ensuring continuity of shock compression data across the coupled boundaries between the FEA and CFD models. In the coupling process, intermediate individual FEA and CFD solutions are obtained in turn with dynamically updated boundary conditions. To avoid exceptional dead lock of the individual CFD simulations, appropriate maximum numbers of iterations are assigned for each CFD model.

IV. Outlook

There are a variety of approaches in implementing the coupled FEA/CFD analysis. One is generally called "‘strong coupling"’, where data have to be transferred between ANSYS Autodyn and ABAQUS in every single time step. A "‘semi-strong coupling"’ can get along with a smaller set of date, using mathematical interpolation for a sufficient approximation. The third concept is a "‘weak coupling"’ solution. Here, neural networks and deep learning can be used to replicate blast effects on different vehicle structures. These approaches are going to be tested in a next step.

Furthermore, a larger blast loading data set has to be created in ANSYS. This will allow a more accurate illustration of blast effects on vehicle structures. Smaller time steps will enable a linear interpolation with a higher accuracy. Different explosives are going to be tested to expand the data base. The next step will be a model for the reflection of blast waves and dynamic changes of pressure values. Using a full vehicle model will provide important information about the behavior of armored structures under blast effects. But to validate the results of the simulation, more ballistic trials are needed. Based on the difficulties of full vehicle model simulations, the implementation of an automatic surface detection has to be taken into consideration. This could be helpful if a large number of different vehicles are investigated. In order to create a user-friendly interface it is possible to generate the script as a plug-in which can be started from the Abaqus user surface directly.

By using pre-defined blast data to create forces as vectors on our vehicle structures, the proposal can be generalized. Then, FEA analysis can be done with other software suites as well. Right now, the concept is not applicable to other systems. This is a major disadvantage and part of our future work. Furthermore, a parallelization of the problem should be considered.

V. Conclusion and Future Work

A technique for efficiently coupling FEA/CFD for the simulation of blast effects is described. An interface between ANSYS and Abaqus was created to provide blast data sets. The data sets from ANSYS include snapshots from the blast simulation saved at different points in time. The interface is coded in Python and also contains the possibility to use linear interpolation on the data sets.

A good agreement of blast load test data and simulation results was observed. Furthermore, it is shown that the coupled solutions can be obtained in sufficiently short turn-around times for use in design. These solutions can be used as the basis of an iterative optimization process. They are a valuable adjunct to the study of the behavior of vehicle structures subjected to high-velocity impact or intense impulsive loading. The combined use of computations, experiments and high-strain-rate material characterization has, in many cases, supplemented the data achievable by experiments alone at considerable savings in both cost and engineering man-hours.

References

[1] A. Ramezani and H. Rothe, 'Investigation of Solver Technologies for the Simulation of Brittle Materials,' *The Sixth International Conference on Advances in System Simulation* (SIMUL 2014) IARIA, pp. 236-242, Oct. 2014, ISBN 978-61208-371-1

[2] J. Zukas, 'Introduction to Hydrocodes,' Elsevier Science, February 2004.

[3] A. M. S. Hamouda and M. S. J. Hashmi, 'Modelling the impact and penetration events of modern engineering materials: Characteristics of computer codes and material models,' *Journal of Materials Processing Technology*, vol. 56, pp. 847-862, Jan. 1996.

[4] D. J. Benson, 'Computational methods in Lagrangian and Eulerian hydrocodes,' *Computer Methods in Applied Mechanics and Engineering*, vol. 99, pp. 235-394, Sep. 1992, doi: 10.1016/0045-7825(92)90042-I.

[5] M. Oevermann, S. Gerber, and F. Behrendt, '*Euler-Lagrange/DEM simulation of wood gasification in a bubbling fluidized bed reactor*,' Particuology, vol. 7, pp. 307-316, Aug. 2009, doi: 10.1016/j.partic.2009.04.004.

[6] D. L. Hicks and L. M. Liebrock, '*SPH hydrocodes can be stabilized with shape-shifting*,' Computers & Mathematics with Applications, vol. 38, pp. 1-16, Sep. 1999, doi: 10.1016/S0898-1221(99)00210-2.

[7] X. Quan, N. K. Birnbaum, M. S. Cowler, and B. I. Gerber, 'Numerical Simulations of Structural Deformation under Shock and Impact Loads using a Coupled Multi-Solver Approach,' *5th Asia-Pacific Conference on Shock and Impact Loads on Structures*, Hunan, China, pp. 152-161, Nov. 2003.

[8] N. V. Bermeo, M. G. Mendoza, and A. G. Castro, '*Semantic Representation of CAD Models Based on the IGES Standard*,' Computer Science, vol. 8265, pp. 157-168, Dec. 2001, doi: 10.1007/ 978-3-642-45114-013

[9] IEEE 100 - *The Authoritative Dictionary Of IEEE Standards Terms*. NYC, NY, USA: IEEE Press. pp. 574-575, 2000. ISBN 0-7381-2601-2

[10] "ANSYS", 2016, URL: http://www.ansys.com [accessed: 2016-04-01].

[11] "Abaqus CAE", 2016, URL: http://www.3ds.com/products-services/ simulia/ products/abaqus/abaquscae/ [accessed: 2016-04-05]

Modeling and Analyzing Enterprise Architectures to Examine the Feasibility of Network Centric Operations

Oliver Kröning and Hendrik Rothe
Chair of Measurement and Information Technology
Helmut Schmidt University / University of the Federal Armed Forces
Hamburg, Germany
Email: oliver.kroening@hsu-hh.de, rothe@hsu-hh.de

Abstract—**Military forces of NATO states are often constrained to perform missions within the framework of Network Centric Operations (NCO) due to a joint and multinational environment requiring a high level of interoperability. The transformation and development of respective capabilities and systems are often tied to financial and time based expenditures. Thus, models of real NCOs are necessary to analyze risks, problems and development needs. Enterprise architecture models of a certain organization provide views from different perspectives to examine various aspects with the aim of supporting problem solutions. This work presents an approach to apply two different architecture frameworks for modeling NCOs examining various layers of a model for interoperability. Furthermore, analysis methods are introduced to assess the feasibility of NCOs.**

Keywords – Enterprise Architecture; Network Centric Operations; UML modeling; analyzing methods; TOGAF; NAF.

I. INTRODUCTION

The importance of acquisition and evaluation of information has become an essential component of military operations. Thus, military forces endeavor to optimize the information flow and to minimize technical and operational errors. Among the "classical" operational factors – forces, space and time – information is considered as the fourth decisive factor of successful warfare [1].

Coincidentally the introduction of new technological capabilities to gather, exchange and process information offers new opportunities of efficiency enhancement and optimization of resources.

In the late 1990s, the principle of NCOs (also called Network Centric Warfare) was developed to achieve information superiority, as well as firepower and command superiority involving an optimized mission execution [1][2]. The attainment of these benefits requires an essential transform in thinking and acting of respective military forces. Organizational, structural and technical changes are necessary as well. Furthermore, just like any other new development, there are risks and problems to face.

Since a couple of years the German Federal Armed Forces have used scientific approaches to analyze and document the forces' progression and transformation with the objective to realize NCOs. In this paper, the modeling and analysis of NCOs using the method of architecture are described. Thereby architecture supports interoperability, cost effectiveness and a common understanding of the concept of NCO.

The paper is structured as follows: Section II defines the term of NCO and discusses its advantages, risks and problems. Section III introduces the architectural approach and gives an overview of the architecture frameworks. Section IV describes the modeling of NCO and the usage of architecture tools applied to a model of interoperability. After that analysis methods of architecture products are presented followed by best practice hints and lessons learned in Section VI. Section VII contains the papers conclusion.

II. NETWORK CENTRIC OPERATIONS

NCO is a military warfare doctrine with the aim to optimally bring available forces and means into effect. The concept of the Federal Armed Forces [3] presets the theory of NCO as the groundwork for all missions of the German forces. Therefore, all missions are performed by reconnaissance, command, joint fires and support networks in all dimensions (land, air, navy, space, cyber).

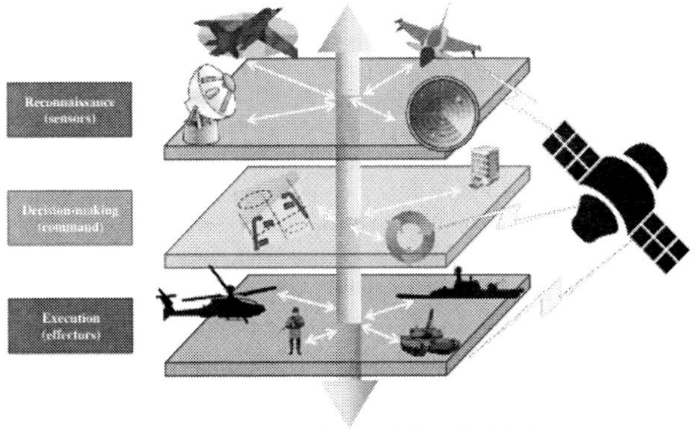

Figure 1. Scheme of Network Centric Warfare.

This requires a joint, cross-departmental, national, combined, interoperable and secure information and communication network embracing all levels of command. All units, duty stations and facilities together with sensors and effectors have to be connected using multinational and interoperable means to achieve a fast and efficient operation.

In contrast to a "Platform Centric Warfare" a network connecting multiple sensors, decision-makers and effectors as depicted in Figure 1 is able to create synergy by coupling system functionalities [4]. The information structure is based on a Common Operational Picture (COP) collecting and merging data from connected sensors. This improves the common situational awareness, informational superiority and command superiority in respective command facilities resulting in a fast, quick-response and effective use of effectors.

NCOs also contain some risks military forces have to avoid or reduce. The complexity of the COP could lead to an information overload especially on lower levels of command. However, a high level of detail could result in micromanagement on higher levels of command. Furthermore, the forces also have to provide a high quality of interoperability - operational and technical. Other risks might be the threat of cyber-attacks and vague responsibilities. Problems in the development of a NCO capability are the expensive costs of new technologies and a high financial and practical effort during the transformation.

III. ARCHITECTURAL APPROACH

A. *Enterprise Architecture*

An Enterprise Architecture is described as a well-defined practice for conducting enterprise analysis, design, planning, and implementation, using a holistic approach at all times, for the successful development and execution of strategy [5]. The basic idea of architecture is the systematic and structured description and analysis of a real and complex system by methodically disassemble the problem into smaller and simpler models of the reality without disregarding coherences and dependencies between these components. The definition of architecture terms and elements can be found in [6].

Architecture offers the opportunity to document complex sociotechnical systems. Thus, it is a reliable methodology to

- Verify operational deliberations and document an operational context,
- Deduce special user commands from the operational context,
- Design a technical solution to fulfil operational requirements,
- Abstract and document the internal structure of a technical solution as well as its inclusion in an overall system or network and
- Manage system and product dependencies.

Thus, enterprise architecture provides decision support of defining how resources will be used to support enterprise strategy and helps to achieve goals and objectives [7].

B. *Architecture Frameworks*

Due to the requirement of a structured and systematic development, architecture holds standardized patterns and process models for developing and using architecture products. Architecture frameworks contain valid conventions and guidelines for architecture preparation to ensure the models' and/or sub models' compatibility, integration, uniformity and reusability.

The variety of architecture frameworks is large and there are many different approaches. An overview of frameworks is given by Urbaczewski et al. [8]. Architecture frameworks used within military applications are compared by Jamjoom et al. [9].

The latter reference examines frameworks by focusing on their support of the Service Oriented Architecture (SOA) paradigm, which contains needs and capabilities and their distribution between stakeholders. With regard to Jamjoom et al. [9], the NATO Architecture Framework (NAF) strongly provides SOA features, such as interoperability and reusability, to implement NATO capabilities in complex operational environments.

Due to these benefits, the modeling of architecture products is based on rules and standards which are defined in the NAF Version 3.1 (NAFv3.1). Further on, an architecture development process is introduced in Section III.C by using The Open Group Architecture Framework (TOGAF).

C. *Architecture Development Method*

The development of enterprise architectures is guided by referenced process models to ensure a standardized, comprehensible and consistent way of projecting, implementing, analyzing and governing architectures. TOGAF characterizes a comprehensive approach to realize these requirements.

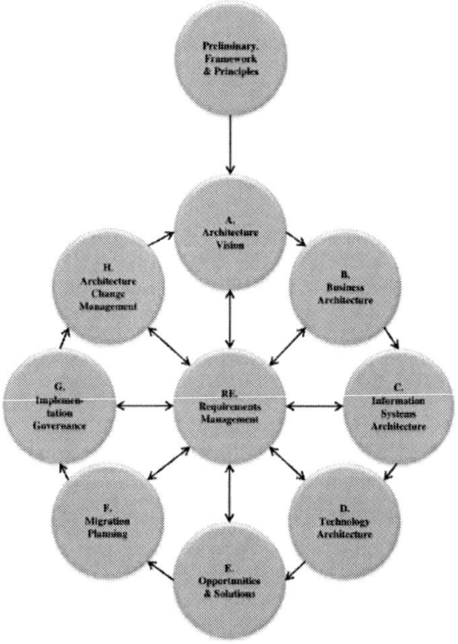

Figure 2. ADM correspondent to TOGAF [11].

Figure 2 shows the Architecture Development Method (ADM) designed in TOGAF to support the production, use and maintenance of enterprise architectures. This iterative cycle contains several activities and phases to realize an Enterprise Architecture in a controlled manner in response to business goals. Phases compliant with TOGAFs ADM are as follows [10]:

- Preliminary Phase: Initial phase to evaluate organizational frame for enterprise architecture, to analyze stakeholders and to identify affected organizational elements,

- Phase RE: Requirements engineering to survey, formulate, validate and manage requirements in every phase of the project.
- Phase A: The architecture vision validates capability requirements, organizational principles and business goals by developing an operational basic concept which defines the scope and relevant stakeholders of the architecture as well as key business requirements.
- Phase B: The business or operational architecture describes organizational, process and information aspects of the operational environment. This phase derives an operational and organizational structure by developing distributions of responsibilities and an information exchange process between authorities.
- Phase C: The development and implementation of data and application domains are part of the information systems architecture. The objective is to describe the support of business processes by information technology.
- Phase D: The technology architecture describes systems, system interfaces and dependencies for communication and interoperability aspects to support operational processes.
- Phase E: This phase evaluates and selects implementation options, identified in the development of the architectures developed in ADM before, by assessing dependencies, costs and benefits to generate a migration strategy and detailed implementation plans.
- Phase F: The objective of the migration planning is to prioritize projects to finalize a detailed implementation and migration plan.
- Phase G: The implementation governance formulates recommendations for realizing the implementation plan and manages the governance of the overall implementation and deployment process in the terms of capability improvement.
- Phase H: The phase of architecture change management establishes procedures for managing changes to initiate the development of a new architecture, thus a new iteration of the ADM

D. Views and subviews of the NAFv3.1

The NAF in Version 3.1 [7] proposes an elaborate content framework to model architecture products. It provides a range of convention and modeling rules on how to describe and document an architecture model. Therefore, the NAF defines "views" to consider an enterprise from an individual perspective. Dividing an individual view into a set of "subviews" supports the development of single architecture products, which can be analyzed easily by respective stakeholders. The views of the NAFv3.1 are:

- NATO All View (NAV): NAV describes overarching aspects and provides information, which are pertinent to the entire architecture including scope and context.
- NATO Capability View (NCV): The enterprises vision, goals and capabilities are modelled within the NCV by building e.g. taxonomies and dependency descriptions.
- NATO Operational View (NOV): The NOV conducts descriptions of derived tasks, activities, operational elements as well as information exchange processes that are necessary to fulfil missions.

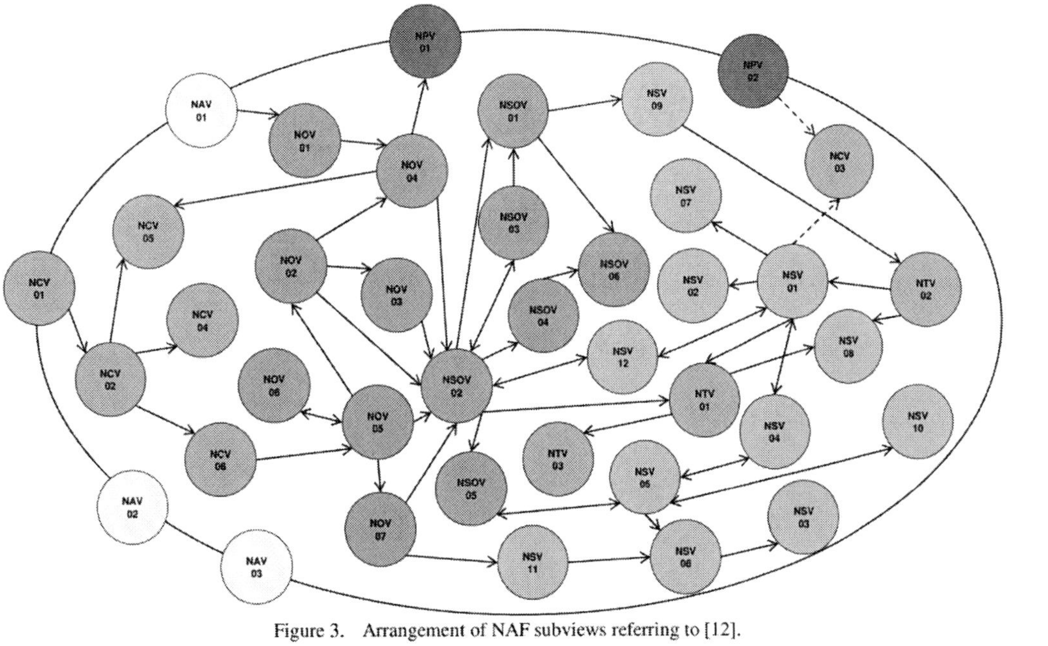

Figure 3. Arrangement of NAF subviews referring to [12].

- NATO Service-Oriented View (NSOV): The concept of SOA is fundamental to the NATO Network Enabled Capability (NNEC). The NSOV contains a description of services, which the provider provides as a useful result to a consumer to directly support the operational domain.
- NATO Systems View (NSV): The NSV contains subviews to describe the structure, interfaces and interconnections as well as functionalities of technical resources. Systems can provide services and support operational activities.
- NATO Technical View (NTV): Technical Standards, implementations and conventions are parts of the NTV.
- NATO Programme View (NPV): Products of NPV describe the relationships between capability requirements and implemented programs and projects.

The subviews are presented in a detailed manner in chapter 4 of the NAF [7]. In Figure 3, the subviews are arranged to show their dependencies within the structure of the NAF. On the left hand side (in green and blue), we have the perspective of the consumer, who performs operational activities and thereby consumes services to realize enterprise capabilities. On the right (yellow and grey), there are descriptions of technical systems providing functionalities to support operational processes. Both sides are connected by service-oriented views (purple) decoupling operational views from system views.

IV. MODELING NCOs

NCOs are, e.g., military evacuation operations. Therefore, forces of all military domains, especially Special Forces and navy supported by air force units deployed for this operation have to cooperate in a quick-response manner, which requires a high level of interoperability.

But, how can we define and examine interoperability to validate and develop respective capabilities and technology? In Tolk [16], Turnitsa [17] and Tolk et al. [18], a conceptual model abstracting and simplifying the terms of interoperability on various levels is presented, developed and applied. The Levels of Conceptual Interoperability Model (LCIM) introduces different layers of interoperation and describes their relation to the ideas of integratability, interoperability and composability [18]. The seven levels are defined as follows:

- Level 0: No interoperability, i.e., stand-alone systems.
- Level 1: Technical interoperability, i.e., established communication infrastructure allowing the systems to exchange data.
- Level 2: Syntactic interoperability, i.e., application and definition of a common data format to exchange information.
- Level 3: Semantic interoperability, i.e., unambiguous definition of the content of exchanged information.
- Level 4: Pragmatic interoperability, i.e., unambiguous definition of context, methods and procedures to use exchanged information.
- Level 5: Dynamic interoperability, i.e., changing system states and their effects – including the effects of information exchanges – on operation and data interchange are unambiguously defined.
- Level 6: Conceptual Interoperability, i.e., alignment of assumptions and constraints of the meaningful abstraction of reality [18].

NAFs SOA, as presented in Section III.D, has a high degree of support for interoperability, because of focusing on standardization and supporting the need for autonomy of systems [13]. Thus, the NNEC Feasibility Study pointed the SOA as a key to meet interoperability requirements, because

TABLE I. NAF SUBVIEWS ASSIGNED TO TOGAF PHASES (BASED ON [15]).

		A	B	C	D	E	F	G	H
NAV	1	■						▒	
	2		■						
	3					■			
NCV	1	■	▒					▒	▒
	2	■	▒					▒	
	3				■	▒		▒	
	4				■	▒		▒	
	5		■	▒	▒		▒		
	6		■						
NOV	1	■	▒					▒	
	2		■						
	3		■						
	4		■						
	5		■						
	6		■						
	7		■	▒					
NSOV	1		■	▒					
	2		■	▒	▒			▒	
	3		■						
	4		■						
	5		■	▒					
	6		■	▒		▒	▒	▒	
NSV	1				■				
	2				■				
	3				■				
	4			■	▒				
	5			■	▒				
	6			■					
	7				■				
	8					■	▒		
	9					■			▒
	10			■	▒				
	11			■	▒				
	12		■	▒	▒				
NTV	1				■				
	2					■			▒
	3					■			
NPV	1					■	▒	▒	
	2					■	▒	▒	

of its flexible, modular approach for implementing system functional requirements in the form of accessible and utilizable services [14].

To model capabilities, operations and/or missions for the purposes of examining their feasibility within the meaning of Network Centric Warfare on every single level of interoperability, we utilize the presented architectural methodology and content-related conventions from Section III. Referring to Jørgensen et al. [15] "TOGAF proposes an elaborate methodology and a simple content framework, while NAF contains a simple methodology and an elaborate content framework. The two approaches are thus complementary." Combining advantages of both, NAF and TOGAF, we can connect the content-related guidelines of NAF subviews to the compelling development methodology of TOGAF phases. This mapping is visualized in Table I. By using this mapping, we can easily derive guidance for modeling enterprise architecture for NCO by focusing on services. In this table, the initial version of a subview is colored in dark blue. Further developments and/or changes of a subview are expressed in light blue.

We applied Unified Modeling Language (UML) [21] as an object oriented, graphical modelling language by using SPARX Enterprise Architect (SPARX EA) to model single NAF subviews in the prescribed order given by TOGAF. The intent is to examine and analyze every layer of interoperability by modeling processes, systems and services to make a point about the feasibility of respective NCOs. Therefore, existing technical, operational or capability gaps requiring further development have to be spotted and recommendations have to be made.

To express the relationship between architecture views according to NAFv3.1 at application level in SPARX EA Figure 4 depicts an UML class diagram showing single architectural elements and dependencies among themselves.

Starting with establishing a NAV-1 to present the actual problem area and the scope of the architecture, the capabilities, which have to be examined, are described in the form of taxonomies derived from the actual architecture vision in NCV-1 and NCV-2. Additionally, NOV-1 presents the operational concept on high-level. Thus, conceptual interoperability can be investigated.

In phase B, it is necessary to derive *OperationalActivities* from *Capabilities* (NCV-6) and model the placed order in the context of the operation and derived tasks thereof within the "Operational Activity Model" of NOV-05. Process models support the view on tasks and processes to describe real events and activities of the operation. To obtain clarity within the operational model at different levels of abstraction, it is recommended to build an activity hierarchy. Thus, the model can provide a better overview and activities can be structured easily. Operational constraints, states and timing descriptions are arranged in NOV-6 diagrams to support the modeling of dynamic interoperability.

Allocation of responsibilities can be modeled in an "Operational Node Relationship Description" (NOV-2) by mapping identified *OperationalActivities* to involved authorities, so called operational nodes. Furthermore, NOV-2

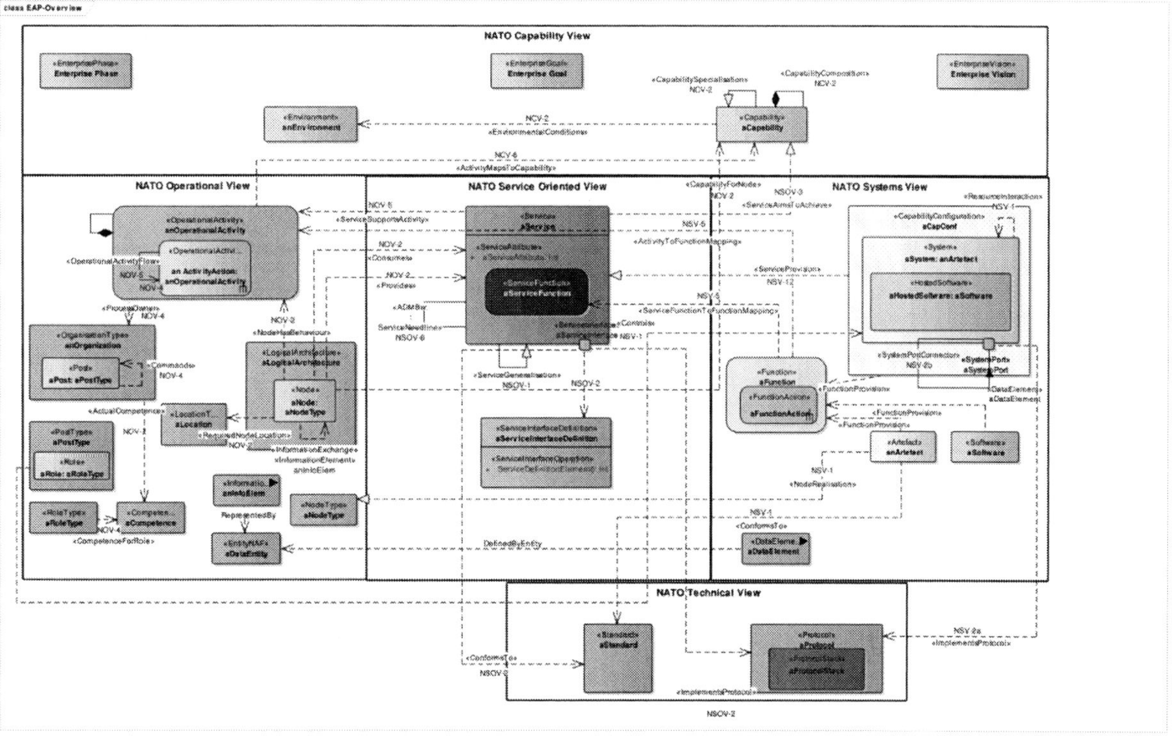

Figure 4. Selection of important NAFv3.1 elements and connections.

describes the information exchange between authorities to model their relationship, dependencies and the requirements according to operational and therefore, pragmatic interoperability. Using SPARX EA one can easily derive an "Operational Information Exchange Matrix" (NOV-3) from NOV-2 models resulting in an easy to read overview of information exchange elements, which can be analyzed significantly better. The actual or intended organizational structure among identified key players including command and control (C2), hierarchical and functional relationships, e.g., required competences, can be modeled in NOV-4. Information content, provision and consumption aspects in NCO have to be explicitly modeled to describe and analyze the level of semantic interoperability. NOV-7 represents an information model that gives an answer to "what we want to know" and "what we want to communicate" [7].

After modeling processes as part of the business architecture, we detected two approaches on modeling services and systems. First we stick to the temporal progress preset by TOGAF identifying and describing required *Services* in the form of taxonomies (NSOV-1) and "Service Definitions" (NSOV-2). Additionally, the orchestration (NSOV-4) and decomposition (NSOV-6) support the classification, structuring and dynamic behavior of respective services promoting interoperability in various domains and on different layers. In NSOV-3, *Services* can directly be mapped to supported *Capabilities* to show their importance within an operation. Further on, one can map these services, supporting *OperationalActivities* in NOV-5 or model service provision or consumption, by using already existing *Nodes* in NOV-2. As a precondition for this approach, the modeler has to have sound knowledge of NATOs C3 (Consultation, Command and Control) taxonomy perspective [19] to identify required services. To proceed to information system architecture (phase C) it is necessary to define *ServiceFunctions* performed by *Services* in NSOV-5. *ServiceFunctions* are implemented by system functions which can be modeled in NSV-5. However, system functions can be described in subview NSV-4 to impose requirements on applicable systems. Thus, this approach might be adapted to design technological requirements for new technological developments to realize interoperability within NCO.

Another approach – departing from the TOGAF methodology presented in Table I – might be suitable to examine the application of already featured systems to realize the required level of interoperability in NCO. In this case, existing systems have to be modeled using a system profile, containing the internal structure or system composition (NSV-1), the system interfaces and communications description (NSV-2) and the already mentioned systems functionality (NSV-4). Additional constraints regarding the systems quality are described in NSV-7. The systems service provision can then be modeled by applying NSV-12 to analyze what services are covered by the application of actual or intended systems. Using system function to operational activity mapping (NSV-5) we can also map the direct realization of *OperationalActivities* by respective system functions and condense system functions to implemented service functions.

Within the technical Architecture, it is possible to examine the feasibility of NCO focusing on the technical and syntactic level of interoperability. For this purpose required resource interactions can be described as a matrix in NSV-3. Furthermore, the data exchange between systems is part of NSV-6. The systems data model (NSV-11) follows the information modeled in NOV-7 (Information Model). Thus, information can be used as an input for modeling required logical and physical data models gaining insights of syntactic interoperability. In the end, technical requirements according technical interoperability are part of the NTV in phase D and E of the ADM.

While compiling the architecture, the development is documented in NAV-1; thus, conventions and recommendations can directly be noted. Additionally, a glossary can be implemented in NAV-2 to put the architecture across.

V. Analyzing Models of NCOs

The model developed in Section IV contains various architecture elements, which are able to be analyzed subview-by-subview or within the architectural context of elements (compare Figure 4). Both variants are capable of examining interoperable processes and technologies of a certain organization to estimate the feasibility of NCOs.

The product-by-product (or subview-by-subview) analysis to examine the different layers of interoperability within the scope of the LCIM is already part of Section IV. The aim of this section is to show several methods to analyze the architecture model as a whole to obtain insights about potentialities, risks, problems and development needs.

SPARX EA's option "*Traceability*" offers an important tool for the cognition of coherences and navigation within the model by revealing all relations with reference to a special element. Thus, this tool significantly facilitates the analysis of the model.

A selection of methods for analyzing an Enterprise Architecture is introduced as followed:

- **Bottom-up analysis**: Starting from the bottom of a tree of elements (ordinarily technical standards defined within the NTV) one can trace the path till the overarching enterprise vision or capabilities. The aim is to obtain knowledge about the importance or redundancy of bottom elements. Thus, you can support decisions about discarding or developing respective technologies or standards.
- **Top-down analysis**: In contrast to the bottom-up approach the top-down analysis starts the examination beginning at the top of the tree of elements (ordinarily capability-based elements within the NCV) and ending at the bottom. The aim is to show effects of cancelling capabilities, which might be obsolete or no longer required, on processes, services and technical systems. Thus, evaluations about savings on the cost of redundant systems and technologies can be done.
- **Risk analysis**: The risk analysis is an important method within in the field of quality management to

systematically identify and assess risks inside processes, organizations or systems. The aim is to find bottlenecks or precarious systems and to validate whose outage. Thus, one can estimate which processes and/or capabilities are influenced by the failure of respective elements and how large a potential risk might be. Furthermore, requirements for the development of new technologies or for redundant systems to minimize respective risks can be imposed.

- **Hotspots analysis**: Comparable with the risk analysis, the hotspots analysis is able to identify and assess elements with major impact on the whole model and thus on the whole enterprise. Hotspots are e.g. single systems, whose functions are accessed by many other systems, or e.g. pervasive technologies. The result of identified hotspots might be the creation or development of redundant systems to improve the distribution of respective system functionalities and the imparting of knowledge about these hotspots.
- **Migration analysis**: Especially in SOA, the migration of services and service functions is very important to apply changes in architectures. The migration analysis supports System Modernization through the identification of dependencies between elements and the reuse of legacy systems [20]. Thus, expenses on the development of technologies can be minimized by providing identified service functions through the usage of existing systems. Migration analysis requires an actual and a target architecture.
- **Capability gap analysis**: The examination of the feasibility of NCOs needs to focus on the covering of required capabilities. The capability gap analysis supports the identification of missing links in the realization of respective capabilities. Thus, required processes, services and/or systems can be recognized in detail and advancements of new technologies can be brought into better alignment to cover needed functions and capabilities.
- **Service composition analysis**: Modularity is one major advantage of SOA. The development of new services can be expedited and improved by analyzing existing and realized services and service functions. Thus, the composition of service functions or parts of other services can generate adjusted services that are automatically related to respective processes and realizing systems.

VI. LESSONS LEARNED FROM ARCHITECTURAL MODELING

There are various problems that can occur in the course of applying enterprise architecture to a particular problem. This section presents some best practice hints and lessons learned, obtained while modeling enterprise architectures to minimize problems in projecting, targeting and performing.

Especially for modeling NCOs it is recommended to apply an architecture model on performed military and/or tabletop exercises. Architects should also take part in this exercise as observers to get a better comprehension of the issue and the opportunity to undertake interviews with Subject Matter Experts (SME). Thus, perceptions and recommendations can directly be included into the model.

The principal investigator of an architectural project is responsible to impose a distinct problem whose resolving shall be supported by architecture products. The issue and the focus have to be precisely and unambiguously defined [7]. Thus, no universal models shall be commissioned. The level of detail with respect to time horizon has to be adjusted too. It is also necessary to provide required and common resources and continuous support by all stakeholders and experts. Reliable architecture modeling should be a result of teamwork requiring a permanent communication between all involved parties, e.g. within workshops.

Methodology specialists are responsible for quality assurance of architecture products. Thus, a constant and intensive support and a quality assurance plan have to be established [7]. Quality requirements for architecture views are e.g. comprehensibility, comparability, consistency and reusability. To ensure content-related and formal requirements it is recommended to adjust the model to the common architecture landscape. This can be realized by establishing and providing an architecture repository or database as well as documenting common architecture conventions for model diagrams and matrices without limiting specific requirements. Conventions should bindingly regulate as much as necessary, but as little as possible. Additionally, architecture repositories should be configured and administered to ensure its quality. Therefore, a central administration has to be responsible for importing, exporting and deleting architecture elements, providing products and applying user and roles concepts to manage access privileges.

According to the iterative character of TOGAFs ADM, the implementation and usage of architecture models have to be carefully planned. Therefore, it is important to familiarize stakeholders that are not acquainted with the method with architecture products by visually editing respective results. Thus, the realization of outcomes can be performed quickly and correctly. Furthermore, architecture models have to be constantly maintained by the architect to populate potential changes and to keep the model up to date.

VII. CONCLUSION AND FUTURE WORK

The feasibility of operations in terms of Network Centric Warfare is dependent on the level of interoperability of the realizing military forces. Today, military missions are frequently performed in a joint and multinational environment, thus, military forces have to adjust their capabilities to the characteristics of NCO.

The LCIM presents a suitable model of the organizations actual and desired interoperability by introducing various layers. The methodology of ADM according to TOGAF combined with the content-related conventions and rules defined in NAFv3.1 are manifested as convenient methods to examine these layers by focusing on different views and therefore, perspectives on the organization.

In this paper, we presented how to use the introduced architectural methods to obtain insights of the organization interoperable capabilities. Layers of interoperability of the LCIM are directly connected to views and subviews of the NAFv3.1 to support the estimation of the feasibility of respective operations. Additionally, analyzing methods have been introduced to assess the actual state relating to the desired condition. It was shown that these methods can be used to focus on special risks and problems as well as to minimize technical and financial effort within the transformation of organization and military forces to develop the capabilities of NCO.

Eventually, risks and problems within the process of architectural modeling have been described and lessons learned together with best practice hints were suggested. These recommendations might help architects and principal investigators to minimize issues while projecting and modeling enterprise architectures.

REFERENCES

[1] D. Lambert, A. Dale, and J. B. Scholz, "A dialectic for network centric warfare". Defence Science and Technology Organisation Edinburgh (Australia) Command and Control Div., 2005.

[2] D. S. Alberts, J. J. Garstka, and F. P. Stein, „Network Centric Warfare: Developing and Leveraging Information Superiority", CCRP Publication Series, 2nd Edition, 1999.

[3] T. de Maizière, „Konzeption der Bundeswehr", Ministry of Defence, Berlin, July 2013.

[4] S. Leuchter and R. Schönbein, „Die Verwendung von Architectural Frameworks als Vorgehensmodell für die System-of-System-Entwicklung", In: C. Hochberger, R. Liskowsky (Hrsg), INFORMATIK 2006. Informatik für Menschen. Beiträge der 36. Jahrestagung der Gesellschaft für Informatik e.V. (GI), Vol. 1, pp. 669-675, Bonn, October 2006.

[5] The Federation of Enterprise Architecture Professional Organization, "A Common Perspective on Enterprise Architecture", 2013. [Online]. Available from: http://feapo.org/wp-content/uploads/2013/11/Common-Perspectives-on-Enterprise-Architecture-v15.pdf. [retrieved: May 2016].

[6] ISO/IEC/IEEE 42010:2011 „Systems and software engineering - Architecture description", ISO/IEC, 2011.

[7] NATO C3 Board, "NATO Architecture Framework", Version 3, 2007.

[8] L. Urbaczewski and S. Mrdalj, "A Comparison of Enterprise Architecture Frameworks", Issues in Information Systems, Volume VII, No. 2, pp. 18-23, 2006.

[9] M. M. Jamjoom, A. S. Alghamdi, and I. Ahmad, "Service Oriented Architecture Support in Various Architecture Frameworks: A Brief Review", Proceedings of the World Congress on Engineering and Computer Science 2012 Vol II, pp. 1338-1343, WCECS 2012, October 24-26, San Francisco, USA, 2012

[10] V. Haren, "TOGAF Version 9.1", 10th Edition, Van Haren Publishing, 2011, ISBN 9087536798.

[11] S. Marley, "Architectural Framework" Applied Sciences Program, Geosciences Interoperability Office, Stephen Marley NASA /SCI, 2003.

[12] BMT Hi-Q Sigma 2010 TOGAF to MODAF Mapping. BMT Hi-Q Sigma, 9th December 2010. [Online]. Available from: http://www.bmt-hqs.com/media/3991716/togaf_to_modaf_mapping.pdf. [retrieved: May 2016].

[13] T. H. Bloebaum, J. E. Hannay, O.-E. Hedenstad, S. Haavik, and F. Lillevold, "Architecture for the Norwegian defence information infrastructure (INI) – remarks on the C3 Classification Taxonomy", FFI-rapport 2013/01729, Norwegian Defence Research Establishment, 2013, ISBN 978-82-464-2294-7.

[14] M. Booth et al., "NATO Network Enabled Capability Feasibility Study", VII version 2.0. Technical report, NC3A, 2005.

[15] H. D. Jørgensen, T. Liland, and S. Skogvold, "Aligning TOGAF and NAF—experiences from the Norwegian Armed Forces", In P. Johannesson, J. Krogstie, and A. Opdahl, editors, The Practice of Enterprise Modeling, volume 92 of Lecture Notes in Business Information Processing, pp. 131–146. Springer, 2011.

[16] A. Tolk, "The Levels of Conceptual Interoperability Model", 2003 Fall Simulation Interoperability Workshop, Orlando, Florida, September 2003.

[17] C. D. Turnitsa, "Extending the Levels of Conceptual Interoperability Model", Proceedings IEEE Summer Computer Simulation Conference, IEEE CS Press, 2005.

[18] A. Tolk, S. Y. Diallo, and C. D. Turnitsa, "Applying the Levels of Conceptual Interoperability Model in Support of Integratability, Interoperability, and Composability for System-of-Systems Engineering", In Journal of Systems, Cybernetics and Informatics, Volume 5, Number 5, pp. 65-74, 2007.

[19] Command, Control, Deployability and Sustainability (C2DS) Division, "C3 Taxonomy Perspective", Allied Command Transformation (ACT), January 2015.

[20] L. O'Brien, D. Smith, and G. Lewis, "Supporting Migration to Services using Software Architecture Reconstruction", Proceedings of the 13th IEEE International Workshop on Software Technology and Engineering Practice (STEP'05), pp. 81-91, 2005.

[21] J. Rumbaugh, I. Jacobson, and G. Booch, "Unified Modeling Language Reference Manual", 2nd Edition, Pearson Higher Education, 2004, ISBN 0321245628.

Effects of Elevated Temperatures on Ballistic Resistance of Ultra High Molecular Weight Polyethylene

Thore Heurich, Arash Ramezani and Hendrik Rothe
Chair of Measurement and Information Technology
University of the Federal Armed Forces
Hamburg, Germany
Email: thore.heurich@hsu-hh.de, ramezani@hsu-hh.de, rothe@hsu-hh.de

Abstract—**In the security sector, the partly insufficient safety of people and equipment due to failure of industrial components are ongoing problems that cause great concern. The temperature resistance of cross-plied oriented ultra high molecular weight polyethylen (UHMWPE) is an important thermomechanical property for using this material under different environmental conditions. Therefore, it is essential for the safety of people inside the armored vehicle to know the ballistic resistance at elevated temperatures.**

Keywords-solver ballistic resistance; elevated temperatures; fiber-reinforced plastics; armor systems.

I. INTRODUCTION

Nowadays, fiber reinforced composites are used in numerous technical areas. In contrast to other materials like steel or aluminum, they have the advantage of the same mechanical strength at less weight.

This work will focus on composite armor structures consisting of several layers of ultra-high molecular weight polyethylene (UHMWPE), a promising ballistic armor material due to its high specific strength and stiffness. The goal is to evaluate the ballistic resistance of UHMWPE composite at elevated temperatures.

While soft armor packages used in body armor have to withstand temperatures up to 70 °C, there are hard armor panels which have to withstand even higher temperatures. Hard armor panels are used in security vehicles where the temperature can reach up to 110 °C. In this study, the temperature dependent ballistic resistance of hard armor panels made of Dyneema® HB26 is analyzed. Therefore, the theoretical background of the thermomechanics of fiber reinforced composite is presented. Furthermore, practical tests were performed to show the influence of temperature on the ballistic resistance. Panels with different thicknesses were shot with three types of ammunition at room temperature (20 °C) and at elevated temperatures (up to 110 °C) to compare their ballistic performance at different environmental conditions.

The rest of the paper is structured as follows. Section II presents the state of the art. Section III introduces thermomechanical principles relevant to this work. Section IV presents and discusses the ballistic trials. We conclude in Section V.

II. STATE-OF-THE-ART

Fundamental studies about the laminate theory were performed in [1]. In this work, Mittelstedt presented calculation methods to describe the mechanical characteristics of laminates. In thermoplastics, the degree of crystallization essentially determines the mechanical properties of the material, which is described in [2, 3].

Further literature describes construction rules, where the influence of the temperature on the material is explained. For example, the coefficients of thermal expansion for different materials are given in [4]. The deformation caused by the change of temperature results in thermal stress, presented in [5].

In order to investigate the thermal effects on UHMWPE, it is essential to know the temperature in the application area of the material. A lot of researches exist in this field, so only the most important are mentioned. First, there are practice tests about temperature variations in automobiles in various weather conditions [6, 7]. Additional simulations in [8, 9] show the highest temperatures under extreme environmental conditions, which are 110 °C at the vehicle roof and up to 165 °C near the exhaust system. UHMWPE cannot be used under these conditions, because it has a too low melting temperature, at around 135-138 °C [10].

Cunniff made important researches to define the ballistic resistance of different materials by adding the Cunniff-parameter in [11]. This parameter correlates well with the limit velocity V_{50}, where 50 % of the bullets perforate the target. Moreover, the dependence of V_{50} and the areal density (AD) of Dyneema® composites is analyzed in [12].

Similar investigations, such as those in this study, are made by Meulmann et al. in [13, 14]. First, they analyze the aging of Dyneema® HB26 in thermal long-term tests, then they performed ballistic tests on HB26 at 90 °C with 7.62×39 mm MSC-projectiles.

III. THERMOMECHANICAL PRINCIPLES

The constitutive equations describe the connectivity between stress σ and strain ε of an elastic deformed body and are summarized in the linear elastic material law. To describe the state of an elastic body under load, the one-dimensional Hooke's Law is needed:

$$\sigma = E\varepsilon \tag{1}$$

where E describes the tensile modulus.

The three-dimensional form depends on the different directions of deformations ε_{ij} and γ_{ij}, of the values S_{ij} of the symmetric compliance matrix and of the stress σ_{ij} and γ_{ij}. Therefore, the first index defines the direction of the surface normal and the second index the direction of the deformation or stress.

$$\begin{bmatrix}\varepsilon_{11}\\ \varepsilon_{22}\\ \varepsilon_{33}\\ \gamma_{23}\\ \gamma_{13}\\ \gamma_{12}\end{bmatrix} = \begin{bmatrix} S_{11} & S_{12} & S_{13} & S_{14} & S_{15} & S_{16}\\ S_{12} & S_{22} & S_{23} & S_{24} & S_{25} & S_{26}\\ S_{13} & S_{23} & S_{33} & S_{34} & S_{35} & S_{36}\\ S_{14} & S_{24} & S_{34} & S_{44} & S_{45} & S_{46}\\ S_{15} & S_{25} & S_{35} & S_{45} & S_{55} & S_{56}\\ S_{16} & S_{26} & S_{36} & S_{46} & S_{56} & S_{66}\end{bmatrix} \begin{bmatrix}\sigma_{11}\\ \sigma_{22}\\ \sigma_{33}\\ \tau_{23}\\ \tau_{13}\\ \tau_{12}\end{bmatrix} \tag{2}$$

The compliance matrix can be calculated out of the tensile moduli E_{ij}, shear moduli G_{ij} and poisson's ratios ν_{ij}. Also, a laminate is an orthotropic material with symmetrical planes, so there are some values in the compliance matrix, which become zero. Besides the deformation caused by mechanical stress, there is a deformation caused by the change of temperature ΔT.

$$\begin{bmatrix}\varepsilon_{11}\\ \varepsilon_{22}\\ \varepsilon_{33}\\ \gamma_{23}\\ \gamma_{13}\\ \gamma_{12}\end{bmatrix} = \begin{bmatrix} \frac{1}{E_{11}} & -\frac{\nu_{21}}{E_{22}} & -\frac{\nu_{31}}{E_{33}} & 0 & 0 & 0\\ -\frac{\nu_{12}}{E_{11}} & \frac{1}{E_{22}} & -\frac{\nu_{32}}{E_{33}} & 0 & 0 & 0\\ -\frac{\nu_{13}}{E_{11}} & -\frac{\nu_{23}}{E_{22}} & \frac{1}{E_{33}} & 0 & 0 & 0\\ 0 & 0 & 0 & \frac{1}{G_{23}} & 0 & 0\\ 0 & 0 & 0 & 0 & \frac{1}{G_{13}} & 0\\ 0 & 0 & 0 & 0 & 0 & \frac{1}{G_{12}}\end{bmatrix} \begin{bmatrix}\sigma_{11}\\ \sigma_{22}\\ \sigma_{33}\\ \tau_{23}\\ \tau_{13}\\ \tau_{12}\end{bmatrix} + \Delta T \begin{bmatrix}\alpha_{11}^{T}\\ \alpha_{22}^{T}\\ \alpha_{33}^{T}\\ 0\\ 0\\ 0\end{bmatrix} \tag{3}$$

In an orthotropic material, only the first three coefficients of thermal expansion α_{ij}^{T} are nonzero, so they cause only a strain state. Because of different coefficients of thermal expansion and orientation of fiber and matrix in the laminate, thermal expansion can result in thermal stress.

Moreover, plastics show three different temperature-depended states, plotted in Figure 1. First, there is the energy-elastic area, where the material shows glassy and brittle

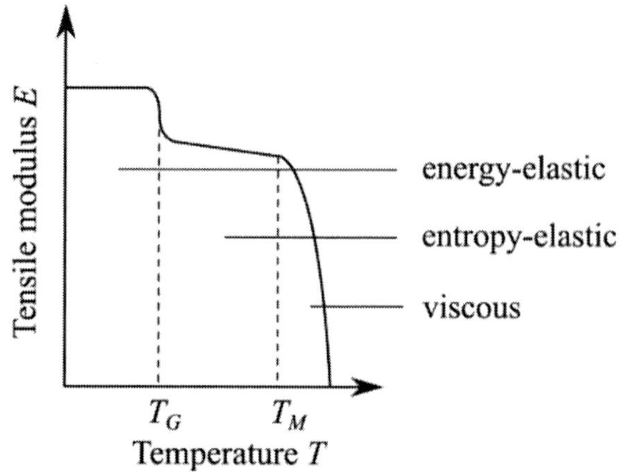

Figure 1. Energy-elastic, entropy-elastic and viscous area of thermoplastics shown at the tensile modulus E as a function of the temperature T.

behavior. In the entropy-elastic area, the material shows tough behavior and the mechanical strength values decrease slowly at higher temperatures. At the melting temperature T_M, the material loses its stiffness so the mechanical strength values fall to zero, which is why this area is called the viscous area.

The temperature also influences the fail-tension σ_f and fail-elongation ε_f of a thermoplastic, shown in Figure 2. Higher temperatures cause a decrease in fail tension and increase in fail-elongation, so the material can be more deformed until it cracks.

To make a connection between the temperature-depended mechanical values and the ballistic resistance of fiber-reinforced plastics, Cunniff introduced the parameter

$$U = \frac{1}{2}\frac{\sigma_f \varepsilon_f}{\rho}\sqrt{\frac{E}{\rho}} \tag{4}$$

which depends on the material parameters of the fibers, like the density ρ. The Cunniff-parameter $U^{1/3}$ correlates well with the limit velocity V_{50}, where the bullet perforates the target by a probability of 50 %.

IV. BALLISTIC TRIALS

Ballistics is an essential component for the evaluation of our results. Here, terminal ballistics is the most important sub-field. It describes the interaction of a projectile with its target. Terminal ballistics is relevant for both small and large caliber projectiles. The task is to analyze and evaluate the impact and its various modes of action. This will provide information on the effect of the projectile and the extinction risk.

A. *Experimental set-up*

To analyze the decrease of the ballistic resistance at elevated temperatures, the test results at room temperature

(20 °C) are used as reference values for the following tests. Therefore, the experimental set-up shown in Figure 3 is used. Ballistic tests are recorded with high-speed videos and analyzed afterwards. Testing was undertaken at an indoor

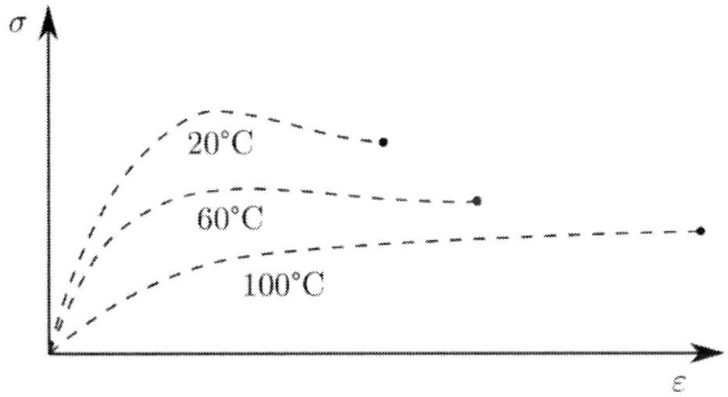

Figure 2. Qualitative effects of the temperature on the stress-strain-diagram of thermoplastics with decreasing fail-stress σ_f and increasing fail-strain ε_f at higher temperatures.

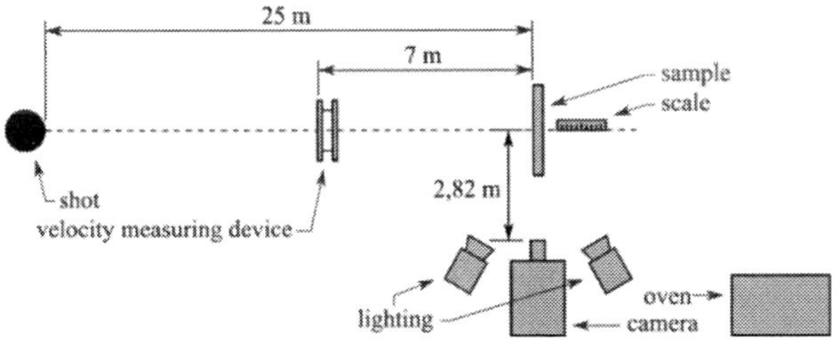

Figure 3. Experimental set-up.

testing facility. The target stand provides support behind the target on all four sides. The camera system is a PHANTOM v1611 that enables fast image rates up to 646,000 frames per second (fps) at full resolution of 1280 x 800 pixels. Because of the short time lapse of about 2ms and the high fps, three powerful plasma spotlights Hive Wasp Plasma Par were used for lighting with nearly 178,000Lx.

The oven Hamilton Beach 22 Quart Roaster Oven has to be placed near the sample to ensure a fast attachment of the panels. Before the test execution, analyses about the cooling rate of the panels with different thicknesses have been performed. For this purpose, the surface temperature was measured with an infrared thermometer Bosch GIS 100C Professional and the core temperature was measured with a temperature sensor Greisinger GMH 3710. These tests have shown that the surface temperature is cooling too fast from the temperature of the oven $T_0 = 125$ °C to the boundary-temperature $T_B = 110$ °C. Nevertheless, it can be ensured that the core temperature of plates made by 40 plies of HB26 is still over 110 °C within the first 2 minutes after removing them from the oven.

B. *Test execution*

As described above, this experiment is based on the results of ballistic tests at room temperature, so three different projectiles were fired at the HB26 plates which stopped the projectile in these reference tests. So, the projectiles 9×19 mm Luger FMJ, 7.62×39 mm Kalaschnikow MSC and 7.62×51 mm NATO FMJ were fired at plates with 20, 40 or 60 plies of HB26 with a core temperature of at least 110 °C. Additional measurements have shown that 20 plies have a thickness of 5.5 mm, 40 plies a thickness of 11.0 mm and 60 plies a thickness of 16.2 mm. It is important that the impact velocity is nearly the same at room temperature and elevated temperature to ensure comparability between both experiments.

The next important fact is that the plates have to heat up in the oven for at least 2 hours. In this way, it is guaranteed that the core temperature reaches the boundary-temperature of 110 °C during the impact.

C. *Test results*

After the ballistic trials at elevated temperatures, the results have to be prepared carefully to compare them with the results of the measurements at room temperature. For this purpose, the following parameters out of the video-analyses and static measurements are used:

1) Impact velocity: The impact velocity v_i will be measured to ensure the comparability between the tests with the same amunition. Besides the enviromental influences, the variations in the amount of propellant in the amunition pose a problem.

2) Perforation: This is the easiest and most important way to evaluate these ballistic tests. Therefore, only the fact of a successful or unsuccessful perforation is used.

3) Remaining velocity or thickness: Based on the previous evaluation of a perforation, there are two more parameters for a comparison. For one thing the remaining velocity v_r after a successful perforation measured in the video, for another thing the remaining thickness of the plate x_r after a unsuccessful perforation measured at the undeformed corner of the plates because of the compression of the material at the impact zone.

4) Buckling diameter and depth: The decisive factor for a real usage is the space taken by the dynamic deformation during the impact, because this space is mostly limited in constructions. Hence, the buckling diameter $\boldsymbol{a}$ and buckling depth $\boldsymbol{b}$ were measured in the video when the buckling is at the maximum, seen in Figure 4.

First, the 9×19 mm Luger FMJ-projectile is fired at plates made of 20 plies of Dyneema® HB26. In Figure 5, the maxima of buckling at room temperature (left) and at elevated temperature (right) are shown to compare the qualitative deformation. The deformation characteristics of both tests show no significant difference. The measured parameters for comparison are given in Table I.

Figure 4. Measuring the buckling diameter a and the buckling depth b at the maximum of the dynamic deformation.

Figure 5. Effect of 20 plies Dyneema®HB26 impacts by a 9×19 mm FMJ bullets at 20 °C (left) and 110°C (right), 507 μs and 774 μs after the initial impact.

TABLE I. COMPARISON BETWEEN THE MEASURED RESULTS OF 20 PLIES DYNEEMA® HB26 IMPACTS BY A 9X19 mm JMF BULLETS 20 °C AND 110 °C.

	Room temp.	Elevated temp.
Impact velocity	348 m/s	316 m/s
Perforation	no	no
Remaining velocity	0 m/s	0 m/s
Remaining thickness	4.5 mm	4.9 mm
Buckling diameter	224 mm	202 mm
Buckling depth	27 mm	34 mm

TABLE II. COMPARISON BETWEEN THE MEASURED RESULTS OF 60 PLIES DYNEEMA® HB26 IMPACTS BY A 7.62X39 mm JMF BULLETS 20 °C AND 110 °C.

	Room temp.	Elevated temp.
Impact velocity	674 m/s	708 m/s
Perforation	no	yes
Remaining velocity	0 m/s	569 m/s
Remaining thickness	10.9 mm	-
Buckling diameter	224 mm	-
Buckling depth	27 mm	-

The test at elevated temperature has shown a 9.2 % lesser impact velocity than the test at room temperature, but a larger buckling depth. The reason for these results is the changing mechanical values, as explained above. In connection therewith the thermoplastic becomes tougher and the fail-elongation ε_f increases at higher temperatures. Indeed, the deformation is a little bit larger at elevated temperature, but the ballistic resistance remains nearly constant for low-energy projectiles like 9×19 mm FMJ.

The second analyzed projectile is 7.62×39 mm Kalaschnikow FMJ. Here, the ballistic tests at both temperatures have a deviation of their impact velocity of 2.9 %. While the bullet gets stopped easily by a 60 plies HB26 plate at room temperature with a remaining thickness of nearly a third of the initial thickness, the ballistic resistance of HB26 decreases critically at elevated temperature. As seen in Figure 6, the bullet perforates a headed up 60 plies HB26 plate and loses only 19.6 % of the velocity trough energy release. Because the buckling has nearly the same size in both tests, it is obvious that the decrease of the fail-tension σ_f is the dominating problem here.

Finally, the standardized NATO projectile 7.62×51 mm FMJ will be fired at 60 plies HB26 plates. Both pictures out of the video analysis are shown in Figure 7 and the measured parameters are given in Table III. Although the impact velocity of both ballistic tests are exactly the same (measuring errors are neglected), there is an obvious difference in the results. The result of the bullet fired at the HB26 plate at room temperature causes initial approaches of delamination at the margins, but has not enough energy for a perforation. At elevated temperature, the bullet does not break up all plies, but causes a fully delamination of the plate. This result gets classified as a successful perforation, because the plies at the far end get detached from the rest and will be accelerated in the firing direction. The reason for the delamination is the failing matrix, which cannot transfer the forces between the fibers because of the decreased strength.

Figure 6. Effect of 60 plies Dyneema®HB26 impacts by a 7.62×39 mm FMJ bullets at 20 °C (left) and 110°C (right), 265 µs and 53 µs after the initial impact.

TABLE III. COMPARISON BETWEEN THE MEASURED RESULTS OF 60 PLIES DYNEEMA® HB26 IMPACTS BY A 7.62X19 mm JMF BULLETS 20 °C AND 110 °C.

	Room temp.	Elevated temp.
Impact velocity	819 m/s	819 m/s
Perforation	no	yes
Remaining velocity	0 m/s	-
Remaining thickness	6.4 mm	4.2
Buckling diameter	144 mm	-
Buckling depth	42 mm	-

Figure 7. Effect of 60 plies Dyneema®HB26 impacts by a 7.62×51 mm FMJ bullets at 20 °C (left) and 110°C (right), 409 µs and 2050 µs after the initial impact.

V. Conclusions

This paper examines the effects of elevated temperatures on ballistic resistance of ultra high molecular weight polyethylene. Therefore, ballistic trials with different projectiles were fired at plates made of Dyneema® HB26 plies.

At the beginning, the thermomechanical principles of thermoplastic composites were presented. Starting from the one-dimensional Hooke's Law, the three-dimensional linear elastic material law was established. After this, the deformations caused by the change of temperature were introduced and added to the linear elastic material law. These deformations can lead to thermal stress in the material.

Afterwards, the temperature-depended states of plastics were explained on mechanical strength values. These include the energy-elastic area, the entropy-elastic area and the viscous area. In connection with this, the effect of the temperature on the stress-strain-diagram of plastic is shown.

Completing the thermomechanical principles, the Cunniff-parameter was presented to connect the mechanical parameters with the ballistic resistance in one equation.

Finally, ballistic trials were performed, where plates made of 20 or 60 Dyneema® HB26 plies were fired first at 20 °C and then at 110 °C. Therefore, the projectiles 9×19 mm Luger FMJ, 7.62×39 mm Kalschnikow FMJ and 7.62×51 mm NATO FMJ were used. High-speed videos were used to analyse the characteristics of the deformation during the impact. Subsequently, the results were qualitatively and quantitatively compared. The results have shown that the ballistic resistance has a low to high lack at elevated temperatures, depending of the type of projectile.

References

[1] C. Mittelstedt, W. Becker. 2012. "Strukturmechanik ebener Laminate."

[2] H. Domininghaus, P. Elsner, P. Eyerer, T. Hirth. 2012. "Kunststoffe: Eigenschaften und Anwendungen," Berlin, Springer Verlag.

[3] A. Franbourg, F. Rietsch. 1990. "Influence of the melt temperature on the thermoplastics crystallization process," in *Polymer bulletin*, pp. 445-450.

[4] H. Schürmann. 2005. "Konstruieren mit Faser-Kunststoff-Verbunden," Berlin, Springer Verlag.

[5] W.Schneider, 1977. "Thermische Ausdehnungskoeffizienten und Wärmespannungen faserverstärkter Kunststoffe," *Kohlenstoff- und aramidfaserverstärkten Kunststoffen*. Düsseldorf. VDI Verlag.

[6] W. Marty, T. Sigrist, D. Wyler, 2001. "Temperature variations in automobiles in various weather conditions: An experimental contribution to the determination of time of death," in *The American journal of forensic medicine and pathology 22*, pp. 215-219.

[7] Volkswagen-AG, 2004 "Vehicle parts - Testing of Resistance to Enviromental Cycle test," PV 1200 Klass.-Nr. 50321.

[8] S. Schlegl, 2016 "Schutzkonzepte für zivile Sicherheitsfahrzeuge," presented at Carl-Cranz-Gesellschaft e.V. in Lichtenau, Germany.

[9] E. T. Hasegawa, 2008. "Simulation der thermischen Ver hältnisse in Motorräumen mit CFD," in *ATZ-Automobiltechnische Zeitschrift 110*, pp. 330-335.

[10] J. P. Attwood, S. N. Khaderi, K. Karthikeyan, N. A. Fleck, M. R. O'Masta, H. Wadley, V. S. Deshpande. 2014. "The out-of-plane compressive response of Dyneema composites," in *Journal of the Mechanics and Physics of Solids 70*, pp. 200-226

[11] P. M. Cunniff, 1999. "Dimensionless parameters for optimization of textile-based body armor systems," in *Proceedings of the 18th International and Symposium on Ballistics*, pp. 1303-1310.

[12] M. J. N. Jacobs, J. L. J. Van Dingenen. 2001. "Ballistic protection mechanisms in personal armour," in *Journal of Materials Science 36*, pp. 3137-3142.

[13] J. H. Meulman, H. van der Werf, S. Chabba, A. Vunderink. 2010. "Ballistic performance of Dyneema® at elevated temperatures, extreme for body armor," in *Proceedings Personal Armor System Symposium*. Quebec.

[14] J. H. Meulman, 2012. "Ballistic performance of Dyneema® at elevated temperatures, extreme for body armor - part 2."

AUTHOR INDEX

Bauer, M. 61
Crcarevska, M. 11
Dijkstra, J. 33
Dodov, M. 11
Ehlers, N. 73
Fent, T. 26
Flourentzou, N. 40
Galeano, R. 46
Gonzalez, G. 67
Gupta, R. 52
Hahn, A. 1
Hansen, E. 73
Heinrichs, D. 56
Heurich, T. 85
Jessurun, J. 33
Jogi, J. 52
Koteska, B. 11
Kozik, R. 40
Krajzewicz, D. 56
Kroning, O. 77
Lozoya-Santos, J. 67
Luque, E. 46
Mendez, E. 67
Mishev, A. 11
Molenberghs, G. 26
Mulder, W. 26
Nakayama, M. 6
Pejov, L. 11
Ramezani, A. 17, 73, 85
Ramirez-Mendoza, R. 67
Rengs, B. 26
Rexachs, D. 46
Ribarska, J. 11
Rothe, H. 17, 73, 77, 85
Salinas, J. 67
Sharma, P. 52
Tudon-Martinez, J. 67
Verbeke, G. 26
Villalba, C. 46
Wu, L. 1
Xie, J. 40